PARTNERS BECOMING PARENTS

The Tavistock Marital Studies Institute

Edited by
Christopher Clulow

JASON ARONSON INC.
Northvale, New Jersey
London

First published in Great Britain in 1996 by
Sheldon Press, SPCK, Marylebone Road, London NW1 4DU

Copyright © by the Tavistock Institute of Medical Psychology and by the authors for
their contributions.

First US printing 1997

10 9 8 7 6 5 4 3 2 1

Library of Congress Cataloging-in-Publication Data

Partners becoming parents / Tavistock Marital Studies Institute ;
  edited by Christopher Clulow.
        p. cm.
  Includes bibliographical references and index.
  ISBN 0-7657-0024-7 (alk. paper)
  1. Parenthood. 2. Marriage. 3. Interpersonal relations.
I. Clulow, Christopher F. II. Tavistock Institute of Marital
Studies.
HQ755.8.P395   1996
306.8—dc20   96-26516

Printed in the United States of America on acid-free paper. For information and cata-
log write to Jason Aronson Inc., 230 Livingston Street, Northvale, New Jersey 07647-
1731. Or visit our website: http://www.aronson.com

Contents

Acknowledgements

As editor, I would like to thank the contributors to this book for making time available to work up their lectures into written form in a climate where there are many competing claims on their time and energy, and for doing all this without financial reward; the royalties from this volume will go to the Tavistock Institute of Medical Psychology, a charitable body. I would also like to thank Joanna Moriarty who, as commissioning editor, encouraged me to go ahead with the project at a time when it would have been very easy for other commitments to take priority, and her colleagues at Sheldon Press for their help in converting the manuscript into a book.

We would like to take this opportunity to thank those individuals and organisations who have given us permission to use and adapt material for this book. Every effort has been made to trace the owners of copyright material, though in a few cases this has proved impossible and we apologize to any copyright holders whose rights may have been unwittingly infringed. We trust that in the event of any accidental infringement, the owners of the material will contact us directly.

An expanded version of Chapter 7 was published in *Feminism and Psychology*, Vol. 5, No. 4, 1995, pp. 511–30. The research described in Chapters 8 and 9 was supported by grant MH-31109 from the United States National Institute of Mental Health. The cartoon in Chapter 8 is reproduced by kind permission of *The New Yorker Magazine, Inc.* Joanna Rosenthall wishes to acknowledge discussion of her contribution with James Fisher, and thanks him for his helpful comments.

Extracts have been reproduced from the following publications:

Batchelor et al. *Understanding Stepfamilies: What Can Be Learned from Callers to the Stepfamily Telephone Counselling Service?* Stepfamily Publications, 1994.

Board of Social Responsibility, Church of England. *Something to Celebrate: Valuing Families in Church and Society*. Church House, 1995.

Bowlby, J. *Charles Darwin: A New Biography*. Hutchinson, 1990.

Dennet, D. *Consciousness Explained*. Penguin, 1993.

Eliot, T.S. 'Little Gidding', Four Quartets, in *The Complete Poems and Plays of T.S. Eliot*. Faber and Faber, 1969.

Giddens, A. *Modernity and Self Identity*. Polity Press, 1991.

Gillis, J. *For Better or Worse: British Marriage 1600 to the Present*. Oxford University Press, 1985.

Greil, et al. 'Sex and Intimacy Among Infertile Couples', in *Journal of Psychology and Human Sexuality*. 1989.

Harrison, F. *A Winter's Tale*. Harper Collins, 1987.

Macfarlane, A. *Marriage and Love in England 1300–1840*. Basil Blackwell, 1986.

McRae, S. *Cohabiting Mothers: Changing Marriage and Motherhood?* Policy Studies Institute, 1993.

Menning, B. 'The Emotional Needs of Infertile Couples', in *Fertility and Infertility*. 1980.

Mooney, B. *From this Day Forward: An Anthology of Marriage*. John Murray, 1989.

Rose, P. *Parallel Lives*. Chatto and Windus, 1984.

Rubin, L. *Erotic Wars*. Farrar, Straus and Giroux, 1990.

Biographical Notes

Penny Mansfield is Director of One Plus One, the marriage and partnership research charity based in central London. She is a family researcher and has written a number of articles. She is co-author (with Jean Collard) of *The Beginning of the Rest of Your Life?* – a book describing the marriages of a group of couples who have been followed since their respective wedding days. A sequel, *Person, Partner, Parent*, looking at the same couples six years later, when most of them are parents, is being produced with colleagues at One Plus One. She has also contributed to other books and television programmes about family life – most recently, the BBC 1 series *Life Stories*. Penny Mansfield lives in London with her husband and their two daughters.

Penelope Leach is a research psychologist specializing in child development and parent education. Her best-known book, *Baby and Child*, is available in twenty-eight languages. She is a Fellow of the British Psychological Society, a Vice President of the Health Visitors' Association, Chair of the Child Development Society, and sits on the professional board of the American Institute for Child, Adolescent and Family Studies. She works on both sides of the Atlantic for parents' organizations concerned with birth, childcare and early-years education, and for various children's organizations – especially those concerned with children's rights. A member of the Commission on Social Justice, and co-author of its issues paper *Social Justice, Children and Families*, her most recent book, *Children First: What Society Must Do – And is Not Doing – For Children Today*, was published in 1994 and is now available as a Penguin paperback.

Marcus Johns is a practising psychoanalyst of the British Psycho-Analytical Society. He is Editor of the *Bulletin of the British Psycho-Analytical Society* and Deputy Director of the London Clinic of Psycho-Analysis. He is a psychiatrist who has worked in the National Health Service with children and families, and is a past Chairman of the Child Guidance Centre at the Tavistock Centre, and Consultant Psychiatrist to the Day Unit for Children.

Lynne Cudmore trained as a social worker after completing her degree, and worked for seven years in an inner-city social services department. She has worked at the Tavistock Marital Studies Institute since 1978, where she is a senior marital psychotherapist, teacher and researcher. Her research interests include the impact of infertility on the couple relationship and the effects of child death on the partnerships of parents. She lives in London and is married with two sons.

Joan Raphael-Leff is a practising psychoanalyst and social psychologist specializing in reproductive issues. She has produced more than fifty publications in this area, including *Psychological Processes of Childbearing* (1991) and *Pregnancy: The Inside Story* (1993). She teaches on a wide variety of training courses for psychotherapists and primary care workers in the field. She is consultant to numerous related projects, and lectures and holds workshops for professionals and parents in many countries worldwide.

Jennifer Johns is a Member of the British Psycho-Analytical Society. She is a medical doctor and has been a partner in general practice, a clinical associate in obstetrics, a training doctor for the Family Planning Association, and has worked in Infant Welfare and Well Woman clinics. She has edited *The Ailment and other Psychoanalytic Essays* by Tom Main, and, with other editors from the Winnicott Trust, the forthcoming collection by Donald Winnicott entitled *Thinking About Children*. She is in private psychoanalytic practice and teaches psychotherapy at University College Hospital. She is married with three grown-up children.

Andrew Samuels is Professor of Analytical Psychology at the University of Essex. He is a Training Analyst of the Society of Analytical Psychology and a Scientific Associate of the American Academy of Psychoanalysis. He is the author of *Jung and the Post-Jungians* (1985), *The Father* (1985), *A Critical Dictionary of Jungian Analysis* (1986), *The Plural Psyche* (1989), *Psychopathology* (1989) and *The Political Psyche* (1993). He also works as a consultant to several political groups and organizations.

Carolyn Pape Cowan is a Research Psychologist at the University of California, Berkeley. She co-directs the 'Becoming a Family Project' for first-time parents and their children, and the 'Schoolchildren and their Families Project' for families whose first child is making the transition into elementary school. Both studies assess the impact of professionally-led couples' groups on the parents' marital quality, parenting style, and the children's adaptation to school. She is co-author, with Philip Cowan, of *When Partners Become Parents: The Big Life Change for Couples* (1992), and co-editor with Phyllis Bronstein of *Fatherhood Today: Men's Changing Role in the Family* (1988).

Philip Cowan is Professor of Psychology at the University of California, Berkeley. He co-directs the 'Becoming a Family Project' for first-time parents and their children, and the 'Schoolchildren and their Families Project' for families whose first child is making the transition into elementary school. Both studies assess the impact of professionally-led couples' groups on the parents' marital quality, parenting style, and their children's adaptation to school. He is co-author with Carolyn Pape Cowan of *When Partners Become Parents: The Big Life Change for Couples* (1992), and co-editor with E. Mavis Hetherington of *Family Transitions: Advances in Family Research, Volume 2* (1993).

Margaret Robinson is a marital and family therapist and mediator who, during her time working at the Tavistock Clinic, gained her experience at the Tavistock Marital Studies Institute (then the Family Discussion Bureau). She taught social work at the University of London for some years. She is a founder member of the Institute of Family Therapy in London, and also set up the Family Mediation Service there. She has written a number of books and articles on divorce and stepfamilies, including *Family Transformation Through Divorce and Remarriage* (1991), and is herself a stepmother. She is in part-time clinical practice, and is interested in combining psychoanalytic and systemic ideas.

Joanna Rosenthall started her career as a social worker after graduating from university. She has taught social work students and is co-author of *The Politics of Mental Health* (1985), as well as being a published writer of fiction. She joined the staff of the Tavistock Marital Studies Institute in 1986 where she practises as a senior marital psychotherapist and teacher. She is currently a member of the Executive Committee of the Society of Psychoanalytical Marital Psychotherapists. She lives in London with her husband and their daughter, and is also a stepmother.

Christopher Clulow started his professional career as a probation officer after graduating from university and completing a social work training. He is Director of the Tavistock Marital Studies Institute where he works as a senior marital psychotherapist, teacher and researcher. He is author or editor of eight books and numerous articles on marriage and family life, including *To Have and To Hold: Marriage, the First Baby and Preparing Couples for Parenthood* (1982); with Christopher Vincent, *In the Child's Best Interests? Divorce Court Welfare and the Search for a Settlement* (1987); with Janet Mattinson, *Marriage Inside Out: Understanding Problems of Intimacy* (1989); and the companion volume to this book, *Women, Men and Marriage* (1995). Between 1986 and 1994 he chaired the Commission on Marriage and Interpersonal Relations of the International Union of Family Organizations. He is married with two daughters.

Introduction

Consider these facts: in the United Kingdom, more than one in three children are currently being born to parents who are not married. This proportion has grown dramatically in the last fifteen years and is set to continue rising. Over half these births are registered by the mother alone or by couples who are living apart. Many couples see no need to marry unless they have children, and sometimes not even then. Of children with married parents, one in four will see them divorce before their sixteenth birthday. There are 1.3 million lone-parent families in the United Kingdom – twice the number of twenty years ago – and they now constitute one in five of all families with dependent children.* When people remarry, children will often precede the forming of a partnership; one family in twelve contains at least one stepchild.

These facts suggest that, within one generation, we have begun to disconnect the practice of child-rearing not only from the institution of marriage, but also from partnership. Is this an accurate conclusion to draw? If so, is it something to be concerned about? What are the issues for partners becoming parents today, and how can we understand what is happening to them?

These questions outline the territory of this book. Following the companion volume that investigated the nature of contemporary marriage (Clulow, 1995), *Partners Becoming Parents* draws on the experience of authorities from different professional backgrounds to examine what is involved in the process of becoming a parent and sustaining a partnership in the closing years of this century. It spotlights the connections between partnering and parenting relationships at the moment when the foundations of family life are being laid, and considers whether they help or hinder in this most important period of change.

Those starting a family initiate a process that will transform their lives. They may think they know what to expect, but nothing compares with the actual experience. In charting a route through the unknown landscape of parenthood, they will draw on how their own families managed, how friends are doing things, and any advice they may read or hear about from books, magazines, radio and television programmes. Their individual journeys will traverse a social and economic landscape that is also changing. This will make it difficult for them to take reliable bearings or to follow the paths that others

---

* In the U.S. there are over 10 million single parent families and approximately 30 percent of all American children are born to single mothers.

have trod. The juxtaposition of personal and social change creates choices and opportunities that were not available to previous generations; by the same token, it imposes a burden of responsibilities that must be discharged without some of the familiar markers and structures that offered their parents guidance and support. Today's new parents are refashioning tomorrow's world; they are not simply handing on what happened yesterday. This is both a tremendous challenge and an awesome responsibility. Are they doing this in a climate that fosters creative choices, or one that promotes potentially dangerous disconnections?

A missing link?

The figures describing family life today may seem alarming. Yet statistical snapshots, as we know, can be misleading. Inert images of the moment discount what happens over time, taking account neither of what preceded nor follows the closing of the shutter. The picture is seldom complete, allowing conclusions to be drawn that can support the prejudices of the most optimistic and pessimistic of social commentators – in other words, the cup is both half full and half empty. It is, for example, just as true to say that the great majority of children continue to be brought up by both natural parents who are married to each other as to cite the facts with which I opened. Yet few would deny that there have been significant changes in the structuring of family life in most, if not all, of the so-called developed countries over the past thirty years. Falling marriage rates, growing numbers of cohabiting couples, high divorce rates, the increase of lone-parent and stepfamily households, male unemployment, the presumption that mothers will have a job as well as be the primary parent at home, and associated pressures for more crèche, nursery education and child-minding facilities are all familiar features of the social, economic and political landscapes of post-industrial countries in the closing years of this century. They represent important changes in the fabric of society which cannot but affect the dynamics of family relationships, and especially the relationship between partnering and parenting.

From the outset of the parenting cycle, informal surrogacy, adoption and medical technology make it possible for people to become parents without being in a partnership. Medical technology, in particular, has transformed parenting possibilities within the space of the last fifteen years. Women can be impregnated without having sexual intercourse and without knowing the sperm donor. They can host ova donated by other women – who may no longer even be alive – and even human tissue taken from an unborn child. What price men in this brave new world? The exchange of bodily substances by technological means, or the placement of actual bodies, can create the appearance of making redundant coupling processes and all the emotional complexities surrounding them. Of course, the supplicant relationship between the adult who longs to be a parent and the donor, or medical team, or placement agency, can stir up intensely powerful feelings associated with infantile dependency and parental authority which may not be so far removed from those experienced within a partnership.

Complicated questions about the connections between kin, the familial roots of children and generational differences are introduced by medical wizardry and social engineering, even before the ethics of the new technology are considered. An important consequence has been to establish a clear distinction between the biological and social role of parent. For example, lesbian women can now have children without going through the pretence of a marriage, the indignity of a one-night stand or the uphill struggle of overcoming prejudice about adoption. While, in these circumstances, there has to be a biological disconnection between partnering and parenting roles, there need be no social disconnection unless public attitudes deem this to be necessary. Then one has to make a judgement about the relative merits of raising children in heterosexual and homosexual partnerships. This, in turn, involves having criteria for fitness to be a parent – no straightforward matter according to the social commentator Mukti Jain Campion (1995); it involves making comparisons and recognizing that conventional partnerships frequently do not measure up to the ideal type we so commonly have in mind when first responding to these issues.

At the microcosmic level of family life, the tension between being a parent and maintaining a partnership has never been easy to manage. The word 'mothering' has frequently been used synonymously with 'parenting', revealing the still-prevalent assumption in most households – in practice if not in attitude – that bringing up children is women's work. For parents whose primary investment is in bringing up children, there is always the possibility that the relationship with spouse or partner will be relegated to the second or third division of priorities. This can create a vacuum in the partnership that inflexible couples might find difficult to fill when the children leave home. At the other end of the spectrum are parents whose primary investment is in their relationship with each other – or, perhaps increasingly, in their work. This can create a vacuum in the parenting relationship – as the old adage goes, 'the children of lovers are orphans'. Either way round, the 'two's company, three's a crowd' mentality can be hard to shake off.

Ironically, the value to children of having an active involvement with both their natural parents has in recent years been recognized and promoted most actively in the aftermath of divorce. The costs – both emotional and financial – of children losing contact with their non-resident parent (usually father) in around half the marriages that end in divorce has influenced recent legislative thinking in relation to children, child support and divorce procedures. The mediation movement has been at pains to draw the distinction between parenting and partnering roles, recognizing how many child-related disputes can be understood in the context of one partner being unwilling to relinquish the marriage, and that a different kind of partnership is needed for joint parenting to go well. Ironic, too, that in the least propitious of circumstances – divorce – some men have discovered themselves as parents in ways that would not have happened had they stayed married. Other men (and women) have found themselves taking up parenting roles in relation to children from other partnerships while simultaneously trying to establish relationships with the natural parents of these children. The circumstances of stepfamily life serve to underline what is true for other families at all stages of life: parenting is primarily a psychological, social and economic activity; biological roots assume significance mainly in relation to these other aspects.

Public interest in family life has reflected the dichotomous thinking about partnering and parenting relationships. Programmes to support parenting still sometimes ignore the partnerships of the parents they aim to assist; occasionally they discount these partnerships and seek to replace them. Programmes to help couples may take little account of the impact of children upon their partnerships. Family research has tended to focus either on parenting relationships or, and to a much lesser extent, on partnerships; only recently have the connections between the two excited much interest. Agencies offering services to couples know only too well from their fund-raising exercises the public prejudice that 'adults ought to be able to look after themselves', or that 'marriage is a private matter'. Casting longing glances at the ability of children's charities to appeal to the hearts and wallets of potential donors, they too must play the child welfare card to secure support for improving the quality of partnerships.

Why is it that it seems so difficult at so many different levels to think about our capacities as parents and the experiences of our children in relation to the partnerships we may or may not be in?·Are these partnerships important, or might parenting be a simpler matter if it was unencumbered by the pulls and pushes of one's partner? Are the inducements of parenthood nowadays insufficient to tempt potential candidates to give up other rewarding aspects of their lives so that the tension is not experienced? Recent predictions that one in five women will remain childless – or child-free, depending upon how you look at it – invite speculation that parenthood may increasingly conflict with the aspirations of a generation that has more choices now than in the past.

The polemic surrounding discussions of parenthood, marriage and the culture of individualism can polarize opinion. When a Conservative politician extols the virtues of two-parent families, it is hard to shake off an Orwellian suspicion that what really is being said is not only that 'two parents are good', but also that 'one parent is bad'. Lone parents have been targeted politically as a problem group and represented as sponging off a welfare system that they have become adept at exploiting. The message can resonate uncomfortably with that of Richard Hermstein and Charles Murray (1994) of the American Enterprise Institute, who argue that illegitimacy constitutes the greatest single threat to the future stability of society. Their solution is to stigmatize lone parents, reduce benefits to people in these circumstances, and encourage the adoption of children whose parents do not have the financial means to bring them up. The prospect of one of the poorest sections of the community – lone mothers – facing reduced benefits and increased financial dependence on reluctant men with whom they have no wish to be associated, and children paying the price for this, offends liberal sensitivities. Labour politicians do not escape the fall-out from these arguments as they adopt the communitarian philosophy of Amitai Etzioni (1995), an American sociologist who similarly identifies liberal lifestyles and the mass re-entry of women into the labour market as contributing to a 'parenting deficit' that threatens future social cohesion.

These arguments for connecting parenthood and partnership in structured and socially approved ways are not without merit. Private choices *do* result in public costs and consequences that need to be acknowledged. There *is* nothing wrong with the principle that men and women should accept the financial and other responsibilities that follow from bringing children into the world. Society *does* need to be clear about who will care for children. Two-parent families often *do* provide a secure and stable environment in which children can thrive. There *is* evidence of aggressive individualism, exploitation and an uncertainty about commonly held values that work against social cohesion, and so on.

Yet marrying or staying together simply for the sake of the children has never been an adequate remedy for the problems between men and women. The 'shotgun' marriage and the 'policing of divorce' have never protected children from the damaging effects of parental conflict, nor have they guaranteed responsible and involved parenting. The two-generational family is a relatively recent invention; it is certainly not a universally adopted structure and its history leaves much to be desired. Nostalgia needs to be tempered with historical reality and a recognition that the two-parent, two-generational definition of family is unhelpfully narrow. And to lay the blame for social ills at the feet of women who abandon their children and their men suggests a particular form of male myopia – a deficit in partnering as much as in parenting – and a failure to grasp the changing socio-economic realities of contemporary life. As feminist commentators have observed, the genie of women's economic, sexual and social independence cannot be put back into the bottle of old-style marriage – and this is because yesterday's institution was usually based on the absence of those things.

In so far as the economic contract lies at the heart of marriage, it can be argued that women are doing no more than exchanging husbands who are becoming increasingly vulnerable as providers for a partnership for their employer or the state. The question is whether these new 'partners' are likely to offer more security and freedom than the husband of yesterday and the 'newish' man of today. Insecurity is a feature of contemporary work environments; jobs for life are very much rarer than marriages for life; and women continue to lose out in relation to men at work in terms of levels of pay and status. On the other hand, while seven out of ten lone parents at any one time will be claiming income support, no one would claim that the provision is generous; the state has no wish to take over family responsibilities. The point is that in so far as there has been a disconnection of partnering and parenting at the economic level, this has relied on new 'partnerships' being established to fill the void. When they fail to do so, we have rumblings of social discontent as well as evidence of personal problems.

Picking up the threads

While much is changing in the fabric of society as a whole, most people register what is happening to them at a personal level. We tend not to look at the big picture of social change in explaining what is happening to us unless events intrude in an unwelcome way. In our efforts to make sense of experience, we seek to integrate what is happening to us now with what has happened to us in the past, and what we expect from and plan for in the future. Coherence in these three domains provides a sense of security and agency. Threads of continuity provide a sense of who we are as individuals and how to think about and manage unfamiliar situations. They define our identity and our strategies for coping with change. Perhaps most important of all, they provide what the social scientist Peter Marris (1974) has called 'structures of meaning'. These are the personal navigating instruments developed over a lifetime that we use to decode experience and plot ways forward.

There are indications, at social and personal levels, that it is becoming more difficult to maintain and modify these structures of meaning in relation to family change. The continuities and connections are sometimes less apparent to us now than they were to our parents' or grandparents' generations. The busyness of modern life provides us with many experiences, but little time to assimilate their meanings – and this is as true for parents (who tend to be the busiest of people) as for anyone else. Thus there is a case for taking stock of the issues facing contemporary couples as they contemplate and embark on the enterprise of becoming parents.

These thoughts lay behind the decision of the Tavistock Marital Studies Institute to put on a series of public lectures in the spring of 1995 to highlight, from different perspectives, what is involved for partners in become parents. The idea was that by studying a particular family transition, ideas might be generated that would illuminate wider questions associated with family change. The particular focus was to be the connection between partnering and parenting, allowing an examination of some of the issues that emanated from this for couples and for the community as a whole. The intention was to move between the realms of private and public experience in the hope that the interplay of mutual influence between the two domains might become clearer. This involved tapping the knowledge of people who had something to say about partnering and parenting issues from different vantage points. We were fortunate in assembling a range of speakers with formidable combined professional experience, each of whom knew about partnerships from their own personal experience (two sets of couples contributed to the lectures, and so to this book) and came with the additional authority of being parents themselves. While the ground they covered was not, and could not be, comprehensive (different speakers would have introduced other perspectives and issues, or covered the same ground in different ways), they did succeed in identifying and commenting on key issues faced by parents today. Their contributions have been assembled in a way that I hope allows the main themes to be stated and re-encountered in the course of tracking a journey from partnership to parenthood and back again. The journey is more circular than linear, reflecting the kinds of truth

that T. S. Eliot (1942) expressed in the last of his Four Quartets, 'Little Gidding': 'What we call the beginning is often the end,
              And to make an end is to make a beginning.'

In times gone by, the connections between pairing, procreation and parenthood were self-evident. The purpose of marriage was to reproduce. The decision to marry embodied not only a commitment to another person, but a statement about the future direction of one's life. In Chapter 1, Penny Mansfield sets the scene for what is to follow by reviewing the purpose of contemporary marriage against the backdrop of early sexual experience, delayed marriage, and the drift towards cohabitation that are prominent features of the marital landscape today. In this she provides a bridge from the earlier volume (Clulow, 1995), which addressed the nature of marriage, to the subject of this book. She argues, from such research as is available, that marriage may be distinguished from most cohabitation by the nature of the commitment partners make to each other, and that this may explain the relative durability of marriage. When married, there are elements of both partnership – a structure of understanding between partners that expresses the purpose of their being together – and relationship – the emotional interaction between partners that sustains them as individuals and nurtures the partnership when things go well. While not contending that marriage provides the only secure foundations for family life, she argues that the considered commitment of marriage and the sense of future implied in it is more likely to provide a secure anchorage for couples than the process of drift that characterizes the background of many cohabiting partnerships.

Children certainly create turbulence in relationships, and will benefit from the anchorage of a secure and loving partnership between their parents. The reasons for the turbulence they bring can be understood in different ways. In Chapter 2, Penelope Leach argues that the way family relationships are thought about in post-industrial societies has introduced a false dichotomy between individual and collective interests which finds expression in the question 'Who comes first?' While traditional folklore represents children as the 'glue' that holds marriage together, the individualistic values that underpin many contemporary partnerships can result in offspring becoming marriage 'solvents' – in other words, children breaking rather than making marriage. Instead of being valued as a resource and related to as future adults who will continue to have a role in the family, children are sometimes perceived as a race apart, a constraint on career opportunities, and are experienced as a drain on family resources; they may even be regarded as transient beings who will grow up to leave their families behind. She suggests the central conflict facing parents and society today is not about who comes first in the family, but between earning and caring. The gendered solutions provided by marriage in the past (he would earn and she would care) are no longer adequate to the circumstances of today. What is needed are family-friendly policies at the workplace and a value system at home that reconciles 'family stuff' with individual preference, recognizing that we are all children first, and it is in our own best interests to invest in children if we have a stake in the future.

An ability to be in touch with the needs of others and to give due regard to one's own needs is a hallmark of maturity. The capacity for mature relating is forged primarily through the experiences children have of family relationships. These experiences provide templates that guide how relationships are thought about in later life. As Penelope Leach makes clear, how we think about relationships frames how we understand the dilemmas of life and what we do about them. Marcus Johns develops this theme in Chapter 3 by enquiring, from a psychoanalytical point of view, how our representations of relationships come about. Addressing the complexities of three-person relationships, he suggests that the illusion of possessive exclusivity is probably the most difficult developmental hurdle to negotiate in life, one that is never completely overcome, and which is particularly likely to reassert itself in times of change and stress. Such an omnipotent illusion encourages a state of mind in which others are required to adapt to the centrality of self. The illusion finds expression in public theories as well as private lives, and he cites the Copernican and Darwinian revolutions as examples of just how much resistance there can be to giving up world views in which we are located at the centre of our particular universes. He outlines the relational circumstances that foster a capacity to give up this illusion and to share with others, to include third persons rather than designate them as convenient scapegoats for all that we do not wish to recognize in ourselves. In particular, he cites the idealization of the pair – with its attendant narcissistic self-aggrandizement – as the biggest obstacle to the development of generous relationships and mutual concern.

The early stages of courtship and marriage are, of course, characterized by the idealization of the pair, and this may be translated into a wish to produce together a perfect third as an expression of the ideal partnership. More frequently, and especially nowadays when child-rearing is being deferred, the decision to start a family will be taken in a context where some proper disillusionment has occurred within the partnership. Yet among the many reasons for wanting children there is always a narcissistic aspect, a wish to reproduce oneself and to create the world in one's own image. Despite the opportunity costs of children, most women want and expect to become mothers at some stage in their lives, most men will assume parenthood as part of their future, and the great majority of marriages will realize these aspirations. Yet what happens when these plans are thwarted?

Lynne Cudmore explores this question in Chapter 4 as she charts the experiences of couples who seek medical help to have children. She captures the distress of those living in a culture that expects children as of right, assumes couples will have them, and denies the increasing difficulties of conception now being registered in many developed countries. Small wonder, then, that infertility has a powerful impact on the sexual identity of women and men, on their feelings about themselves and their partner, and on how they construe their partnership. Medical interventions provide a solution for some, but for the majority undergoing *in vitro* fertilization treatments (from which her experience is drawn) they constitute an additional trauma – endured with hope but ultimately with barren outcome. Cycles of uncertainty and disappointment are borne with different degrees of fortitude, and she highlights a psychological division of labour between partners in expressing their feelings and managing the treatment processes that can help *and* hinder them in making necessary adjustments. Unrequited longing, complicated feelings and pressures to preserve the front of 'ideal couple' to qualify for scarce treatment resources (whether justified in reality or not) may compound the resistance to accepting loss as a creative solution rather than a counsel of despair.

For most couples, mercifully, the road to parenthood will not be impeded by insuperable obstacles. In Chapter 5, Joan Raphael-Leff considers the processes by which fact and fiction, fantasy and reality, past and present, are woven into a tapestry depicting the personal stories women and men construct to describe their experiences of pregnancy and parenthood. These stories, including their elements of fantasy (and, indeed, phantasy – the change in spelling denoting preoccupations that are not in the realms of conscious awareness), shape parenting behaviour and frame the emotional backdrop to early parenthood. From the seemingly endless diversity of stories there are patterns that can be assembled into what she describes as a *placental paradigm*. The women ('Facilitators') and men ('Participators') who organize themselves and their lives around babies contrast sharply with the women ('Regulators') and men ('Renouncers') who expect them to slot into the pre-existing adult scheme of things. Between these extremes are women and men who are more fluid in recognizing and responding to the needs of their children and themselves ('Reciprocators'). These characteristics can combine in different ways within partnerships, resulting in different patterns of interaction between the partners and in relation to their children. The patterns are not fixed attributes, but paradigms that will predominate at different times according to circumstance and predisposition. Each has outcomes and implications for every member of the newly-formed family group.

Some of the most important reproductive narratives are the stories daughters construct when they become mothers. In Chapter 6, Jennifer Johns embarks on a developmental odyssey, tracing an imaginary journey to motherhood undertaken by the heroine of her story. She describes how, right from the beginning of life, gender matters for girls; it influences the kind of response that, first as babies and later as young girls, they will elicit from those around them. In particular, the kind of mothering a daughter receives will be a reliable predictor of how that daughter will behave when she, in turn, becomes a mother. The psychological skin separating mother and daughter is permeable, allowing, in fantasy, the generations to be reversed in ways that can both facilitate and impede development. Fathers, the parental couple and other figures feature in this deliberately conventional odyssey, providing some of the push for both daughter and mother to give up the illusion of proprietorship in their relationship with each other; but it is the cycle of motherhood that is the main subject of this story.

In contrast, Andrew Samuels challenges the gendered distinction between mothers and fathers, asking instead about what is involved in mothering and fathering that requires them to be demarcated on the basis of sex. In Chapter 7, he addresses the *role of fathering*, not the biological entity of fatherhood, in an attempt to counter both the idealization and denigration of fathers and to open the position (and, indeed, that of motherhood) to candidates of either sex. His starting point is the political context of concern about lone mothers which he links with what is sometimes described as the 'crisis in fatherhood'. Both questions point in the same direction for him: reconceptualizing parenting as a role, mothering and fathering can be conceived as different aspects of the same process and, in conducive circumstances, be effectively carried out by one person irrespective of their sex. In so far as roles are social constructions, the gauntlet is thrown down for a re-examination of assumptions still operating from a patriarchal age about the place of women and men in public and private life. In as much as they emanate from professional theories, the challenge is to examine how culture-bound these theories might be. The closing section of the chapter offers a critique of psychoanalytical theory as it applies to fatherhood, and concludes that the archetype of the father is no more – and hence no less – than a cultural construct.

While these arguments emanate from and are highly relevant to the predicaments of the rapidly growing number of lone parents, the majority of children in this country are still born to two parents who are, and will remain, married to each other. That is not to discount the relevance of Andrew Samuels's arguments for two-parent families, but to draw attention to the implications *for the couple relationship* of a newborn baby. In Chapter 8, Carolyn Pape Cowan takes up this brief as she describes the changes that children introduce into their parents' partnerships. From her part in one of the best-documented longitudinal studies of the transition to parenthood yet undertaken, she charts what helps and hinders couples in making the necessary adaptations to this most significant of life changes. Of particular interest is the way children tend to differentiate, along stereotypically gendered lines, the roles that couples take up as parents, and this in even the most egalitarian of West Coast American families. This constitutes one of a number of pressures on the couple's relationship in the early years of parenthood. A group approach to helping couples manage the transition is described in detail. She concludes that in comparison with childless couples, children do keep partnerships together for a time. This stability is enhanced in the short term by the programmes of support she describes. In the longer term, questions are raised about how parents can be helped throughout the child-rearing cycle.

The relationship between partnering and parenting is a reciprocal one. As well as children affecting the nature of their parents' partnership, the quality of that partnership affects parenting styles and child development. This under-investigated aspect of family relationships – except, ironically, following divorce – is explored by Philip Cowan in Chapter 9. From research that assessed parents in terms of their warmth, responsiveness, capacity to set limits and to structure relationships with their children (qualities associated with healthy child development), it was found that parents who were hostile towards each other were less able to function in these ways than couples who were getting on well. A good partnership can act as a buffer to life stresses, and even mediate the hand-me-down cross-generational effects of conflict within the parents' own families of origin. While the correlational research and intervention studies that he reports have demonstrated that the quality of the couple relationship is central to the dynamics of family life, the causal connections have yet to be tracked. But the results thus far make the case for helping couples with the parenting task, and suggest that a parenting focus is more effective than a marital focus in reducing conflict between partners.

While it is easy to slip into thinking of the process of becoming a parent as one that follows the business of establishing a partnership, parenthood often precedes partnerships. This most commonly happens as a result of remarriage, where one or both partners bring children from a previous relationship into their new partnership. In Chapter 10, Margaret Robinson looks at the legal framework that governs partnering and parenting relationships after divorce, as this comprises an important contextual factor for stepfamilies. She examines some of the issues that step-parents have to face in managing the roles of parent and partner by looking at definitions and categories of stepfamilies. Rooted in loss, often extended beyond the confines of any one household, stepfamilies face particular challenges. These require a change in attitude from family members, and from those outside the family who are in a position to provide support, if the particular vulnerabilities of remarriage and repartnering are to be reduced.

Joanna Rosenthall, in Chapter 11, goes inside the structures framing stepfamily life to the psychological processes that shape attitudes and mould behaviour. In particular, she examines the implications of antecedent loss for all the members of the newly formed family unit, paying special attention to the idealization and denigration that serves in the short term as a protective measure against anxiety, but ultimately works against the resolution of loss. She argues that the hatred expressed in fairy tales about stepfamilies needs acknowledging as a reality, and outlines the risks of reliving the Oedipal myth after divorce – a time when the illusion of exclusive possession can reassert itself to console children and their parents. With the creative act of remembering, and the containment that allows ambivalent feelings to be accepted, the dilemmas associated with triangular relationships that are so much a feature of stepfamily life can be managed in ways that provide generous and inclusive solutions. The problems associated with them can also be seen as the spur to differentiation and development.

Different images of family life emerge from the contributions to this book, raising some common questions and themes. Implied in many of the chapters is the assumption of children having two parents who stay together during their upbringing, an assumption that accurately reflects the situation of most children today, but not all. Yet what is the function of the partnership between parents for children, and is it necessary for their healthy development? In the concluding chapter, Chapter 12, I explore this question as a means of drawing together the threads of the book and interweaving them with some thoughts of my own. And if, to continue the lines of T. S. Eliot,

... the end of all our exploring
Will be to arrive where we started
And know the place for the first time,

that constitutes progress.

Christopher Clulow

1
Marrying for Children?

There was a time when the question mark in this title would have been superfluous; pairing and procreation were synonymous. The purpose of marriage was reproduction – the forging of another link in the chain of the family. This was unambiguously expressed in the 1662 Book of Common Prayer, which stated that the primary purpose of marriage was the procreation of children. These days, it is the relationship between spouses that is pre-eminent; in the 1980 Alternative Service Book, mutual comfort, help and fidelity are given as the principal reasons for marriage. If the primary purpose of marriage has changed, is that because the nature of marriage has changed?

Children and the changing nature of marriage

Over the course of the past three centuries, marriage appears to have been transformed. That transformation is commonly described as a shift from institution to relationship. *Marriage in the past* (the past is an imprecise location – it could be as close as the previous generation of newly-weds or as far back as early Christian marriage) is typically defined as a social and economic contract, a public institution. It is contrasted with *modern marriage*, which is described as an intimate private relationship – indeed, *the* relationship. This neat dichotomy obscures the ambiguities and complexities that comprise marriage. Historians cite evidence of the 'companionly ideal' of marriage in a wide range of writings over the centuries, and have taken exception to the caricature of yesterday's marriages (however yesterday is defined) as impersonal loveless arrangements (Macfarlane, 1986). Family researchers express a similar scepticism: looking at the evidence of their contemporary data, they question whether modern nuptiality is inspired *entirely* by romance and whether modern couples are all engaged in highly intimate relationships (Clark, 1991).

If today's marital *relationship* is such a private matter, why do substantial numbers of men and women still seek public recognition of their personal commitment by getting married? After all, cohabitation is rarely disapproved of, and is often recommended as a prelude to marriage: less than 10 per cent of men and women under 45 think that living together is always wrong; and two out of three of them would actually advise a young person to cohabit before marriage

(British Household Panel Survey, 1994). A working party of the Church of England, having reviewed the statistics on marriage and cohabitation, have recently urged the Church to take a more positive approach to cohabitation by abandoning the phrase 'living in sin', and recognizing that 'some people choose cohabitation as a way of expressing their deepest commitments' (Board of Social Responsibility, 1995).

Is the problem, as the historian Gillis (1985) suggests, that we live in a conjugal age when the couple has become the standard bearer for all intimate relationships and therefore we fail to appreciate the wider significance of marriage? Gillis states: 'The marriage process is simultaneously private and public; it is personal but also political. It belongs to that part of life which we, from our twentieth century perspective, like to think of as voluntary, but which is actually subject to substantial constraints and obligations' (p. 8).

The chance survival of a scrap of paper from over 150 years ago throws light upon this process. In 1838 Charles Darwin was 29 years old: he had been back in England for two years after his famous five-year voyage around the world and was contemplating his future. Such thoughts inevitably centred on whether he should marry. The young student of natural sciences approached the question in a highly rational manner by writing down possible outcomes under two adjacent columns, one headed 'Marry' and the other 'Not Marry'. Under each heading he wrote down the pros and cons of each choice (see Mooney, 1989):

This is the question

Marry

Not Marry

Children – (if it please God) – constant companion, who will feel interested in one (a friend in old age) – object to be beloved and played with – better than a dog anyhow – Home, and someone to take care of house – Classics of Music and female Chit Chat – These things good for one's health – (forced to visit and receive relations) – but *terrible loss of time* – My God, it is unthinkable to think of

No children (no second life) – no one to care for one in old age– what is the use of working without sympathy from near and dear friends – who are near and dear friends to the old except relatives – Freedom to go where one liked – choice of Society and *little of it*. Conversations with the clever men at clubs – Not forced to visit relatives, and to bend in every trifle – to have the spending one's whole life, like a neuter bee, working, working, and nothing after all – No, no won't do – Imagine living all one's days solitarily in smoky dirty London House – Only picture to yourself a nice soft wife on a sofa with good fire, and books and music perhaps – compare this vision with dingy reality of Grt Marlb[orough] Str.

expense and anxiety of children – perhaps quarrelling – *Loss of time* – cannot read in the Evenings – *fatness and idleness* – anxiety and responsibility – less money for books etc. – if many children forced to gain one's bread (But then it is very bad for one's health to work too much). Perhaps my wife won't like London, then the sentence is punishment and degradation with indolent, idle fool . . .

Charles Darwin (on a scrap of paper), 1838

Darwin's comparison was of the state of marriage with bacherlorhood, and his concern was *whether* to marry rather than *who* to marry. Running throughout his cost-benefit analysis of marriage is a preoccupation with the future – what would become of him? Children were his primary consideration, for they would provide a purpose in life and an insurance against the vicissitudes of old age. The subject of children appeared first under each of the column headings: Under 'Marry', he wrote 'children', because children would follow marriage just as night followed day (unless the Almighty deemed otherwise); under 'Not Marry', he wrote 'no children', because remaining a bachelor meant childlessness, a lonely and empty destiny; there would be no 'second life', nothing would remain to denote his existence.

Companionship and home comforts were Darwin's next considerations: they were part and parcel of having a wife. Throughout his account, Darwin concentrates on the attributes of *a* wife, not the personal qualities of a particular woman (he does note the feminine influence of a wife). The thumb-nail sketch of married life that emerges is like a scene from a play in which the chief players are carrying out their occupations of 'husband' and 'wife'. There is little sense of an emotional encounter between an individual man and an individual woman. Taken as a whole, this marital balance sheet conveys an acute awareness of the real costs of married domesticity, both economic and personal, in terms of the loss of privacy and individual freedom. Interestingly, Darwin was somewhat ahead of his time in recognizing that having a wife was good for a man's health (McAllister, 1995).

There are fascinating similarities between this young man's contemplations on married life in the nineteenth century and the reflections of newly-wed husbands interviewed as part of a longitudinal study of marriage (undertaken by One Plus One) almost one and a half centuries later (Mansfield and Collard, 1988). Most of these new husbands had opted for marriage at a time in their lives (mid-twenties) when it felt right to settle down; they were *ready for marriage*. Yet that readiness did not spring principally from a yearning to be a partner in a marital relationship; instead, they had experienced a creeping disillusionment with being single: 'I didn't fancy growing old singly . . . on your own . . . and nobody at all . . . no children . . . it's horrible.' Or: 'Thought of myself as an old bachelor. I'm on the shelf and I'm staying there – it did bother me to a certain extent, but I didn't let it get me down.'

In spite of the general portrayal in our culture of romantic love as *the* motive for matrimony, these young husbands had chosen marriage, as had Charles Darwin, because it was part of their logic for living. Marriage made good sense to them because it offered independence and freedom without the drawback of loneliness; the opportunity to settle their own futures and to make their own mark on the world. However, reasons such as these were submerged; the immediate response to the question 'Why did you marry?' was 'Because I fell in love'. As they explored the 'act' of falling in love in the context of other aspects of their lives, it became clear that the conditions had been right for falling in love. In her introduction to a biography of five famous literary marriages, the biographer Phyllis Rose (1984) echoes this theme:

> At certain moments, the need to decide upon the story of our own lives becomes particularly pressing – when we choose a mate for example . . . Decisions like that make sense retroactively of the past and project a meaning onto the future, knit past and present together, and create, suspended between the two, the present. Questions we have all asked ourselves such as Why am I doing this? or the even more basic What am I doing? suggest the way in which living forces us to look for and forces us to find a design within the primal stew of data which is our daily experience (p. 5).

Marriage represented loss, or at least restrictions, for many of the men and women we interviewed, yet this was what they sought. The binding of commitment and the limiting of personal choice were the same thing. An outline to their lives and a sense of direction were their objectives. A powerful sense of the future permeated much of what they talked about in their interviews; as one husband put it: 'Getting married is where it all starts. You're not a kid any more, you're branching out on your own. It's the beginning of the rest of your life.'

Five years later, in the mid-1980s, when most of these couples were parents, they were re-interviewed and asked to look back and imagine what would have happened had they *not* married. Only a very few could view this positively. For most, husbands especially, life without marriage or their particular spouses (it was not always clear which) would amount to a solitary and lonely existence: 'I couldn't take the loneliness of being single', or 'I don't really have a lot of time to myself, whereas before I got married I had plenty of time to myself. I do look back on that and think it would be nice, definitely, but then again would it? I don't know, you can end up very lonely that way.'

In his comprehensive study of marriage over five centuries, Macfarlane (1986) identifies the fear of loneliness as the inspiration for marriage, and he explains how marriage specifically combines the institutional and the relational, the public and the private:

> The loneliness which Milton, Donne, Shakespeare and others diagnosed at the heart of love led many to marry. The examination of this emotion, impulse, inclination will provide us with a final indication of the way in which people were propelled into marriage through the centuries. The marriage contract was something more than other contracts. In an extraordinary way, what began as an artificial exercise of will, an almost linking of two bodies, minds and personalities, became the most important and, paradoxically, the most natural of all relationships (p. 173).

This was certainly Charles Darwin's experience. On the reverse of the piece of paper on which he had summarized the advantages and disadvantages of marriage, he scribbled further thoughts about the timing of marriage, and concluded: 'One cannot live this solitary life, with growing old age, friendless and cold, and childlessness staring in one's face, already beginning to wrinkle – Never mind, trust to chance – Keep a sharp look out – There is many a happy slave – ' (Mooney, 1989).

About a year later, Darwin married his cousin, Emma Wedgewood, who bore him ten children. Decades later, in a letter to his sons, he wrote these words about their mother, his wife:

> You all know your mother and what a good mother she has ever been to all of you. She has been my greatest blessing . . . I marvel at my good fortune, that she, so infinitely my superior in every single

moral quality, consented to be my wife. She has been my wise adviser and cheerful comforter throughout life, which without her would have been during a very long period a miserable one from ill-health. She has earned the love and admiration of every soul near her' (p. 274).

Comparing Darwin's anticipation of matrimony with his report of the experience of many years of being married to Emma enables us to appreciate the complex process of becoming a couple – how, in Macfarlane's words, 'what began as an artificial exercise of will became the most natural of all relationships'. The concepts of marriage as both a social and economic unit (institutional) and an intimate relationship (relational) are ever present; it is surely the emphasis we place on one rather than another at a particular time that distorts our perception of marriage as *either* an institution *or* a relationship.

If we consider a *particular* marriage over time there will be variation too. The relational aspects of marriage may be more pronounced when the couple are 'in love'; more institutional aspects hold sway when children are born; and another more relational form predominates when the children have left home. At any one period, marriage will manifest both institutional and relational aspects, and within any given time span there is also likely to be variation of emphasis upon one or other aspect according to class, religion and ethnic group.

The fundamental nature of marriage has not altered in the sense that it was once one thing and is now quite another; there is great continuity over time in what constitutes the elements of marriage. However, the place of marriage in the sequence of growing up and reaching independence has changed considerably in the past three decades. Once, marriage was the launchpad of adulthood. The marriage contract consisted of an exclusive package of rights that gave status, and therefore meaning, to an individual's life. However, marriage no longer has the monopoly when it comes to those benefits that Darwin listed.

The social pressure to confine sexual activity, domestic partnerships and childbearing within legal marriage has diminished dramatically. The National Survey of Sexual Attitudes and Lifestyles (Wellings *et al.*, 1994) shows that the age at first sexual intercourse has declined (for women born between 1931 and 1935, the median age at first sexual intercourse was 21; for women born between 1966 and 1975, it was 17), while the age at marriage has increased (in 1971, the average age of men marrying for the first time was 22; today it is 27).

So, both men and women are now sexually active at younger ages and for longer periods outside marriage than thirty years ago. In England and Wales in the late 1950s, two-thirds of women claimed to be virgins on their wedding day; fifteen years later, in the early 1970s, only a quarter of brides made that claim. In this period, 1950–70, strong disapproval of sexual relations outside marriage was coupled with economic prosperity; in other words, there was a strong incentive to wed and the means to do so. Not surprisingly, the age at marriage fell significantly. This was the golden age of marriage, 'never before had so many married, and with such ceremony' (Gillis, 1985, p. 289).

Comparisons with the past usually refer to the immediate past. In much of the contemporary debate about family values, it is the pattern of family formation in the post-war period that has been used as the yardstick for judging change in the 1990s. A longer perspective reveals conflicting evidence. Sexual behaviour in previous centuries was not scrutinized by social surveys, but historians are able to investigate the records of marriages and births to establish the incidence of pre-marital pregnancy and illegitimacy:

> The incidence of pre-marital pregnancy rose rapidly from the 1750s onward; and so too did illegitimacy, which accelerated at a rate unprecedented in the known history of the British population. While a certain amount can be attributed to seduction and abandonment, recent studies suggest that a very large part of the rise was the result of the simultaneous increase in the numbers of common-law unions, whose offspring were recorded as bastards (Gillis, 1985, p. 110).

Sexual relationships did occur outside marriage, but that did not mean they were casual relationships. Indeed, there were many stable, non-marital procreative unions which often attained the status of legal marriage. Until the middle of the eighteenth century and the passing of the Marriage Act of 1753 (intended to prevent clandestine marriage), sexual intercourse after the promise of marriage converted a betrothal into a marriage (McRae, 1993): 'At the very least, recognition that the private ordering of family relationships is likely to have always existed alongside the public ordering may provide a salutary lesson for those who view today's cohabiting mothers as having fallen somehow from a 1950s paradise of wedded bliss into disorder' (p. 8).

Lilian Rubin's study of the sexual histories of almost 1,000 heterosexual people in the United States aged 18–48 in 1989 reveals the way sexual licence for the young has altered the context in which personal commitments are established today. She describes the study as 'a tale of change of almost staggering proportions in relations between men and women' (Rubin, 1990). Changes in the sexual behaviour and attitudes of girls were much more pronounced than among boys. In particular, the link between sexual intercourse and commitment had altered, redefining the nature of commitment. One 16-year-old respondent explained her sexual relationship with her boyfriend thus: 'We love each other so there's no reason why we shouldn't be making love.' She was then asked to what extent she saw her tie with him as long term: 'Do you mean are we going to get married? The answer is no. Or will we be together next year? I don't know about that; that's a long time from now. Most kids don't stay together for such a long time. But we don't date anybody else as long as we are together. That's a commitment, isn't it?' (Rubin, 1990, p. 61.)

While there is great continuity in what constitutes marriage, perhaps the greatest change has been in the expectation of continuity in marriage itself. It is still regarded as a life-long commitment, but the experience of the past three decades, when divorce rates have soared, has gradually turned the expectation of permanence into a 'fingers-crossed' hope. If marriage is becoming impermanent, can it offer escape from a pointless and lonely destiny, a promise that it once appeared to guarantee? Young men and women who are thinking about commitment today have grown up in a divorcing society, and may have experienced their own parents' marital disruption and divorce. Deciding on the right time to settle down, and the right person to settle down with, is a precarious procedure nowadays. In all his musings on marriage, Darwin did not ask 'Will it last?', although he did venture the thought that he might quarrel with his wife.

Cohabitation – an alternative basis for parenthood?

British couples, especially those living in England and Wales, are resisting marriage. In 1993, the number of marriages in England and Wales dipped below 300,000 for the first time in fifty years. The media reaction was predictably doom-laden: 'Marriage on the rocks' and 'Love and marriage now as dated as a horse and carriage' were two of the headlines. So does the current disinclination to marry signal a preference for living alone?

There was an appreciable increase in 1987–93 in the proportion of women aged under 50 living outside a partnership. For men, too, there was a corresponding increase, although the growth has only been about half of that for women in the same period. However, the category 'living outside a partnership' does not necessarily translate as 'living alone'. In 1993, 32 per cent of women aged 18–49 were not living with a partner, yet 23 per cent were lone parents or 'a child within a family'. Teenage women who became pregnant before abortion was legally available tended to marry before the birth of their babies (almost half such women in 1971), but ten years later only one in five unmarried teenagers who became pregnant had 'shotgun weddings': they were more likely to have a termination or to have the baby on their own. We cannot assume that all the women living outside a partnership have *chosen* not to be a partner. Statistics are like snapshots: they capture people at one moment in time. However, things change: some women may yet enter a partnership; others have left previous partnerships and may go on to repartner in the future.

The popularity of marriage is declining, but living as a couple remains highly attractive. It has been the youngest age groups, those in their twenties, that have shown the greatest changes in pairing behaviour. Living together before first marriage has become the practice of an increasing majority, and couples who do cohabit are doing so for longer periods. If we want to understand the declining popularity of marriage, we need to look further at cohabitation.

In the golden era of marriage, when marriage rates were at their highest, cohabitation was largely regarded as the predicament of an unfortunate minority who were unable to marry (because one or both partners was not yet divorced) or the choice of an exceptional few who were unwilling to wed. During the 1970s, when pre-marital sexual activity was reported to be more common for women, a new form of cohabitation came to the fore. This has been termed 'nubile cohabitation' and refers to young people who live together as a prelude to, or as an alternative to, marriage (Kiernan and Estaugh, 1994). This type of cohabitation has increased dramatically over the last two decades: seven out of ten first marriages in the early 1990s were preceded by pre-marital cohabitation, compared with only one in ten in the early 1970s.

During the 1970s, it seemed that nubile cohabitation was essentially a final phase of courtship and that childbearing would continue to be confined to marriage. Instead of marrying and postponing parenthood, couples were delaying marriage until they wanted to start a family. While that is still the practice of the majority of young cohabitants, an increasing minority are not marrying when the woman becomes pregnant or before the birth of a baby, although they may marry at a later date. Since the beginning of the 1980s, the number of children born outside marriage has tripled to about a third of all births. Eight out of ten of these births are to single women. These never-married mothers are either living without a partner (on their own or in their parents' home), or they are cohabiting. When a birth is registered by both parents living at the same address, it is assumed that they are cohabiting. About three-quarters of births outside marriage are registered jointly, and in just over a half of joint registrations the mother and father give the same address. Cohabiting unions tend to be short-lived – around two years. They either convert into marriages or they break up (Haskey, 1995).

While two out of three cohabitants are men and women who have never been married, the remaining third are people who have been married previously; in the main, they are divorced or separated rather than widowed. Predictably, these cohabitants are on average older and more likely to be living with a partner who has also been married before. Separated and divorced cohabitants are more likely to have a child or children from a previous marriage or partnership.

One way of looking at the emergence of nubile cohabitation is to see it as an opportunity for testing out a partnership. The hope then is that there will be fewer mistakes; incompatibility can be recognized before taking the plunge. Concern about marital (and partnership) breakdown has grown as evidence mounts to show that divorce, and the conflicts and disruptions that precede and accompany it, can have long-term negative effects on many children (McAllister, 1995). In 1992, half of all divorces were granted to couples who had been married for less than ten years; and 57,000 children under the age of 5 experienced the divorce of their parents – an increase of two-thirds in just fifteen years. If pre-marital cohabitation can promote marital stability, should it be encouraged for couples who are ultimately 'marrying for children'?

In *Something to Celebrate*, a report of a working party of the Board of Social Responsibility of the Church of England (1995), the evidence that couples marrying in the 1980s who had first cohabited were 50 per cent more likely to have divorced within five years than those who had not, evoked the following comment:

> Children born to parents who marry after cohabiting may therefore be at more risk of going through family breakdown. However, the research in this area is difficult to interpret, as the evidence does not necessarily mean that cohabitation before marriage *causes* breakdown. It may reveal that those who cohabit and then marry are likely to have a different commitment to marriage than those who do not. It also seems that some cohabiting couples who are having relationship difficulties go on to marry because they think that this may ease their problems. For all these

reasons, those who enter cohabitation with a commitment to marriage, in order to test out the partnership and their compatibility before marriage, may be deluding themselves (p. 114).

There is often an assumption that couples who cohabit are 'committed', when compared with men and women who are sexually active but not living with a partner. The 16-year-old girl in Rubin's study said that she was committed to her boyfriend, but not because she expected to be with him in the future; her commitment was based on the existing state of their relationship. In surveys such as the General Household Survey, unrelated adults of the opposite sex are classed as cohabiting if they consider themselves to be 'living together as a couple'. Peel back that label and a variety of situations unfold:

- Ian and Sarah are both in their late twenties. They met at work four months ago and very soon afterwards started to sleep together. Sarah's flatmate found a job in another city so she needed someone to share her flat. As things were going well with Ian, it made sense for him to move in. Marriage? They've never thought about it. Neither of them would say that they are committed to each other, but each of them expects the other to be faithful – at the moment.

- Rob is in his early thirties and Jane is 29. They met two and a half years ago when Rob's marriage was breaking up. When Rob's home was sold, he bought a flat and he and Jane moved in together. Marriage? Rob is waiting for his divorce to come through, but 'after what I went through' he is not sure that he would marry again. Jane thinks it's unimportant; they are 'as good as married'.

- Peter and Jenny met in their second year at university when they shared a house with a couple of other students. By the end of that year, 'we were regarded as a couple'. After graduation they found jobs in the same city and rented a flat together: 'there was no reason not to stay together'. Neither of them is sure about the future. Jenny says she would marry when they have children. Peter is considering a big career move and does not know if he ever wants children.

- Annie and Kurt are both in their late forties. They have lived together for nineteen years and have two teenage sons. When they started living together they were sure 'this was it'; that they wanted to be together for 'as long as we could imagine'. Marriage was not considered because they both felt it was too conventional. After a year they decided to buy a place of their own. They nearly married in order to qualify for a mortgage, but in the end it was not necessary. When Annie was pregnant with their first baby (a pregnancy they planned), there was the odd comment from family and friends about 'getting married', but they 'just kept on going as we were'. They don't rule marriage out: one day they might marry quietly 'just to sort out pensions and things'. They hope to be together 'till death do us part'.

- Sue is in her mid-twenties and Matthew is a couple of years older. When they met, the relationship was immediately 'very intense'. As they were sleeping together, they spent a lot of time staying over in each other's flats. Matthew wanted Sue to move in with him, but she did not want to give up her flat. Three months later, Matthew proposed to Sue: 'it was the right time in our lives to marry'. Both their families wanted a big wedding, which meant waiting another year. In the meantime, the couple went ahead with buying a flat and moved in together. 'There didn't seem any point in living apart if we were getting married in a year's time.'

- Lesley and Anthony were both in their early twenties when they met on holiday. They lived in different parts of the country and saw each other whenever they could. Both of them were shocked when Lesley became pregnant: 'we'd only been going out for a couple of months and didn't have any idea about the future'. Lesley knew she did not want a termination, but neither of them felt they could commit themselves to marriage – so they decided to move in together and see how things went. That was three years ago. Their daughter is now 2 and Lesley would like another child, but she would like to be married before getting pregnant again. Anthony can't see the point of marriage; things are fine as they are.

All these couples are likely to be classified as cohabitants. In a year's time some might appear as 'married', others as single, others as cohabiting, but possibly with a different partner. For, as these vignettes of cohabiting life illustrate, there are varying levels of commitment *within* partnerships as well as *between* the different couples. Perhaps the most interesting feature of these brief descriptions is the sense we get of the *drift* into cohabitation (apart from Sue and Matthew, who made their wedding plans before moving in together). In some instances, a sexual relationship slides into a domestic living arrangement; and as long as the relationship is satisfying, it continues. The couple stay together because there is no reason to leave, but the matter of the future may not be discussed, or even considered.

In a study of a group of cohabiting mothers, Susan McRae (1993) captures some of this sense of drift. Of the 228 cohabiting mothers in her original sample, seventy-seven were still cohabiting four years later. Some sixty-two women married *before* their babies were born, and fifty-seven married *after* the baby's birth. She comments:

> ... there appears to be a steady flow out of cohabiting motherhood into married motherhood. Therefore if we had carried out our interviews one year later, for example, or six months earlier, the numbers included in these two groups (those continuing to cohabit and those who married after the baby's birth) would have been different (p. 20).

These mothers were asked about the factors that influenced their decision to cohabit. Among the mothers who had married *after* the baby's birth, half stated that the pregnancy had influenced their decision to cohabit; their pregnancies were largely unplanned. Housing availability also had a marked influence upon the decision to set up home together. For those women who went on to marry their partner after cohabiting, about a quarter said that they had cohabited as a trial marriage. For the mothers who continued to cohabit, McRae remarks that *not* marrying was not necessarily the outcome of a deliberate or calculated decision: 'Rather, couples who live together (like married couples) simply may accept the day-to-day contours of their lives and not act to change them. Time passes surprisingly quickly, and unless there are compelling reasons to marry, marriage just might not happen' (p. 45).

Among the long-term cohabiting mothers, only 21 per cent declared opposition to marriage (they were the most likely to be the women who had cohabited for the longest time). Divorce (their own, their partner's, parents' or friends') had deterred 30 per cent of the women from marriage; 30 per cent said there was no advantage in marrying; 26 per cent said they could not afford a wedding; and for 19 per cent marriage had been delayed (they did not want to be pregnant at their wedding). For those mothers who married *after* the baby was born, the most important reason given was 'to ensure the security of their children'. Two-thirds of these mothers gave that reason compared with 28 per cent of mothers who married *before* their baby was born; for them, the most important reason had been to 'make a commitment' (53 per cent). Marrying for children, perhaps?

McRae also obtained information from one hundred married mothers who had *never* cohabited, but had gone straight into marriage. The family lives of these wives were little different from those of the cohabiting mothers: they were as likely or unlikely to share household tasks, leisure, problems and views on a range of social and family issues; and they were as happy or unhappy as other mothers. However, when McRae asked all the mothers in her sample to consider a 'second-chance scenario' – 'if they could live their lives over again, would they choose the same partner?' – only one out of two cohabiting women said 'yes', compared with three out of four of each of the other groups of married mothers (those who had not cohabited before marriage; those who married before their baby's birth; those who married after the birth of their baby). McRae considered that this lack of commitment to the partner suggested a degree of instability in cohabiting relationships. Maybe the key difference lies in the decision to marry crystallizing a sense of the future, a commitment for life which, according to John Eekelaar (Eekelaar and Katz, 1980), is the crucial characteristic that distinguishes it from cohabitation: 'Even a cohabitation formalised by declaration appears to operate on a different level to marriage, for it can be no more than a declaration of an existing state of affairs with no implications about future conduct, which still remains the essence of marriage' (p. 454).

Stable unions – partnership as an anchor

In our study of British newly-weds, the influence of future orientation upon action in the present first became apparent when we examined their retrospective accounts of courtship (Mansfield and Collard, 1988). In particular, we noticed that there were clear differences in the way couples planned and organized their lives before marriage and in the timing of the wedding itself. One group stood out dramatically: men and women who were not merely planning *what they would do* with their lives, but *who they would be*. Marriage provided a framework within which to become a certain kind of person and to maintain a particular way of life. Their orientation to the future was similarly apparent when they discussed their expectations of and attitudes towards becoming parents, their attitudes to change, and their hopes and fears about the future. Talking about children, especially in the abstract, is usually a mechanism for talking about the future. Charles Darwin was 'marrying for children'. Yet his vision of family life did not convey a fondness for children, even a desire to be a father; instead, he used 'children' as shorthand, a way of expressing that cocktail of hopes and fears that is 'the future'.

For the newly-weds in our study, falling in love had been the common explanation for matrimony, yet when further details emerged a purpose to marriage was discernible. The purpose was different for different people. Some wanted to have a family, others wanted to build a home together, and others wished to create a lifestyle in which the partners could flourish as individuals. Whatever the purpose, it was distinct from, although related to, the way in which the spouses got on with each other – their relationship. For many couples, the purpose was highly social. They had a sense of marriage existing outside the two of them; it was almost as if they had joined the 'Marriage Club' and, as a result, were 'doing married things'. Yet for the rest, marriage was a highly individual arrangement. The whole point of marriage was *being* married. The legal formalities of marriage meant simply that the specialness of 'our partnership' was recognized by others. In early discussions, we referred to the two groups as the 'M's and the 'm's.

We could detect more structure to the 'M' than the 'm' marriages. These couples had more clearly defined objectives. Sometimes they were expressed in familial terms: a desire to have a 'family of our own' or to provide another branch of *the* family. They were different from the 'm' marriages, where one or both spouses stressed their relationship as being of central importance and yet valued independence from one another as well. There were, then, two elements to these marriages: the partnership and the relationship. The type of partnership appeared to suggest the type of relationship and vice versa. The link between partnership and relationship is provided by the concept of meaning.

Peter Marris explored the concept of 'meaning' in his classic work *Loss and Change* (1974). He regarded meaning as a crucial organizing principle of human behaviour, a structure that related purposes to expectations so as to organize actions. Structures of meaning were defined as 'organized structures of understanding *and* emotional attachments by which grown people interpret and assimilate their environment'. Such a definition seems to be highly applicable to marriage. An 'organized structure of understanding' encompasses the sense of two individuals moving towards the future with shared goals (the partnership); and the 'emotional attachment' describes the relationship between the spouses. Marriage, then, comprises two interdependent elements: *the partnership* and *the relationship*. The partnership provides an anchor for the relationship, while the relationship absorbs and defines the structure of understanding, thereby sustaining the partnership.

At times when the relationship is under strain, the partnership is crucial, since it articulates the commitment (the reasons for staying together), thereby *anchoring* the relationship. At times when the partnership is changing (and children are particularly significant in this regard), the relationship will be a key factor, for if the partners are getting on well there is greater potential for revising the partnership to accommodate change, and thus to reach a new equilibrium between partnership and relationship.

A relationship without a partnership has no anchor, since commitment is articulated solely in the present. In Eekelaar's and Katz's (1980) terms, it is no more than 'a declaration of an existing state of affairs'. The relationship is kept going as long as it is satisfying to both partners. According to Giddens (1991), the use of the term 'relationship' for marriage indicates that in modern times the tie is freely chosen, and sought only for what it can bring the partners involved:

> Marriage becomes more and more a relationship initiated and kept going for as long as it delivers emotional satisfaction, to be derived from close contact with another. Other traits – even the seemingly fundamental ones such as having children – tend to become sources of 'inertial drag' on possible separation, rather than the anchoring features of the relationship (p. 89).

All marriages are partnerships in so far as partners have made a commitment to each other for the future. However, partnerships come in different forms (Mansfield, Collard and McAllister, 1996), and over the 'life' of a marriage the couple may move through a range of different partnership types. When the partnership breaks down, the structure of shared understanding collapses – that anchor is lost – and the marriage is unlikely to survive. Yet at times when the couple's relationship is not going well, the partnership may provide enough of an anchor to weather the storm.

The more that we investigate the physical, emotional, social and educational needs of children, the more we become aware of the importance of the environment within which they mature. There is a growing literature on the influence of the marital relationship on parenting attitudes and behaviour, and consequently upon child development. In large measure, ecological and family systems theory, and research, support the idea that the quality of the marital relationship and the relationship between parent and child are interdependent (Hinde and Stevenson-Hinde, 1988).

Marriage (or a 'committed' partnership), where there is an absence of serious conflict and where the partners are supportive of each other, is good for children. Yet the child-rearing years may be bad times for a marriage. The child's arrival can disrupt, or even weaken, the relationship that should cradle his or her upbringing. Having children together makes parents of couples; it does not necessarily create partnerships.

Legal marriage is not essential to the creation of a partnership, but recognition of the partnership by others, particularly people who matter to the partners, may be significant in helping the couple *articulate* their future commitment. Couples without any religious belief or a sense of tradition may seek new rituals to reinforce their notions of conjugality and to reassure themselves about the future:

> . . . ritual is endemic in situations of change, at those times in the life of an individual, group or society when there is greatest uncertainty and when people have difficulty in expressing their ideas and feelings in a more direct way. In fact, ritual is dynamic and creative, because it allows people to handle situations that are otherwise troubling and disruptive. Ritual not only brings order out of chaos, but relieves people's fears about their personal and collective futures (Gillis, 1985, p. 7).

The 1989 Children Act enables an unmarried couple who have a child to make a 'joint parental responsibility agreement'. For the small but growing group of cohabiting parents who make such agreements, this is a way of expressing their commitment to each other as *parents*. But the commitment is only as parents; while not a commitment to each other, and not 'marrying for children', it is, at least, a shared commitment to their child in the future.

Penny Mansfield

2
Who Comes First –
Partner or Child?

Love as a burger

Marriage, or committed cohabitation, is often idealized as a relationship in which each party can take it for granted that they come first with the other. It is in those terms that individuals describe what they want from a future or current partnership, while society endorses the physical and emotional exclusivity of marriage (and increasingly cohabitation) through law and folklore. Everyone assumes that such duos need, and are entitled to, protection from competing relationships with third parties – and such competition need not be sexual. Men's mothers (women's mothers-in-law) are presented as only marginally less dangerous than other kinds of Other Woman, and couples are also seen as vulnerable to same-sex friendships, especially to what goes on – in reality or fantasy – when either partner has a 'night out with the boys/girls'. It is as if partnerships require so much of people's relationship-potential – let us call it love – and the supply is so limited, that any they give outside their partnership must be stolen from it. Love as a burger: a bit for you, a bit for you; does that leave enough for him – and me?

It is not only in adult relationships that we play portion-control; we do it in children's relationships too. A mother asks herself: 'Will my child love the nanny more than he loves me? How can I arrange for him to love her just the right amount: enough that he'll be happy with her when I'm not there, but not so much that he'll miss her when she's not there and I am?' Amid many families agonizing about making childcare arrangements that are sufficiently warm and long-lasting, there are always a few whose concern is to prevent them becoming too much so. One woman employs a succession of non-English-speaking au pairs on short-term contracts: 'That way, there's never any question who the children prefer and look forward to. I enjoy my work enough that I don't mind spending money to be able to do it, but it's not worth one bit of my children's love. That's all mine.' And then, of course, there are the 'second-helping' families: stepfamilies. Can a child find a second helping of love for a stepfather or will that leave his natural father short? Can a step-parent be expected to love children who are not 'her own' when she – or he – already has children who are?

The traditional folklore of parenthood did not suggest that a mutually wanted baby was a threatening third party to his or her parents. Indeed, it was so widely assumed that 'a baby brings a couple together' that some couples conceived babies to serve as marital glue, and many were surprised when their offspring drove a wedge between them. Increasingly, research findings concerning the transition from couple to parents is overwriting that folklore. In the long run, children *do* deepen and enrich the relationships between most pairs of parents, but initially children drive many couples apart: 'No matter how much they love each other, no two people share the same values or feelings or have the same perspective on life, and few things highlight these personal differences as pointedly as the birth of a child' (Belsky and Kelly, 1994, p. 12).

New folklore does present a child – especially a first child – as an outsider to the parent-duo, and an outsider who, on the assumption that 'two's company, three's a crowd', is especially threatening because he or she is totally dependent and ever-present. To pursue the metaphor, children are represented as demanding an especially large bite of a relatively small burger. Babies now are often depicted as closer to marriage-solvent than marriage-glue, and parents – especially mothers – are alerted to particular behaviours that might intensify that threat and advised of ways to modify them. Although there is some truth and utility here, as there is in all folklore, this is not only simple to the point of being simplistic, but also based on a wholly false premise.

The undoubted, and increasingly well-documented, stresses of becoming parents do not arise because the child is an outsider and third party to the couple, but specifically because he or she is *not*. A child – especially a first child – is not something or somebody external to the parents, but the child within each of them as well as their joint product (Brazelton and Cramer, 1991). That being the case, it is pointless to ask whether individuals should put their partners or their children first. Distinctions are not clear-cut, and if mother, father and baby make up any kind of triangle, it certainly does not have objectively measurable and voluntarily alterable distances between its vertices. Unfortunately, the question is as popular as it is wrong-headed, and answers are as widely debated as they are unhelpful.

Popular advice suggests that while the action of the moment should be flexibly tailored to individual needs, partners' overall policy should always be to put each other (and themselves) before their children. The main rationale is that parents who behave in this way will keep each other happy; that if they are happy, it is more likely that their marriage or partnership will remain intact, and that only an intact partnership can assure security and happiness for the children. Secondary arguments in support of this judgement are not so much in favour of priority for partners, as against priority for children. In essence, these suggest that to put a child first is to 'spoil' him or her. Such a child will fail to learn that he or she 'is not the only pebble on the beach'. Furthermore, parental indulgence is 'no kindness' because however happy it may make a child in the short term, it will inevitably lead to parental resentment, and therefore to unhappiness for the child in the long term.

This message is especially targeted on mothers. They are exhorted to ensure that they give their own needs priority over those of their children because personal time and space will make them better mothers and, crucially, better partners. It is certainly true that self-care and mother-care are enmeshed. Being cooped up alone all day with a mother who is depressed and feels isolated is as serious a threat to a child's development as to a woman's mental health. It is also true that, far from being a gift, self-sacrifice often places a burden of guilt on the recipient, even if gratitude is not overtly demanded. Nevertheless, these exhortations are based on unquestioned assumptions that need questioning. It is widely assumed, for example, that a woman would not *want* to be with a child as much as her child might want to be with her. That, in turn, has led to some absurdly extreme positions such as the presumption that a woman will *necessarily* be a better mother and wife the more time she spends fulfilling other roles that enable her to 'be herself'. In parts of the United States, most notably Manhattan, women who regard themselves, and are regarded, as devoted mothers, are encouraged to spend almost all their time submerged in adult life and to emerge to be with their children for only an hour or two of 'quality time'. Spending one superb hour with a mother who is 'highly fulfilled as a person' (and presumably highly fulfilled as a wage-earner) is supposed to do more for a child than a mother could do if she were around for hours of that ordinary old family stuff, like making meals and jokes, cleaning up faces and language, squabbling and hugging. Of course, the one good hour is better than none, and also better for all concerned than a whole bunch of *bad* ones. But is that hour as good as two or three? And who says a bunch *would* be bad? When surveys ask large numbers of American mothers what they need most to ease working lives that tend to be even more stressful than in Europe, it is not 'time for myself' (or even 'affordable childcare') that heads their list (though both may appear on it); the leading item is almost invariably 'more time to spend with the children'.

For some women (although not all), at some stages in their mothering (although not perpetually), exhortations to put themselves before their children are meaningless because their link with a child is so all-embracing that there is no separately identifiable adult person whose personal gratifications need protecting from family demands. Their self-sacrifice may be more apparent than real. Women often do what their children want primarily because they themselves are incapable, for the moment, of wanting to do anything different. Many women, for example, almost always stay at home in the evening when their children are small. Some of those women would like to go out but, balancing their own pleasure against the thought of their children's unhappiness if they woke, stay in for the children's sakes. But others actually prefer to stay at home, not because they have lost their taste for parties, or movies, or their partners' company, but because the thought of the children's unhappiness if they woke makes them too uncomfortable to enjoy themselves.

The image of women sacrificing themselves to their children is as often in the eyes of uncomprehending beholders as in the behaviour of observed mothers (Leach, 1987), and it is an image with a sexist sub-text. The sub-text says that women should put their partners before their progeny and never allow themselves to become so absorbed in motherhood that they neglect the partnership that gave rise to it. Extraordinarily sentimental messages on this topic emerge from every level of the media, including advice columns of serious intent: 'Look after your romance and your husband's sexuality. Take care of your man. Your child may not like being left behind while the two of you go out for evenings, away for weekends, or vanish behind doors that demands for drinks of water will not unlock, but such measures "keep the family together" and are therefore in everyone's long-term interests.' This text is printed in bold if the man in question is a stepfather. His adult (romantic/sexual) needs demand even more pointed priority from his partner since the children 'aren't even his own'.

The absence of matching exhortations to men to put partners before children is certainly sexist, but is also realistic: more women are more likely to submerge themselves in mothering their babies than men are in fathering them. Biological gender-differences are real, and significant even before differences in socialization and cultural expectations are grafted on to them. However, the notion that a man who is struggling with the move from couple to threesome can (and should) be 'kept sweet' in this calculated way is not only sexist, but also risks reducing the extent to which the partnership operates as a mutual support system under the stress of parenthood, trivializing the real conflicts it faces and infantilizing the father. It also risks exacerbating the special difficulties of step-parenting relationships by suggesting that mothers try to behave as if they were exclusively adult partners, and that these were just some children they happened to have around who would make no difference. Children *do* make a difference. In fact, that is probably the only universal truth about them. No attempt to pretend that they will not, or do not, can ever help family relationships. So any woman who feels that a man does her a favour by 'taking on her children' may be well advised to remain head of a single-parent household, and any man who feels that way may be well advised to let her.

For women and men, whether they are parents by blood, marriage, adoption or conviction, escape or respite from children may strengthen or revive their couple-relationships, but it will not make them more of a family; and it is in the family that they are, or must learn to be, partners.

Changing families

The transition from couple to parents, twosome to threesome, is almost always difficult. One day, most children will enrich their parents' sense of 'us', and therefore their partnerships and their lives, but there is this day, and a lot of other days, to be lived through first – and for some couples, 'us' will be out of date before those days are over. Many of the difficulties are doubtless inherent in the business of becoming parents, and especially in the bio-social differences between mothers and fathers. However, some of these difficulties may be caused, or made intransigent, by particular demands and risks that face people who are having children here and now; conflicts that are not only part of the deeply personal business of becoming a parent *per se*, but are also embedded in the wider social context in which that transition takes place.

Far-flung societal change has altered the meaning and the experience of 'family', defining both almost exclusively in terms of the 'nuclear family' – parents and their dependent children. Since the relationships between these are the most important in our lives, we expect a great deal of this residual 'family' – more, perhaps, than it can easily provide without a significant wider family to be the nucleus *of*. Lacking a supportive infrastructure outside, and the dilution of multiple generations and individuals inside, nuclear families may be so fragile and intense that both their man–woman and parent–child relationships are vulnerable.

The concept of family as an institution created by marriage, or by the birth of a woman's first baby, and primarily for and about children, is both recent and Western. Of course, children have always been integral to concepts of marriage and family everywhere in the world. But in most times and places, 'family' is a top-down model, starting from the most senior, the grandparent generation or dead ancestors, with young married couples low down the hierarchy and children at the very bottom. Such families are not primarily concerned with children and childish matters, but with adults' needs and adult concerns – with property and wealth, great or small; with position, status and obligation; and with political and religious allegiances. Marriages, of course, often enlarge and enrich family networks, and are often contracted to do so, but in most of the world, marriages and the children born within them do not *create* families, and the concept of 'nuclear family' is so foreign to many cultures that it is untranslatable. To us, it is obvious that biological parents and their natural children form unique, and to some extent exclusive, social groups. Yet to people reared in other parts of the world it is equally obvious that they do not (Gelles, 1995).

Children are no less important to top-down, adult-oriented families than to Western nuclear ones, and no less wanted by individual parents. However, the nature of children's importance does vary from culture to culture. One important difference between the post-industrial West and much of the rest of the world is that, however much we may want children, we do not need them in any practical sense – but are burdened by them. Elsewhere – and depending exactly where – children may be needed to validate marriage settlements and inheritance arrangements, and to broaden kinship ties through their own betrothals and marriages. They may be needed to work, to help adults work, or to free adults to work by taking over the care of younger children and animals. Above all, they may be needed to ensure support for the parents and their generation in old age.

Being needed is clearly a mixed blessing for children. Being associated with child labour, it may mean that they cannot be spared for education – or even that they are trapped in wage-slavery. It may mean an early, arranged, even a personally unwanted, marriage. But although needed children may often find themselves tragic pawns in adult games, knowing that they are an integral and necessary part *of* those games, and of the adult world that plays them, may nevertheless give them a kind of respect and self-respect that many of our children lack, and protect them from adult concern that can sometimes be so intense that it is smothering. Children's childishness is universally accepted and enjoyed (when there is time), but most of the world sees children as potential adults, and the play and learning of childhood as part of their apprenticeship to the adult world. The West, on the contrary, sees children almost as a separate species from adults, and childhood as an end in itself. This often makes childhood successes and failures disproportionately and painfully important in the present, and difficult to leave behind in a future requiring self-confidence and high self-esteem.

Most adults want to reproduce themselves. People in all parts of the world who have been asked why they want children have given similar answers, irrespective of their control over their own fertility and of whether children were a necessity or a luxury in their lives – wanted *and* needed, or only wanted. The answers best translate as 'for pleasure and for fun' (Goodnow and Collins, 1990). So it is not surprising that Western adults, who can usually choose whether to have any children or not, mostly choose to have at least one. They have them because they want them, and they are not unique in that. Yet they have them despite personal costs that *are* unique in human history. Children ruin post-industrial Western lifestyles and careers – especially women's careers. They restrict the individuality and autonomy that our culture values so highly; limit the sexuality we rely on to keep our relationships glued together; and cost more money than anyone can comfortably afford. It is estimated that any woman, rich or poor, who has and keeps a child, will thereby lose half the lifetime income she could otherwise expect to earn, irrespective of whether she works for a wage and pays for childcare, or takes time out of work and does the caring herself.

Inevitably, the extraordinarily high costs of Western parenthood are matched by unrealistically high expectations of its compensatory pleasures. A young woman, nearing the end of a longed-for pregnancy, explains: 'Once I have a baby of my own, there'll always be one person in the world who loves me best whatever I do', while a first-time father attending his baby's six-month developmental check expostulates with the doctor: 'Don't tell me he's normal. I don't want him to be normal. I want him to be best.' All parents everywhere have a substantial investment of self in their children, and all over the world some demand gratitude from children who did not ask to be born: 'After all I've done for you . . .' However, when parents have (and expect to lose) several children, there is at least some pleasure in a child's continuing survival irrespective of his performance, and a chance that when one child disappoints the parents, another will please them – or at least distract them. In one- or two-child nuclear families there may be neither refuge nor escape from the emotional firing line.

Being the focus of so much adult attention and care in childhood would have a great deal to recommend it if it was the foundation of close familial ties that were lifelong. Yet Western children only have this degree of importance *as* children, and they are not encouraged to stay around once they are adult. As soon as they reach some marker of maturity, such as the end of compulsory schooling or higher education, they are expected to leave home and prove themselves in a workplace. Most children are their parents' heirs, but few grow up with any sense of apprenticeship to an adult world they will grow into and then take over. And the few who do – being destined, perhaps, for family businesses – evoke a mixture of envy and sympathy. In this culture, young adults are supposed to see themselves as separate, autonomous individuals rather than as links in a continuing family chain; to 'grow out of' their families of origin rather than into them; to move away from roots and from the older generation; and to prove themselves as enterprising individuals. No wonder the scarcity of jobs, student grants and benefit entitlements that is keeping more and more young adults at home and dependent on parents is causing family friction.

Life without family, though, can be very lonely, even if individual enterprise is successful – and desperately depressing if it is not. We are, after all, group animals. Like young lions ejected from the pride, young people team up with their contemporaries, grouping together around the college bar or pub if they have college places or work and money; on street corners and waste ground if they do not.

Sexual partnership and 'starting a family of your own' is the socially approved way out of that isolation, but most sexual partnerships are conducted *in* a kind of social isolation that puts them under tremendous strain. Although extended families play a larger part in people's lives than commentators usually suggest, and an ageing population means that many adults have their own parents still alive, few have extensive networks of aunts, uncles and cousins. And even where there is no actual scarcity of extended blood-and-marriage relationships, there may still be a shortage of intimacy because it is not acceptable – or certainly not admirable – for young adults to turn to older family members for emotional support. In a recent Gallup survey of 1,000 couples, 'Living apart from in-laws' was listed as the fifth most important factor contributing to a successful partnership. For every woman who lives apart from her in-laws, there is a man who must live apart from his parents and his siblings, and therefore a niece or nephew or two who are deprived of an uncle . . .

However much two people 'love' each other, romantically, passionately; however much they also like each other and complement each other, it is a lot to expect of a woman and a man that they should meet each other's needs for many different kinds of relationship with many different people. To be satisfactory to each other as lovers, companions and friends is demanding enough, but can the woman also be her partner's mother or sister when those are the relationships he needs? And when she is the one who needs her mother, can he fill that role for her too? There are many sexual partnerships today that previous generations would have considered exceptionally close, but current divorce rates suggest that they are also exceptionally prone to failure. Our high expectations and demands probably contribute to both extremes, and the birth of a child may often mark the point at which asking a lot of a relationship sours into asking too much of it. Is it reasonable to expect a couple to incorporate a child emotionally, and absorb the enormous extra responsibilities of parenthood, with neither a major upheaval in their relationship nor a substantial increase in its external supports?

Pressures on parenting

Incorporating children into adult lifestyles is more difficult now than it used to be in Western societies, and than it still is in many others, because the paid work that fills parents' lives cannot be shared with children, and responsibility for children's day-to-day lives is not automatically shared with other family members. International statistics suggest that the time children spend with a parent – whether or not they are interacting – has dropped by 40 per cent in this generation (Mattox, 1990). The principal reason, of course, is that mothers now spend fewer hours at home with children and more hours at work, while fathers have not changed their hours to match. They do spend an infinitesimally increased amount of time with their children, but in most industrial countries they spend very little less at work. So despite all those exhortations to mothers, there seems little real risk of children *or* partners being given priority. The question that dominates the daily lives of many parents is not 'Who comes first, my partner or my child?', but 'Which comes first, my job or my family?' Becoming a parent often means the beginning of serious conflict between caring and earning – a conflict that may become even more acute as the waning dependency of children overlaps with the dawning dependency of their grandparents. Once the first adaptation to parenthood has been made, it is not so much competition between child and partner that troubles people as competition between the personal and the professional, the private and the commercial. Time is money. Which is more important: time to earn money to spend on children, or time to spend with them?

Earlier generations adopted a gendered approach to such issues, but did not thereby avoid or solve them. Traditional divisions of labour tended to mean that men put the job first and had money but little time, while women put children first and had time but no money. Neither had free choice. If children benefited – and it is likely that for the comparatively privileged children of the middle classes, at least, life following the Second World War and into the 1970s *was* more stable – they did so at women's expense. It was, after all, female discontent with the 1950s version of family values that powered the women's movement and thereby changed the world.

In an idealized modern Western partnership, these issues are not gendered. Just as men and women are supposed to be equal in bed, in the bank and in the boardroom, so fathers and mothers are supposed to be interchangeably 'parents'. Unfortunately, none of those kinds of equity has been fully achieved, and certainly not the parenting kind. Growing numbers of men are increasingly involved in parenting their children, and even more say they would like the chance to be. Yet children are still primarily a women's problem, and one with which they must cope without the traditional network of widely extended family, by blood and marriage, that made a safety net for children. Women expect – and are expected – to take an equal part in what was traditionally a male world of paid work, and because jobs may be more readily available or better matched to females, they sometimes take the greater part. But men still seldom expect – are almost never expected, and may not even be *allowed* – to take an equal part in the traditionally female world of child-rearing.

Men-who-are-fathers bear a heavy responsibility for the double burden carried by women. Women-who-are-mothers are likely to be blamed by *somebody*, however they divide that load. Those who spend most of their time at home with children are indicted for 'living off other tax-payers' or 'letting themselves go', while those who spend most of their time at work are accused of selfishness or neglecting the children. And if nobody else blames them, then mothers, who are spread so thinly between opposing responsibilities that nothing they do ever feels like quite enough, will blame themselves. Policies matter, too (Leach, 1994); and since this is a democracy, every one of us must share responsibility for the absence of family-friendly policies as a whole as well as for specific disasters, such as a Child Support Agency that does not support children, and the rejection of paternity-leave legislation after months spent stressing the importance of fathers to families. What really matters, though, is not who is to blame for our overall lack of family-friendliness, but what is happening to the only people who are clearly blameless. The privileged children of rich Western nations are not having an easy time.

Whatever is done to make society more friendly to today's children will also make it better for yesterday's children – us – and for tomorrow's children – theirs – because, parents or not, we are all children first. Nationally and internationally, assigning children a new social, economic and political priority as apprentices and heirs to the adult world would open up policies of benefit for everyone. Priority for children's care and education would cost less than the wasted potential and the clean-up costs of present neglect. Appropriate employment policies could enhance efficiency while giving parents choice and time. True gender equality in caring as well as earning would benefit men as well as women.

Yet giving children priority at the familial and personal level is a very different matter. I do not believe that the conflicts suggested by the title of this chapter can be addressed by answering 'children'. Indeed, I do not believe that the question, 'Who comes first – partner or child?' can have a useful answer, because anyone who asks it is already deeply in the kind of trouble that such an answer is supposed to prevent. It may be life-and-death trouble – as in 'Which shall I rescue first from this burning building, my mate or my/our child?' It may be temper-tantrum trouble – as in 'Shall I devote the rest of this Sunday afternoon to helping my partner mend the car or helping my child finish her model?' It may be trivial trouble – as in 'Baked beans which he loves and she hates, or peas which he hates and she loves?' But even the most trivial of such troubles is troublesome because bringing the question into consciousness means that the questioner is distancing herself from both partner and child and each of them from the other; seeing them as objects and manipulating them in relation to her separate self. And if that happens often, however she usually answers, her next question to herself is likely to be: 'What about *me*?'

A functioning family does not coldly calculate its members' rights, constantly checking: 'Do I *want* to do this?' 'Is it fair that I have to do that?' A family that is run by such calculations is not functioning. Institutions only work if they are greater than the sum of their individual parts, and families are no exception to that rule.

This woman does not look forward to a wet Sunday afternoon walk. Her partner would much prefer a Sunday afternoon nap. Their child is always happy to watch a video. None of them wants to go out, so why are they all putting on wellingtons? Because what they do on

Sundays is family stuff, and although no one of them would choose a wet walk, all three will enjoy it . . .

Penelope Leach

3
Why Are Three-Person Relationships Difficult?

Everybody needs a 'somebody'

The genesis of this chapter coincided with a particular weekend when I was acutely conscious that my own family structure had altered considerably. My eldest son qualified, so his increase in salary would enable him to leave the top room in our house; my daughter returned to a remote marine station; my other son disappeared off to university; and, after fourteen years of faithfulness, our dog died. I was reminded of the old theological debate as to when life starts: the Catholic arguing for the moment of conception, the Nonconformist for the moment of birth, and the Rabbi for the day the kids leave home and the dog dies!

Hence, thirty years on, we were left with just the two of us in the house. This of course meant that 'somebody' had to go – the 'somebody' who is that useful adjunct in so many households. 'Somebody' has tidied my papers away. 'Somebody' has finished my shampoo. 'Somebody' has left all the towels wet. 'Somebody' didn't let the cat out. 'Somebody' has moved my toolbox. 'Somebody' has taken my dressmaking scissors. A 'somebody' is, of course, that indispensable container of thoughtlessness, selfishness, forgetfulness and general life deficiencies that interrupt our smoothly running, perfectly laid plans – the plans that would certainly come to fruition in abundance if it was not for the impingement of others who are so disruptive to the plans' completion!

The possible bodily manifestations in which 'somebody' could materialize were now reduced to two. Would we find it essential to have a third, or several 'thirds', in order for us to preserve some conflict-free fantasy of our own self-esteem? Would the responsibility of accepting the limitations of memory, selfishness and thoughtlessness in oneself and others be manageable, and would we be able to regard these with all the necessary regrets and humour?

The change I am describing is a different developmental hurdle to that of partners becoming parents. It is, rather, the reciprocal, when parents, becoming partners again, make new adjustments, experience losses, and re-find freedoms with old and new pleasures. However, the change does serve to emphasize the importance of the different capacities necessary for three-person relationships as distinct from two-person relationships, both in their actuality – the concrete interaction of one person with another – and also in their internal mental representations – the emotional foundations that are the bases for constructing all relationships. Although partnerships need to renegotiate interactions and behaviours when children leave home, one hopes that the internal mental set of the individuals will be primarily that of three-person relationships, so that the children are not dismissed, forgotten or distorted out of all recognition of themselves by parental fantasies. However, if the internal mental sets are primarily two-person, then the absent 'third person' will become the embodiment of all imperfections that are disavowed by the couple and that oscillate in uneasy tension with equally unrealistic idealizations.

The same problem occurs in those parents who, for whatever reason, are separated. They have to maintain a relationship with the absent figure, in reality and within their mental representations, both for themselves and for their children. Separations can be necessary because of training needs, business commitments, wars or availability of work. These times of disrupted relationships, which are temporarily unsupported by the presence of a third person, do put strain on the capacities necessary to maintain relationships. Under strain there is a tendency to return to the mental set of a two-person relationship, a mental set governed by mutual idealization, exclusivity, denigration of outsiders and fear of persecution. These frames of mind result in social isolation, with a limited and repetitive mental life that is constricted by having to maintain the fixity of a vulnerable self-perception. Unacceptable shortcomings that are reflected in the mirror of our own self-perception must rapidly find some way of being placed outside ourselves and attributed to another; we require that other to reflect back to us only our ideal image. This mirroring of self is discussed by Felman (1993) when commenting on a man's requirement for the woman to reflect his self-image, to be a mirror for his narcissistic gain. She quotes Virginia Woolf, who wrote, 'Women have served all these centuries as looking-glasses, possessing the magic and delicious power of reflecting the figure of a man at twice its natural size' (p. 36).

The usefulness of a receptacle for deficiencies of the self depends on the receptacle, the third person, 'somebody', accepting the function of being such a container. Physical absence clearly does not allow the recipient to refute the misattributions, so the absentee is most useful. When the intended container is present, they may be unable to refuse the role because of uncertainty about their own motivations, deliberate attempts to confuse their understanding (as parents can so easily do to children), or they may be colluding with the misattributions because of their own conscious or unconscious gains.

When the misattributions are refused, then something else has to happen to those imperfections. They could be accepted back as part of the giver's own imperfect self, but the pressure to maintain an ideal self-image does not so easily allow such reintegration of unwanted thoughts, impulses and behaviours. They do not conform to that wished-for ideal and do not confirm the self-esteem that is based on that ideal. Hence, what is likely to happen within the two-person relationship, the partnership, is that various shared ideas and fantasies that are agreed on as if they were fixed, absolute and matters of fact, are repetitively rotated through differing receptacles – a sound recycling process serving to conserve the *status quo*. This mutual sharing and confirming of ideas occurs at conscious and unconscious levels. It is aimed at protecting self-esteem and reducing conflict within the individual, while at the same time protecting the rules of the partnership and, supposedly, giving a conflict-free zone that can be shared by the partners to cement the relationship.

Here, concepts of self and of partnership are clearly intimately related. Individuals will have ideas about what a partnership means to them, and how any partnership should be constructed in order to maintain their personal self-esteem. The partnership inevitably contains a lesser or greater amount of idealization. Sensual pleasure and genital sexuality are usually essential elements in creating and maintaining adult partnerships, but along with physical attraction and desire comes the mental luggage – the essentials 'wanted on voyage' – which makes the journey possible, together with the 'excess baggage' that impedes the well-planned journey. The essentials we need to take on board are the concepts that an adult partnership is possible, that it will be alive, adaptive and lead to creativity. When these essential concepts are deficient, then the partnership must, of necessity, have limitations. This does not mean that a partnership started on some idealizations as the basis for mutual delight cannot mature and develop into a more realistic and time-lasting stability; this is what happens in most partnerships, but it is no easy voyage. It is generosity that allows and welcomes the intrusion of third persons such as babies, allowing them to be experienced as what they are without excessive resentment and jealousy of them for joining the partnership.

Losing our illusions

In order to have a reasonable chance of a successful partnership, the individuals concerned will have negotiated conflicts in their own psychological development. Those negotiations will allow them to see themselves, at some point in time, sharing the creation of a new life and being able to manage the inevitable rivalries, frustrations, hurts, disappointments, jealousies and envies that the loss of exclusivity provokes.

The loss of the illusion of possessive exclusivity as of right is probably the most difficult developmental hurdle to be negotiated in life. The illusion is, perhaps, never fully relinquished; it reappears, or is reawakened, in all the wishes to have special rights to possessions or activities that exclude others. Others are excluded from clubs, from lands, from humanity itself, because they do not have those special qualities, supposedly possessed and owned by the excluder, which are promulgated in the rationalizations made for having possessive rights. Rationalizations are often based on religion, or social class, or education, or history, or ethnic origins. There are a whole range of spurious reasons that can be used to distance others, deny them their human qualities, and fix on them all the imperfections of humanity while claiming all purity for the excluder.

This is not to minimize differences. That is a route that opens up the false affirmation that all things are the same. Such a falsehood, in itself, becomes a rationalization for denying any ownership by another of what rightly belongs to them, so that the plundering of what correctly belongs to another can be justified, whether it is of the mind – honesty, sanity and intelligence – or matter – land, jobs, even transplant organs. The differentiation of 'mine' and 'not mine' depends on a secure sense of self, a security based on knowing that what is given by the other under their impulses of thoughtfulness, kindness, generosity and love is not a submissive response to the self's imperative for exclusive possessiveness, but given freely and independently without duress.

The illusion of exclusive possessiveness is an appropriate state of mind for the small infant in mother's arms who, during feeding, is both firmly locked on to the nipple and has the sense that mother's mind is engaged with him or her. Her primary maternal preoccupation (Winnicott, 1956) with the feeding process incorporates both the physical experiences – sucking, digestion of milk, gut movements, hand movements, body movements – and mental experiences – the states of mind of eagerness, anxiety, passion, delight and frustration. This psychological attentiveness of the mother is conveyed to the infant by gesture, speech, tone and facial expression, so that the infant develops a sense of 'at-oneness' both with the breast and with the mother's state of mind. The mother's state of mind is able to be used by the infant to confirm its own states of mind, but is also maturely separate from it (Bion, 1963). This capacity to be temporarily identified with the child while remaining separate is the basis for real empathy which, in turn, leads to appropriate responsiveness. It is not uncommon for the older infant, who is discovering a capacity to give and take back, at some stage to proffer a biscuit or rusk to mother as if to feed her. The empathic mother realizes that the child is not at a stage to be able to be so generous and self-depriving, and will only pretend to nibble the biscuit, while at the same time emotionally accepting the practice generosity and 'pretend' self-deprivation. However, I have seen the 'pretend' gift being accepted as real, with someone gobbling up the biscuit to the utter shock, incomprehension and wailing grief of the child.

We know that the children of mothers who have suffered from puerperal depression can have great difficulty in developing ordinary social interactions with other children when they reach school age (Murray, 1994). They find it difficult to share games and playthings, or to be content with what they have chosen when playing alongside other children. If they see another child with something different from that which they have, then they want to have what the other child has, or to have the other's toy as well as their own, or to take all the toys that should be for shared play. Sharing for them does not just seem difficult, but actually appears to threaten their very existence and stability. When playing games, they find it difficult to take turns and endure the least setbacks, even when they are winning. It is as if, as in a game of snakes and ladders, any snake is a disaster and no ladder safe enough. It is possible that the sad lack of maternal attentiveness occurring within a puerperal depression may be experienced by the infant as the premature intrusion of a third person who is felt to occupy mother's mind, disrupting the normal stage-appropriate, mother–child exclusive possessiveness. If this is so, it could prematurely excite early jealousy as well as envy, at a time when the infant does not have the mental capacity to deal with such feeling states. The infant may then invoke excessive and inappropriate demands for exclusive and total possession, the frustration of which results in increased envies and jealousies, with a vicious circle of felt deprivation and unsatisfied demand. The premature sense of the intrusion of a third person during the feeding event creates anxiety that later interferes with the normal development of coping with the frustrations of sharing, taking turns and overcoming setbacks.

In contrast, the infant who experiences developmentally appropriate physical and psychological attentiveness is gradually able to accommodate the experience of frustration and its attendant feelings. The child is then not devastated when it becomes aware that the breast belongs to mother, that mother is separate and functions independently, that she has relationships with father, other adults and with brothers and sisters. Nevertheless, the wish to retain some sense of one's own central importance is part of the human condition. Much of the development of human thought and science can be seen as reflecting the gradual relinquishment of the omnipotent view that man is the centre of the universe, that it is his place by right and excludes all others.

The origin and development of the individual sense of self is echoed in the history and development of the mass, phylogeny following ontogeny. Greek astronomy held the view that the Earth was the centre of a great rotating sphere, with all the heavenly bodies orbiting around it. This was accepted for 1,400 years until it was challenged by Copernicus and his notion that it is the Sun that is the centre and the Earth just a planet which, along with other planets, circles the Sun. The illusion of centrality was not to be surrendered lightly. Martin Luther dealt with Copernicus summarily in terms of Holy Writ saying, 'This fool wishes to reverse the entire science of Astronomy; but sacred Scripture tells us that Joshua commanded the Sun to stand still and not the Earth' (Golding, 1965, p. 39), as if this confirmed that the Sun did revolve around the Earth. The advent of the astronomical telescope enabled Galileo to confirm the Copernican system, but Galileo's book was banned by the Church. He was summoned to Rome by the Inquisition and forced to recant his views.

Similarly, prior to Darwin, man was regarded as having a unique and superior place in the universe. Darwin, though, destroyed man's view of human centrality with his evolutionary theory. His theory aroused bitter controversy because it did not agree with the literal sense of the Book of Genesis. It was deemed unphilosophical and degrading to the dignity of human nature. Thomas Huxley, defending Darwin in debate with the Bishop of Oxford (Samuel Wilberforce, son of William Wilberforce who abolished the slave trade), was attacked by the Bishop with the contemptuous query as to whether it was on his mother's side as well as on his father's that Huxley was descended from the apes. Huxley's devastating retort was that he was not ashamed to have an ape for an ancestor, but would be ashamed to be connected with such a man as the Bishop, who used great gifts to obscure the truth (Bowlby, 1990).

As the child's view of its own universe widens, it allows the recognition that it is only one of many people orbiting others. The strains and conflicts involved in relinquishing illusions of exclusive possessiveness are softened by the possession of the comforters: silky, blanket or teddy. These transitional objects (Winnicott, 1958), which the parents know are imbued with special qualities and exclusive ownership, help to ease the pain and sorrow for the child when he or she is not the centre of the world. Mother does not orbit around the child; it is the child who is satellite to the mother. Holding on to a security blanket enables the child to tolerate the tension of losing the illusion of possessing the breast, which belongs to mother, and losing exclusivity. The child is then able to tolerate the idea of the breast being given to other babies, whether real or imagined. The child's loss of centrality is accompanied by the realization of mother's relationships with other siblings, as other planets in orbit around her, along with the father who, like a comet, puts in brilliant, though perhaps occasional, appearances! The awareness of the special and sexual relationship of the parents creates rivalry with the parent of the same sex and rivalry with the children – both real and imagined – produced by parental intercourse.

Two-person relationships are based on the paradigm of exclusive possessiveness by one of the other as of right. Maintaining these two-person relationships depends on sharing idealizations, of themselves and of each other, along with consequent denigrations of those outside the closed relationship. The essential change needed to develop three-person relationships is a diminishing reliance on idealization. Diminishing idealization lessens the demands for perfection within the other and within oneself. It then enables deficits and imperfections to be acknowledged in oneself and within the partnership without denigration or contempt, avoiding that pernicious trick of magnanimity where the supposed acknowledgement of one's own faults is more condoning than genuinely regretful. Diminished idealization lessens the need to find fault with others, while at the same time reducing the need to be perfect oneself. Partners look at themselves in a more realistic way; a 'third person' can be admitted into their orbits and also have a realistic identity of their own. This ultimately leads to the development of wider social contacts and a fruitful life of interpersonal relationships.

Individuals stuck within the framework of two-person relationships are under tremendous strain. They have to make sure that what they consider to be bad thoughts and feelings stay outside them and are firmly located in others, while at the same time maintaining in themselves a standard of perfection which is demanded in a reciprocal way as part of the system that excludes blemish. These strains are often exacerbated as a partnership develops towards parenthood. Winnicott (1960) tried to help lessen these strains with his concept of the 'good enough' mother. He wanted to replace the strain of an idealized, perfect motherhood with a more realistic and functional ideal: an ideal that allowed imperfections and misalignments without precipitating savage, persecuting guilt for any failures in attaining perfection. Such failures are inherent in impossible idealizations.

Realigning the universe

Many years ago I was asked to see a young woman who was expecting her second baby. After the birth of her first child, she had experienced quite a severe puerperal depression which had necessitated psychiatric treatment. Her doctor wondered if there was anything I could offer that might help to ease things for her in this second pregnancy. I saw her, together with her husband, and listened to her plans for the birth. I listened to a eulogy for her own mother, next door to whom she still lived. This grandmother was presented as a paragon of grandmothers who would provide all the supports possible for the forthcoming event; my patient thought it would be impossible to contemplate the birth without her. By now, the increasingly restless father could contain himself no longer and burst out with 'Your mother's an old bat!' It was then possible to address the imperative idealization of motherhood that was imposing such an impossible strain on this young mother. She subsequently negotiated the birth successfully with a more realistic attitude towards her own mother, who could be helpful, while gaining greater confidence in her own capacities and ordinary limitations. This illustrates the strain of idealizing the two-person state, and also the usefulness of having a partner who, when two-person states of mind are exaggerated because of doubt and anxiety, can utilize their capacity for three-person relationships to help another to manage developmental conflicts in a better way.

The development from two-person to three-person relationships is not easily achieved because it involves many repeated blows to self-esteem and the ensuing sadness that one is never quite so special, never quite so unique, never quite so exclusive, never quite so much in possession of strength and goodness, as one had always wanted to believe. We never achieve that illusory state of being an idealized child of a virgin mother and an impotent old father, a child hailed as the rightful saviour of the world. In the ordinary run of events, human development is a struggle with the conflict between retaining a special place in the order of things, by hook or by crook, and at the same time trying to be in touch with the realities of life, including the strengths and limitations of oneself. The struggle with this conflict continues throughout life, with its own unexpected twists and turns never delivering *exactly* what was ordered.

Maintaining the illusion of exclusive possessiveness as of right is a very powerful adhesive for creating and sustaining relationships between couples. However, when this superglue is weakened, without the more mature capacities of three-person relationships being in place, partnerships are threatened with breakdown and disastrous disruption. In couples whose mental sets are predominantly two-person, then not only are other adult relationships problematic, but also the advent of a child is likely to impose excessive strain. The relationship of the child with either parent may produce feelings of resentment in the other that their needs or rights are being ignored, and not properly attended to by the partner. The wounding of a fragile self-esteem may be intolerable, and reactions to it can disrupt the mutual and appropriate idealization between infant and mother.

When this ordinary developmental stage is satisfactory, the infant and mother gradually separate, allowing awareness of other relationships – such as the presence of a potent and sexual father. The infant is then strengthened by the experience of how the couple relate to each other and include the child in their own and other relationships. The child unconsciously takes into itself, and makes its own, the ways that the parents relate to each other, whether it is with mutual concern or selfish self-righteousness (Balint, 1993). Even in later life, when a child may consciously decide that he or she will never be like a particular aspect of a parent and never carry out some piece of parental behaviour that was abhorrent, the problem of the unconscious identification with the parental relationships will continue to bedevil expectations and demands of partnerships. These unconscious identifications with apparently unwelcome aspects of the parents will be battled with, but they will become especially apparent at times of stress. At these times, the stressed adult may, unexpectedly and distressingly, find themselves behaving in a similar fashion to the way they experienced some parental behaviour that they thought wrong or misguided, although they may now start to justify it in themselves.

Relationships between couples are never easy, and the strain of idealizing two-person relationships imposes difficulties in accepting and accommodating disappointments, limitations, faults and defects, both in oneself and in others. Any spoiling of idealizations can cause the relationship to degenerate into expressions of savage cruelty, righteousness and selfishness. Hopes and idealizations that are not sustained or achieved through the ordinary life process can precipitate bitter resentment and recriminations.

In Strindberg's *The Dance of Death* (1991), a couple, whose children have left home, are anticipating their twenty-fifth wedding anniversary. He is the garrison commander on a small island and has not progressed beyond the rank of captain, despite his age. She was an aspiring actress who married him as a route to social status with privilege, but this did not come about. Now that their children have left home, their disappointments with each other expose the failures of the idealizations of those two-person relationships that sustained their union. They now live in almost complete isolation; he regarding all and sundry as 'Scumbags, the lot of them'; she, unable to have normal relationships with the servants and resenting his involvement with them, unconsciously forces them out by her abuse of them. The marriage to be celebrated is now one of mutual cruelty, contempt and denigration. The mood changes with the realization of imminent death, and a visitor, an old friend, Kurt, intervenes. Kurt tries to bring some sense of reality into the situation as a third person, but the forces of the two-person relationship are so powerful that he is dragged into the righteous, cruel possessiveness of the marriage. He eventually leaves in order to resist their unreality and preserve his own integrity and sanity. His own capacity for three-person relationships, his care and concern for both his friends, his considerations for his own children and his separated wife, are all threatened by the couple's idealizations and cruel denigration of failures – the superglue of their fragile self-esteem and unhappy marriage.

The play presents the power of two-person relationships which, by their idealized righteous possessiveness, superficially appear to be easy and self-contained, but in fact can only lead to isolation, impoverishment of mental life and restricted social activity. Three-person relationships are more difficult because they allow the realization that a mother does not orbit around her children, but that her children and others orbit around her. Like the planets, they can be closer or further from her, depending on their varying elliptical orbits, but she has a special sexual relationship with the father from which they are excluded. These realizations mean that children have to relinquish their view of themselves as central to the universe and the fount of all goodness. Cherished idealizations are sadly abandoned, but there is enrichment by taking in and identifying with the capacities for interpersonal relatedness of others who live on the same planet and in the same universe. It is then that mental life can be sane and social interaction creative. While the difficulties and blows to self-esteem that occur on the route to mature three-person relationships are painful, the losses to narcissistic self-aggrandizement are outweighed by the gains in enrichment of interpersonal relationships.

The work of relinquishing omnipotence in favour of reality is lifelong; changing, developing, regressing, fluctuating with successes and failures. There is a constant tension between mastering the pain of disillusionment that is encompassed in the three-person relationship and the lure of adhesive idealizations of the two-person mental set. The blows of reality, the stresses of life, the success and supports of self and family, sway the system one way or another, and always there is the hope that at some time or in some way there will be a re-experiencing of the heavenly state of infant bliss.

Marcus Johns

4
Infertility and the Couple

The infertile condition

It is estimated that between one in seven (Houghton, 1984) and one in ten (Menning, 1984) couples have difficulty conceiving a baby. The American Fertility Society defines an infertile couple as one that has not achieved a successful pregnancy after a year of sexual relations without contraception. It is believed that the number of couples who face problems conceiving is on the increase. Four main factors are thought to contribute to this: an increased incidence of sexually transmitted diseases often leading to pelvic or tubal infections (Kapstrom, 1981); environmental hazards that affect sperm adversely (Alexander, 1982); an increased usage of medication; and the decision some couples make to delay childbearing until the woman is in her thirties and past her most fertile period (Pebley, 1981; Bongaarts, 1982).

When faced with a possible infertility problem, some couples will decide against seeking help, and there may be many reasons for this. Some will decide that this is what nature intended. Others will fear and resent the intrusion into their bodies and personal areas of their lives, such as their sexual relationship, that infertility investigations and treatments inevitably bring. Yet others may fear a definite diagnosis of there being something wrong with them.

However, an increasing number of couples *are* seeking medical help when they find they have difficulty conceiving. The last fifteen years have seen some significant treatment developments in this field and these have given hope to many couples. Moreover, the path to parenthood through adoption is increasingly difficult, as fewer and fewer babies become available – no more than 1,000 children are adopted annually in England and Wales, and agencies have become markedly less willing to regard adoption as a service for childless people (Blyth, 1991).

The willingness to seek help may also reflect changing attitudes to infertility. In the 1950s, research in this area was primarily concerned with drawing up a psychological profile of women who were infertile. The results suggested that infertile women were fearful of childbirth, were in conflict about their femininity, and demonstrated psychosexual difficulties (Pantesco, 1986; Wright *et al.*, 1989). More recent studies have compared patients with unexplained infertility with those whose infertility can be organically explained; such studies found no substantial evidence of personality differences (see, for example, Edelmann and Connolly, 1986). Thus current understanding suggests that infertile patients cannot be depicted as a group of psychologically disturbed people. Moreover, scientific advances and sophisticated diagnostic procedures have identified more organic causes of infertility in men and women, so that the current distribution of cases in which infertility can be attributed to a particular cause are 30–40 per cent fallopian tube factors, 10–15 per cent cervical factors, 10 per cent anovulation, and 30–40 per cent male factor problems. Only around 10 per cent of cases remain unexplained (Sadler and Syrop, 1987).

From earliest times, societies have been preoccupied with fertility, for fertility of people and of land was necessary for survival. In many cultures, fertility was considered a gift from the gods and childlessness believed to be a curse from spirits or enemies (Berk and Shapiro, 1984). The concept of reproduction has gradually shifted away from being seen as the gift of gods (although I think much superstitious and magical thinking regarding fertility persists today, both at a conscious and unconscious level) to an area of personal choice and control. This has been made possible by the development of easily available birth control and abortion. Until they start thinking about having a child, couples are more concerned with controlling fertility than the possibility of infertility. Couples assume they will be able to decide *when*, not *if*, they have children. Thus it is not surprising that current writing is focusing on the emotional repercussions on men and women of that assumption being challenged by a diagnosis of infertility (Sadler and Syrop, 1987; Berg *et al.*, 1991; Wirtberg, 1992).

Although family patterns have become more diverse and an increasing number of couples decide that they do not want offspring, the majority of married couples do eventually have children. Parenthood is seen by most as an essential part of adult life, an important adult goal. Children provide a sense of purpose, of continuity and of belonging. They are seen as a way of life. For couples whose marriage has been arranged, there may be more of an assumption than for others that children will follow. Again, the emotional implications of finding a second marriage infertile after a fertile first marriage can be very unsettling and undermining of a new relationship. Whatever the circumstances of the marriage, the effects of infertility on the couple are likely to be significant. They are also little explored.

Although having children is seen by the majority of couples as the normal predictable course in life, I do not wish to suggest that the desire for a child is without more complex reasons. Many factors affect motivation for parenthood. In addition to social pressures, such as pressure from family and friends, a child may be wanted to patch up a difficult relationship, to avoid the pain of a bereavement, to fill an inner emptiness, or to make up for an unhappy childhood (Ramu and Tavuchis, 1986). These motivations will be there for couples who conceive easily as well as for those who find it more difficult. The range of meanings, both conscious and unconscious, of having children, or of not being able to have them, will be unique to each individual and to their relationship.

The trauma of treatment

Recently, I carried out some research with colleagues (Pengelly, 1995; Pengelly *et al.*, 1995), the first aspect of which was to find out about the couples' experiences of investigations and treatments prior to receiving *in vitro* fertilization treatment (IVF). For many couples, the period of investigation and treatment had been a lengthy one. When conception was taking longer than a year, it was usually the woman who initiated discussion about the possibility of there being a problem. Initially, the couple set about tackling the problem them-selves, usually by scheduling intercourse at the time in the month when they believed the woman to be most fertile. Pressure on the sexual relationship began to build up. They began to worry, usually to themselves but sometimes as a couple, that there might be something wrong with either or both of them. The couple then had to decide whether to seek medical advice. They sometimes found they had different views on this, and even different attitudes towards having children now that it looked as if there might be difficulties.

It is easy to underestimate how big a step going to the doctor is for many couples. Involving an often unknown third person means going public with a problem that has previously been kept secret. In general, the women in our sample initiated contact with their doctor, and their partners accompanied them. I describe the situation in this way because, even at this early stage, women assumed a responsibility to do something about the problem and took charge. Sometimes the doctor would advise the couple to keep a temperature chart, but more often s/he would refer them to a specialist centre where other investigations could be carried out. They had now become 'infertility patients'. From the desire to have a baby to becoming a medical patient is quite a leap. Most people who seek help for infertility are healthy; to identify oneself as a patient can be difficult and confusing.

Hospital investigations usually generated more stress and tension. Temperature charts to establish ovulation, post-coital tests and semen analysis were all routine procedures for the hospital, but they were highly charged emotionally for the couple. It was common for couples in our sample to report having sexual problems, as intercourse often had to be scheduled to coincide with peak fertility.

Pressures on the sexual relationship during infertility investigations have been recorded in other studies:

> It was at times frustrating when you would say, 'hey, not today, it's tomorrow'. But I think even more frustrating was saying, 'it has to be today, it's not tomorrow'. You know you go to bed and you go, 'oh God, I'm so tired', and 'no, you can't be too tired now. Wake up, let's go' (Greil *et al.*, 1989, p. 127).

For most couples, the need to plan something that ought to be spontaneous brought communication problems and emotional pain. As one woman in the same study said:

> I don't remember there ever being any hurt feelings before. But now, all of a sudden, there were hurt feelings. I was afraid to tell him sometimes that this was a good night, because I knew he wasn't in the mood or that he was too tired. I could always tell he was doing me a favour.

When entering the medical world of infertility investigation and treatment, the couple formalize, publicly, the fact that they are trying to have a baby. The most intimate area of their life is opened up to the scrutiny of others. As one woman in our study remarked, 'suddenly we are three in a bed'. Temperature charts to establish the timing of ovulation (Berg *et al.*, 1991) symbolize this invasion of privacy. Several women told me how they put extra 'x' on their temperature charts to show how often they were having sex, when the reality was that the sex was becoming less frequent as the couple became more depressed. As one woman said: 'There'll be no babies in our house unless the storks visit.' The following account taken from another research study is typical:

> There is no inner recess of me left unexplored, unprobed, unmolested. It occurs to me when I have sex that what used to be beautiful and very private is now degraded and terribly public. I bring charts to the doctor like a child bringing home a report card. 'Tell me, did I do well? Did I ovulate?' 'Did I have sex at all the right times as you instructed me?' (Menning, 1980, p. 315).

It was common in our study for men to describe periods of

impotence as they felt under pressure to perform. During therapy at the Tavistock Marital Studies Institute, some men have described feeling resentful that they have to perform on demand for a partner who seems primarily interested in becoming pregnant rather than interested in them. Similarly, women have described feeling resentful at their dependence on their partners' arousal. For many couples, a diagnosis relieved the pressure, as they knew there was no possibility of conceiving naturally – although this diagnosis was shocking and brought much grief and anger in its wake. However, for the couples in the group whose infertility remained unexplained, there was a particular ongoing pressure as there was always a chance that conception could take place.

The process of diagnosis was often time-consuming. For example, women who suffered from endometriosis were put on drug programmes. The side-effects of these drugs were often uncomfortable, and included menopausal symptoms, weight gain and depression. Several women complained to me as a researcher – but not to the doctors – that they had not been warned of such side-effects. Other women had undergone tubal surgery, laparoscopies and other intrusive medical procedures. There were periods following such treatments when couples were left wondering if the interventions had worked – long periods of being in limbo and not being sure if they were fertile or not. Several studies have referred to the 'roller coaster ride' of infertility to describe the peaks of hope reached one week, only to drop to the depths of despair the next when the woman's monthly period arrived (Mahlstedt, 1985). This experience of being confronted with the possibility of infertility and its attendant loss of parenthood meant that many couples entered a period of their lives that was highly ambiguous. On the one hand, their difficulty conceiving might mean they were going to be childless for ever, and this would involve a massive readjustment of their life plans. On the other, there was a possibility that they might be able to have children and their imagined future would unfold as planned. In the meantime, uncertainty, the not knowing for sure what they were facing, could be very confusing and stressful.

As part of the diagnostic procedures, all the men had to produce samples of sperm for testing. Many men described their discomfort and embarrassment about this, as they often had to masturbate in the hospital toilets. One man described his humiliation when he handed a young nurse his sample. She held it up and asked in a loud voice, 'Is it fresh?' Other men were worried that they had not produced enough. This very public exposure of the problem could stir up feelings of being inferior, of not measuring up and of humiliation. (Such disclosures were more likely to be made in a therapeutic context than in the hospital setting.) Several men were found to have very low sperm counts, or sperm that were low in motility. The range of treatments for these conditions was limited. Two men in our research agreed to take part in drug trials, but the experience was of hopes being raised and then disappointed. Both said they felt like guinea pigs, but their responses were very different. One remained enthusiastic, describing with some pride 'This machine that can spin the sperm so that all the good ones would come out and could be collected. There's only three in the country.' The other was angry and disillusioned, having gone through eight years of treatment.

For some of the couples in our sample, the inability to have children followed a more clear-cut but traumatic event. For example, several women had suffered ectopic pregnancies and subsequent damage to their fallopian tubes. These partnerships had had to deal with the double grief of losing a much-wanted baby as well as their infertility. For some, there was an urgency to replace the baby who had died. As Joan Raphael-Leff has described, 'The abrupt diagnosis renders the couple powerless, feeling marginal and dependent, seemingly bereft of a future and so much at odds with past expectations, hopes and life plans' (Raphael-Leff, 1986b, p. 28).

Across our sample, it was more common for men than women to express anger with the doctors, hospitals and treatment centres involved in investigating their partners and themselves. Although many women had fears and doubts about the programmes – for example, worries about the long-term effects of drug programmes, or feelings about being treated as objects for research rather than as whole people – these feelings were rarely shared with the medical team. They were good patients, co-operative, quiet and grateful. The medical team were in a very powerful position, as they had the means to perform a modern-day miracle. Couples were anxious not to spoil that relationship in case they jeopardized their position in the programme.

Women, men and infertility

It is common to call couples who are experiencing infertility 'infertile couples'. In this way, emphasis is placed on trying to see infertility as a problem shared by the partners, despite the reality that most investigations and procedures are directed towards women. The problem is certainly one that involves both partners. However, a shared problem does not necessarily mean the same problem. Men and women have very different stories to tell (Wirtberg, 1992).

The majority of women made it clear that with improved contraception and the opportunities open to women they had expected to choose *when* to have children. The denial of choice was experienced as devastating. Some women described having mixed feelings about children before they discovered their infertility, but the denial of choice had made them single-minded in their pursuit of fertility. For many, having children at some point in their lives was seen as a pillar of their female identity. Their inability to achieve this desperately desired state resulted in a serious threat to their idea of themselves as a person and a woman. Infertility had threatened their core identity.

Many expressed the belief that a woman's capacity to create, bear and nurture a child was the very essence of womanhood. One lady described feeling that she had 'not come up to scratch as a woman', another said she felt 'less than a woman for not having a child'. Many invoked the belief in a biological, maternal instinct. As one woman said, 'It's why we're here, why we're put on this earth.' Some longed to be pregnant; others longed for a baby. Many showed what Raphael-Leff (1992b) has described as 'a passionate attachment to biological motherhood'. Two of the sample had adopted children, but this had not resolved their feelings about their own infertility.

For many infertile women, pregnancy and motherhood were idealized and desperately envied. In contrast, they denigrated themselves as women. As this state of mind was so powerful and all-embracing, it intruded into other areas of their lives: into their roles as wives, daughters, sisters, friends and work colleagues. Many previously high-achieving women felt depressed, lacking in self-esteem and creativity. Some women found themselves going back over their lives to find evidence of 'badness' that might account for the way they felt cursed by infertility. Infertility felt like a judgement. Guilt about previous abortions and, for one woman, guilt about giving a baby up for adoption, was particularly hard to bear. This particular woman had not been able to tell her husband about the baby she had once had. There were few pain-free zones. As one woman said: 'The infertility is always there, casting a shadow over everything in my life.'

For men, the experience was in many ways a different one. There was a small group in our sample who knew their sperm was low in number or motility. It was thought unlikely that they would be able to father a child, but much depended on their sperm count on the day IVF took place. This group said that their partners had offered reassurance and support, but this had not removed their feeling that their identity as men had been undermined. They also found their experience much more difficult to talk about than had the women.

They gave glimpses of their shameful feelings under cover of jocularity and bluffness: 'Oh yes,' said one man, 'the old male ego certainly dropped. You get angry, but there's nothing you can do about it, it's a personal thing inside.'

Their female partners described to me, as a woman, how the men had felt devastated when they realized there was a problem with their sperm, but these men made no reference to such feelings when talking with my male researcher colleague. One was able to confide that he felt 'less than 100 per cent man, I'm shooting blanks'. And several male friends had not helped by joking that they would 'go and sort his wife out'. It was rare for these men to talk about their feelings, and their partners would protect them by covering up for them, telling family and friends that the infertility problem was theirs. This is a common finding in research on the emotional effects of male infertility. For example, a recent study of the emotional factors associated with male infertility revealed that men suffered very poor self-esteem, and that this continued over time with an adverse affect on their marital and sexual functioning (Slade *et al.*, 1992). For some men, infertility can denote a lack of virility and masculinity, and it is this aspect that is often more troubling than the denial of an opportunity to parent.

Many men were almost inarticulate about their desire for children. Of these, the childless man was much harder to get to know than the husband of the childless wife. Some seemed to know more about their parents' feelings than their own. One began by saying: 'My wife desperately wants children more than anything in the world', then adding, 'I desperately want children too, but I don't show it.' For others it was something they had never questioned: 'Everyone wants children' or 'I haven't really thought about not having any' were common replies.

A few men said they felt they had a dynastic duty to their families. One explained that his parents had only female grandchildren, so there would be no one left to carry on the family name – a sentiment echoed by the phrase 'I'm the last of the line'. A similar idea was put in biological terms: 'I'm put on this earth to reproduce, to carry on my genes.' Some expressed the longing in more personal terms, and almost explicitly as an extension of the love between themselves and their partners: 'A child in the image of its mother, a child that looks up to you, it almost hurts.' However, generally speaking, while there were few pain-free zones for women, men seemed to be able to compartmentalize the problem; work and leisure activities could be preserved as pain-free zones.

Communication and the couple

There were a small number of couples who were able to talk openly together about their problem, with both partners revealing their hopes as well as their disappointments. They could share the problem. These couples also found it less difficult talking to others about their predicament. Perhaps by receiving support from others they were helped to support each other; the marriage did not have to do all the work. They differed from couples who *said* they shared their doubts, frustrations and disappointments, but who were also at pains to point out that there was no conflict or tension in the relationship. This group seemed preoccupied with presenting themselves as a 'good couple', their assumption being that 'good couples' did not have difficulties.

As I have already observed, a shared problem does not necessarily mean the same problem. Some couples found themselves in difficulties when their feelings and ways of coping were different, but felt they should be the same. It may be that because these couples felt less than perfect in their inability to have children, they wished to be seen, and to see themselves, as what they imagined to be the perfect couple. There might also have been a fear that only 'good' couples would be thought worthy of being accepted on a treatment programme, a fantasy that ascribes parental power to the role of professionals. For this group of couples, the timing and context of the research interviews, which coincided with their second visit to the hospital, inhibited what they felt they could safely say to a researcher. Couples seen in a therapeutic context have confirmed the fantasy that their relationship is assessed before a decision is taken about treatment.

Other couples described talking only minimally about their infertility. Very often the woman would express all the longing and distress and her partner would try to manage this without getting too caught up in it himself. As one man said, 'One minute she wants to come here, the next minute she doesn't. I take no notice of that. I keep going. I keep her going. Without me she'd crack up completely.' In these partnerships, there was a psychological division of labour whereby the woman experienced the emotional pain of the couple's predicament and the man supplied the support and energy to keep the quest for a solution going. While this way of organizing the relationship had been a resource through the stressful quest for conception, there was a danger that, under the increasing strain of the treatment programme, what had been a functional division could become a dysfunctional split, leaving the partners isolated from each other.

Many of the women felt depleted of confidence and very unsure of their worth. They felt anxious that their parents would either abandon them if there were no children or remain with them resentfully. Although they had been reassured, they were still frightened. Some women were aware that their partners wanted children very much, but were apprehensive about encouraging them to talk about this because it felt hurtful to hear these feelings being expressed, and they feared it might put their husbands more in touch with their disappointment.

The pressure on the couple to provide support for each other was intensified by the lack of social support. Most women had found it difficult to talk to anyone about the difficulties they were having conceiving, and for the most part had kept their infertility a secret. Theirs was an invisible problem. Many did not share their predicament with others, because they could not bear to receive the sympathy or, worse still, the pity of others. Their envy of friends or family members who had produced children could feel unbearable, and several women dropped previously important relationships with other women because of this. Some women were lucky enough to have families who they could talk to; others felt that their parents were so anxious about the problems themselves, and so desperate to have grandchildren, that talking to them only increased their sense of failure.

Men communicated with others even less. Several spoke of their fear of humiliation among other men at work or in the pub if they were to reveal their predicament, or even if their childlessness was remarked upon. 'The prod is always there', said one. Others had been the butt of jokes about whether they were 'firing blanks'. For many men, the research interview was a first opportunity to talk about their predicament – and there was a reluctance to use it.

Thus couples were desperately in need of support, but did not feel that others could understand the extent of their pain. Anger, envy and rage towards those with children provoked violent and powerful feelings which, in turn, evoked self-disgust and a withdrawal from social contact. The absence of support and the difficulty couples had of sharing this most sensitive problem with others may be one of the reasons why infertility seems such a difficult problem to come to terms with.

We left our couples in the research project as they were about to embark on IVF treatment, and so we have no idea which couples achieved a pregnancy. When we left them, they were full of optimism and desperately hoping that the treatment would work. Thoughts of failure and the subsequent loss of their imagined future were kept at bay. They sought to avert the loss not only of their physical reproductive capacity, but also of the profound personal meanings of having children that were felt to be fundamental to their core identities both as individuals and as a couple.

However, couples can find it difficult to stop the treatment programmes. There is always the chance that if one programme fails, the next will be successful. For some couples, there will be continuing uncertainty, even if treatment is terminated, because a conclusive diagnosis is never reached. There could be a spontaneous pregnancy in any cycle. The moment for grieving is elusive, and the couple holds back grief for a moment of certainty. Possible loss – even probable loss – is not *actual* loss. As one woman said: 'It wouldn't be so difficult if I had an explanation. I could manage then. Deciding whether to go for another attempt at IVF is so difficult. Will I become pregnant on the next attempt? It hurts because however long I live, I'll never know. It will always be a mystery.'

Mahlstedt (1985) has compared the nature of grief for the loss resulting from infertility with that for a soldier missing in action. Nothing is definite in either case, and hope enables survivors to avoid pain. The loss of fertility is different from grieving an actual loss. There is no funeral, no wake, no grave to lay the flowers on. Family and friends may never have known that there was a problem, so cannot offer solace and support. The loss for an infertile couple is a loss of potential: the never-to-be-born child, the imagined child, the imagined future, genetic continuity. Barbara Berg (1981) entitled the account of her own infertility *Nothing to Cry About*. In one sense, this is wrong; there is much to cry about. But in another sense, the title is accurate. How can you mourn the loss of someone who has never been conceived, let alone born? The fact that there is nothing tangible to represent the loss can intensify pain and make the loss more difficult to bear.

We are only just beginning to understand why this is such a difficult process for couples, and why it is different for different couples. In the absence of a supportive network, and with the often intense pressures on the marital relationship, some couples will find counselling or psychotherapy helpful. Through a therapeutic process, painful feelings may be explored, thought about and come to terms with. Accepting childlessness can be a creative solution, and not simply a counsel of despair.

Lynne Cudmore

5
Reproductive Narratives of Pregnancy and Parenting

Personal stories

> Our tales are spun, but for the most part we don't spin them; they spin us. Our human consciousness and our narrative selfhood, is their product, not their source (Dennett, 1993, p. 418).

Human beings are story-tellers. From earliest times in human existence people have produced stories to answer questions about the creation of the world, our own origins, and differences between the sexes. In almost every known society, legendary epics build up an enduring quasi-historical record of formative events such as migrations, invasions, dynastic changes and social reforms; and for any given society, mythological stories reinforce moral values, explain cultural customs, and justify institutional policies.

Equally, families evolve their own legends. We see how, from a very young age, children use story-telling to make sense of their subjective worlds, reviewing and constantly revising daily happenings by inventing and inviting stories about them and theirs. Neonatal research shows that in a search for meaning, even pre-verbal infants appear to construct a narrative-like format that helps to co-ordinate diverse components of their experience into a coherent whole (Trevarthen, 1979; Stern, 1994). In addition, stories are used as a means of personal communication, and form an important part of our social interaction – reproducing, manufacturing and extending a domain of shared understanding. Jointly created narratives can become a playful way of conveying rich cultural information in palatable form. Family myths serve as an aid to long-term memory, highlighting particular aspects of kinship history. These dramatic narratives – featuring familiar personae, uniting time, place and process – also have wider implications as they facilitate the exploration of motivations, emotions and meanings underpinning human give and take.

Furthermore, through the personalized stories we each tell ourselves, we reconstruct external realities internally, thereby evolving an inner sense of an 'experiencing self', a core of continuity that unites the multiplicity of experiences of our own sense of being. Conversely, by externalizing internal sagas, we re-present ourselves to others. Sharing deep concerns and having them recognized and affirmed by participants outside ourselves, enables us to become known. We also come to know ourselves through this process, making use of people outside ourselves to release inner experiences and, through them, articulate, enact and give expression to often unknown aspects of our internal worlds. Thus, we use others both as 'vehicles of wish' to fulfil our desires, and as 'sources of "transformation" to elicit and elucidate our own inner "self-experience" ' (Bollas, 1992, p. 27).

Unconsciously, we each draw on a wide repertoire of personal stories. The particular themes evoked at any one time, and the specific version selected from a host of simultaneous renderings, or 'multiple drafts' (Dennett, 1993) of each subjective depiction, vary, depending on context. Our narratives, never static, are subject to continual revision. Stories are retrieved through experiences, objects and people we happen to encounter, or through those we seek out, and they are elaborated through their collaborative or intrusive input to the dialogue. For our 'others' are not passive listeners. Neither merely audience to the play nor critics, nor even interpreters, they are active contributors to our personal narratives. Every inside story's cast of characters includes significant others who not only set the scene and perform vital roles in meeting our needs, but often, in addition – although appearing as observers, stage managers and actors in their own right – represent constituents of the self and are ascribed projected agency, intentionality and motive.

Each separate narrative strives towards internal consistency and a scenario that hinges on vital characteristics of the main protagonists. Spinning stories to substantiate dimly perceived happenings in our internal realities, we are also 'spun' by them. Our perception is altered by provisional validation, as gaps are closed, rents tentatively repaired, the irrational rationalized and inconsistencies embroidered. Anxiety drives creation of good plausible plot by supplementing understanding gained through our senses with selective memories, dream fragments, fantasy formulations, imaginary ideas, conflation or intellectualization, as we use every means available both to access and to block further acquaintance with the hidden meaning of our unknown inside stories. For it is difficult to contend with chaos and uncertainty. Surprised by revelations of strange forms of self-experience, we tend to avoid cognitive dissonance by denial and splitting, normalizing the unacceptable, disclaiming ambiguities or amending the facts. By conscious and unconscious reworking, our transmuted stories may at times be altered to the point of self-deception. In addition to rectification, we spend much of our lives repeating. Through action, words and silent representation, familiar stories are reincarnated. Personal parables are recapitulated in revised form, and infantile conflicts are reframed in the new tale that we recount. Figures outside us, unwittingly primed to personify internal figures, come to realize our revivified wishes, as time and time again we force our subjective stories to materialize, reiterating the same old themes in fresh guises. Our life-texts are a patchwork of revisions, rewritten clauses, explanatory subclauses, footnotes and unannotated conjectural elaborations.

In this chapter, I shall tell some stories – 'inside' stories of pregnancy and parenting as told by 'him' and 'her'. My data originate from thousands of hours of listening to narratives of feelings, fears and fantasies throughout twenty years of specialized clinical work with over 150 self-selected childbearing people seen individually, one to five times per week for two to twelve years each in psychoanalysis or psychoanalytic psychotherapy; a further forty-five women seen in weekly therapy or discussion groups through pregnancy and the first year after birth; plus some thirty couples or families who had brief therapy during the course of childbearing. This material is supplemented with data from interviews in pre- and post-natal surveys of people attending childbirth education classes during pregnancy and post-natally, and three modest retrospective studies conducted at one-year intervals in a large community centre playgroup, wherein I also made longitudinal observations of interaction between twenty-three mother–baby couples (Raphael-Leff, 1985a, b and c; Raphael-Leff, 1986a).

Telling 'inside stories' of such emotionally laden subject-matter is no simple task. Although unconsciously motivated to communicate, we humans are 'unreliable narrators' (Schafer, 1992), censoring even in the most receptive conditions, driven to restrict, modify and embellish the storylines of our known psychic realities. And, far from there being one story to be told, even a single narrator on the psychoanalytic couch recounts many stories about numerous complex inner 'selves'. As I see it, the story one hears is a compromise formation of a multitude of voices vying with each other to tell their own story filtered through the biased ears of the listener. As such, while retelling the stories of others, my narration here undoubtedly bears my own imprint.

In sum, as authors, heroes, agents, witnesses and speakers of our own and others' lives, we try to make autobiographical sense of our experiences through mental reconstructions that exploit fantasy to bind anxiety. Unconsciously funnelling them through the medium of storymaking, we struggle on the one hand with our own internal conflicts and incongruities, and on the other with inexplicable external forces and multiple meanings of daily happenings. Groping towards emotional coherence, not only are ongoing stories enhanced by smoothing out irregularities, but futuristic tales, as yet untold, are already pre-structured and invigilated by long-held expectations and distorting preconceptions. This becomes of crucial importance in relation to childbearing, when the future relationship with the baby is being formulated.

During pregnancy, as at other times, lived experience is continuously reinvested with subjective significance, coloured by past expectations, self- and other-representations and the emotions of the moment. Realistic appraisal depends on the degree to which, at any one time, a person can acknowledge his or her implication in life-events, capacity for bedevilment and need to make reparation. With each fresh portrayal of past narratives, habitual incapacitating patterns are further adumbrated. Detection of rigidity and pre-formed layers underpinning repetitions may lead to insights enabling a freeing-up of stasis, and a reinterpretation of defensive meanings in the light of new evidence. When therapy is required, the 'transformational dialogue' of a psychoanalytic exchange offers opportunities for free-associative retelling of life stories, which, by destabilizing established narratives, deconstructing their internal contradictions and defamiliarizing historical accounts, can introduce positive change (Schafer, 1992). In cases where fixed representations of the baby and/or parenting augur badly for the future relationship, therapeutic interventions, whether offered to the pregnant woman on her own or conjointly to the couple, can be extremely effective in working through some of the underlying issues before the birth.

Clearly, then, our stories do not begin at birth; nor do babies begin with conception. The fantasy baby a pregnant woman elaborates is embedded within her own ongoing narrative, that of her extended family, and of her partner if she has one, its symbolic semi-existence heightened by desire and the conscious or unconscious pledge to reproduce. Where the process of baby-making is arrested or highlighted in slow motion, as during fertility treatments, the multi-varied strands from which a dream-baby is fashioned become apparent (see Raphael-Leff, 1992a). Needless to say, the babies conceptualized by partners as the product of their union do not necessarily coincide, since the imagined infant is a cumulative production of each individual's psychic history and lifelong wishes. And fantasy depictions of later-born family members bear traces of preceding babies and the investment of siblings as well as parents.

Once conception occurs, a paradox operates at the heart of pregnancy: although physiologically closer than any other inter-change, the relationship between a mother and her foetus is marked by obscurity. The womb's interior is an intriguing mystery that has long defied understanding, as Leonardo da Vinci's 500-year-old investigations attest. Recent technological advances, such as ultra-sound imaging and foetoscopy, allow glimpses of real-time foetal activity. Nevertheless, the live baby's shape and movement within the womb merely serve as receptacles for the observer's subjective hopes, fears and expectations.

Socio-cultural stories

The unique story each pregnant woman constructs in the context of her family is clearly influenced by the socio-cultural milieu in which she grows up and gestates her baby. However, underpinning her own

Table 1   Procreative anxieties

Mysteries of FORMATION	anxieties about abnormality
Mysteries of PRESERVATION	anxieties about maternal ability to
	– contain
	– sustain
	– protect
	– nourish
Mysteries of TRANSFORMATION	of – 'seed' into foetus
	– pregnancy into baby
	– bodily fluids into milk
	– fantasy into reality
	– woman into mother
Anxieties about SEPARATION	– primal dis-union
	– risk of depletion
	– the price of pain
Anxieties about the BIRTH PROCESS	– moment of disclosure
	– fears of damage
	– loss of control
	– depersonalization
	– humiliation
	– death

Source: Adapted from Raphael-Leff, 1985c.

personal narrative are some universal themes that are embedded in the common experience of pregnancy and our shared numinous reactions to having all been gestated inside a woman's body. I have delineated in Table 1 some of these age-old feminine mysteries, and the related anxieties that seem to preoccupy pregnant women wherever they might conceive.

Clearly, pregnancy is both a universal phenomenon and a unique personal occurrence. As old as womankind, it is eternal and seemingly unchanging. Yet it varies across cultures, surrounded by different beliefs about conception and growth, rituals and avoidances to ensure the sex or health of the baby, and talismans, rites and prohibitions to protect the pregnancy from witchcraft and spirits, and the woman from the evil eye. In traditional societies (as illustrated by anthropological studies, and works of art such as eighteenth-century Japanese prints of communal bath-houses), girls grow up surrounded by a community of women of all ages, closely in touch with the bodies of others and aware of female physical development at all stages, from infancy to old age. In many cultures, fertility stories are imbibed from earliest childhood – a freely expressed feminine folklore pertaining to beliefs about conception and pregnancy, miscarriages, labour practices and ceremonial transactions around confinement, birth, placental disposal, care of the newborn and lactation. This is a very different situation from that of a Western woman who, having grown up in a nuclear family, has usually never before seen a naked pregnant body, or watched a woman breastfeeding, or held a newborn baby until she is handed her own with full responsibility for its survival, often in isolation and lacking even a partner to help her. So although pregnancy is universal, the specific experience of childbearing depends not only on each woman's psycho-history and physiological condition, but also is much influenced by cultural context – geography, demography, accessible services and childcare expectations.

Similarly, although seemingly eternal, the facts of life have themselves altered dramatically. In the West, improved contraception has unhitched sexual activity from impregnation. Conversely, new reproductive techniques have enabled conception to occur without intercourse. Some pregnancies are the result of consistent efforts to conceive; some are accidents; some may follow prolonged fertility treatment. The baby may be the joint product of an intimate couple, born of a surrogacy pregnancy or adopted from the unknown. Although gestated within the partnership it may be conceived through donor sperm and/or egg and have no genetic connection to the expectant parent/s. A woman may be on her own or have a male or female partner. Conception may follow a considered decision in a marriage, a close or loose arrangement with a consciously or unconsciously chosen baby-father or self-insemination with semen from a carefully selected or unknown donor. Or a woman may conceive unintentionally, whether within a permanent relationship, a passing one, an extramarital affair or through casual sex.

Estimating the number of conceptions in any given society and year is complicated. Many end in miscarriage either well into the pregnancy – or so early as to go unrecognized as such. Some end in secret abortions. Others may be terminated due to social circumstance or foetal abnormalities. Yet others do not survive the pregnancy, or die following birth. But whatever the conditions of conception, in the absence of objective knowledge and with only minimal clues presented by the unknown baby whose identity is largely concealed, socio-cultural provisions, traditions and expectations augment parental fantasy to form the core of the inside stories of pregnancy.

Trans-generational stories

Like all transitional phases of the family life cycle, pregnancy reactivates previous conflicts, necessitating new resolutions and reintegration. From earliest childhood, in the continuous interweaving of internal and external realities, we tend to actualize some of our most insistent stories, at first within the family and then outside it, by unconsciously recruiting significant others unwittingly to re-enact our essential scripts while we, in turn, unwittingly imbibe and participate in their unconscious preoccupations. The reproductive process of 'storymaking' will be influenced by how each embryo is conceived, both physically and psychically. The issue is not merely whether the baby was planned, is timely, wanted, permissible and healthy. Unconscious imagery around the gestation, whom the baby represents in each expectant parent's family of origin and psychic reality, what emotional and other resources they can call upon in their internal and external worlds, will affect not only the experience of pregnancy but also patterns of caregiving once the actual infant is born. Parenting itself will be much affected by the degree of resolution achieved in the various psychological processes engendered by the transition to parenthood.

If the woman has a cohabiting partner, the shift from a dyad to a triad resulting from a first pregnancy commonly raises controversial issues around gender, inclusion and exclusion, autonomy and dependence, possessiveness and possession, and longings for and fears of fusion, separation and loss. Within a heterosexual childbearing couple, pregnancy, which demarcates female and male divisions so clearly, will trigger revision of partnership 'contracts', gender expectations and sexual habits (see Raphael-Leff, 1991). The tale each partner recounts around childbearing comes to be constructed from intertwining past and present narratives and unconscious fantasies. This personal 'inheritance' brought to reproduction by each expectant parent consists of the emotional constellation of childhood households, shared family myths, obstetric legends, beliefs about babies and patterns of parenting – a 'lineage' of symbolically pre-structured reproductive narratives – some reaching far back into the archaic past, culled from a pool of positive influences and unresolved ancestral conflicts in their respective extended families. Out of these, each parent constructs a philosophy of parenting.

Given trans-generational and socio-cultural components within idiosyncratic narratives, we must assume that there are a multitude of inside stories. Indeed, in each pregnancy there are as many narratives as there are men and women involved – and, in some cases, as many as there are days of gestation. Researching the 'inside' story of reproduction is therefore fraught with methodological difficulties and, as noted above, 'stories' are themselves affected by contextual influences in the telling. Nevertheless, after relating some stories, I shall propose a model that tries to abstract some common denominators underpinning a variety of possible configurations.

Her story

A pregnant woman's experiential image changes as her shape swells and bulges beyond her control, her senses become acutely keen and hypersensitive and her emotions volatile. Even temperature maintenance cannot be taken for granted, the centre of gravity alters, and her feet become invisible to her. Inevitably, primitive anxieties are reactivated about having herself been a foetus inside a woman's body, with attendant fantasies of fusion, confusion, imprisonment, violation, exploitation and reparation (Raphael-Leff, 1991 and 1993). Essentially, carrying a baby within her, as she herself was carried in the womb of her mother, evokes a fluidity of identifications that she may welcome or resist. Pregnancy forces upon her a reappraisal of identity, a re-evaluation of her own creative and destructive capacities, and an exploration of significant relationships, including those in her family of origin. Within the contradictions of her emotional turmoil, the narratives she evolves will, as ever, strive towards internal consistency.

Narratives vary according to the unconscious meaning each woman attaches to the baby and herself as expectant mother. One woman may be both very identified with her baby and excited by her condition, experiencing it as a culmination of her feminine identity. As one mother-to-be says:

> I feel very turned on and tuned in all the time, and want everybody to know I'm pregnant, even though it doesn't show yet. I feel round and abundant and wonder-full. I absolutely refuse to buy anything unless it sparkles and has pearls – I want to be glitsy, to wear satins, to be pink and smooth and soft and start all over again ... in fact, my skin has become incredibly sensitive and my man treats me as if I'm ever so delicate.[1]

Luxuriating in an idealized state of symbiotic unity with her baby, she feels privileged in comparison with her partner who has only indirect access to the foetus. Once movements are experienced, she revels in immediate communion, never alone, enriched by the internal presence as with an imaginary friend. Needless to say, a woman who thus glories in pregnancy will be saddened by the thought of losing such unimpeded intimacy. Idealizing her baby's stay in the womb as blissful, and herself as lavish provider, she will be eager to reinstate this idyll post-natally, making the transition as smooth as possible. The 'Facilitator', as I have called the mother who wishes to facilitate her baby's every wish, tends to treat the birth as an orgasmic event, a reunion and self-reincarnation in her closest relative ('I am my mother giving birth to me'). She therefore resents intervention in labour, hoping for as *natural* a birth process as possible, and resisting any separations from her newborn. Believing she is primed to care for her baby by their biological connection in pregnancy and breastfeeding, she opts for exclusive full-time care of her infant, feeling she is best qualified to interpret the baby's every need – which she intends to gratify as it arises.

At the other end of the spectrum is the woman who regards pregnancy as a rather tedious means of getting a baby. Determined that pregnancy shall affect her lifestyle as little as possible, she is reluctant to engage in introspection or to invest the foetus with any personality, trying to remain detached 'in case something goes wrong'. As one such woman says:

> It's a very strange feeling – having something alien moving inside me. At first I felt invaded by this eavesdropping creature, listening in to every word I said and exploiting me, rotting my teeth and

draining my energy. Now [eight months] that I've been given a crib and some clothes, it's beginning to be real . . . The main hurdle now is the labour . . . I'm not one of those women who want to squat on the floor; I don't want a caesarean because of the scar and I'm put off an epidural because I can't endure the thought of a forceps delivery – those horrible big metal things – so I'll just have drugs. And after it's born, well, they can go and weigh it, and then they give it to you, don't they, or do they hang on to it? I don't know, I suppose it depends . . . I think I'd like them to bring it to me cleaned up. Maybe I'll just say, 'God, I'm so exhausted, give it to me when I wake up'. Only thing is they might get them muddled up in the nursery. But I shall put myself in their hands and probably stay in there as long as I can.

Unlike the woman who experiences labour as an intimate passage, the 'Regulator', as I have called her, tends to regard labour as a potentially humiliating and painful medical event, to be controlled and curtailed by analgesic drugs, epidural or technological intervention. Clearly, what she wants is not a *natural* birth, but a *civilized* one. As her baby has been unknown in pregnancy, she feels post-natally that it will take time to get to know him or her. Her internal representations of baby-care as a skill that may be learned also means it may be shared. Furthermore, since she believes that newborns are incapable of differentiation between care-givers, she resolves to introduce other carers early on. To her, the pre-social baby requires socialization, which can best be achieved through adapting the baby to a regular household routine. This regime can also serve to create continuity between carers.

Between these positions we find the 'Reciprocator', who enjoys her pregnancy as a preparatory time, but is also keen to have it end so she can meet the child she is carrying:

I think about the baby a lot of the time [says one woman in her sixth month of pregnancy]. I feel more plugged in, full of energy, and my thought processes are bound up with the baby so I seem rather vague to other people, not a separate individual . . . I am very happy looking forward to getting to know this baby. I don't feel anxious, although I do worry about sleepless nights and my own capacity to mother. As to the pregnancy – it's welcome inside and I feel happy it's there. I invited it to be there – I feel it has taken over creatively not invasively. The baby doesn't demand of me in a way which is unreasonable – it's a benevolent feeling. I become increasingly bound up with this creature moving around and also observe him responding to things – like certain pieces of music. I make an effort to be dispassionate. I don't want to fantasize to the point of disappointment. This baby is a Person with his own responses and a personality which I am genuinely curious about. I don't want to foreclose it by injecting my personal expectations in – I'd rather wait and watch and get to know as these qualities begin to unfold over a period of time as he grows up. As to the birth – I feel quite ignorant, haven't started ante-natal classes yet – got a lot to learn. I'm not particularly brave physically, but don't have fearful dreams or feel drained by other people's horror stories. It will just take place and I'll do what I can at the time.

Clearly as a 'Reciprocator' this woman has her own set of internal beliefs about the baby and herself that guide her ability to tolerate uncertainty and to negotiate each instance rather than having a policy of adapting herself to the baby or the baby to the household.

These three differing orientations towards pregnancy, motherhood and babies illustrate a few of the many multi-determined stories imaginable and their underlying assumptions. Starting from pregnancy, I suggest a model I have termed the 'placental paradigm', which abstracts some of the common denominators underpinning the variety of possible themes and configurations.

Inevitably, the live foetus poses a threat. Pregnant, the woman is no longer an individual; she is part of a tandem. A pregnant woman is confronted by the bizarre situation of two people in one body, one inside the other. Not unlike a transitional object (Winnicott, 1958), the embryo is separate yet part of her psychic world, real but intangibly fantastic, already gendered, but – to her – as yet of unspecified sex, unknown but already a transferential locus resonating with primary internal figures. As she struggles to overcome the ambiguity of this indeterminate 'other' by mentally conceiving a symbolic representation of it, her conception becomes a mental receptacle for reproductive concepts gleaned over her lifetime. Thus, psychic configurations take shape, engendered by the inexorable trajectory of gestation – blastocyst developing imperceptibly into embryo, moving foetus, and irreversibly growing towards the reality of the birth of a baby.

According to one psychoanalytic story, mothers are regarded as emotional 'containers' for their babies, containing and 'metabolizing' infantile anxieties (Bion, 1962). I suggest that this maternal processing function has a precedent during pregnancy, as a mother-to-be actually serves as a physical 'container' for her baby and, through the placental system, not only provides nutrients, but processes the baby's deposits

– breathing and excreting for her foetus with every pulse of her heart beat. For some women, having a live being growing inside them, feeding off their resources and pumping waste into them, is a frightening idea. The baby is only partly hers; it is in part a foreign body which under other circumstances her immunological system would reject. Indeed, complications of pregnancy, miscarriages and some maternal illnesses have now been attributed by biological evolutionists to disruption of equilibrium in the internal battle between maternal and paternal genes. Psychologically, too, the baby may feel foreign. So, different positive or negative aspects of the placental exchange of 'good' and/or 'bad' substances may be emphasized, depending on the woman's self-confidence in her own internal provisions, her view of the archaic mother of her own gestation and infancy, the baby she imagines herself to have been, and whether her foetus is envisaged as a benign or malevolent force within her. In other words, how a woman relates to the pregnancy will reflect her own self-esteem, representation of mothering and imagery of the baby within her. In addition to her psycho-history, she will also be affected by current psycho-social factors, such as whether she has a partner, the degree of emotional and practical support available, her economic situation, career status, whether she has other children, how many, their ages and age-gaps, their degree of dependence upon her, and so on.

The model of the 'placental paradigm' delineates various permutations of affects, focusing, for simplicity's sake, on maternal self-esteem and representation of the baby (although, clearly, the paradigm need not be restricted to these and could be expanded to include

Table 2 *Placental paradigm – women's representation of self, internal mother, baby and baby self.* [+]=positive; [−]=negative

	Self	*Mother*	*Baby*	*baby-self*
dyad I (Fac)	'good'	[+]or[−]	'good'	[+]or[−]
dyad II (Reg)	'good'	[+]or[−]	'bad'	[+]or[−]
dyad III (Fac)	'bad'	[+]or[−]	'good'	[+]
dyad IV (Reg)	'bad'	[+]or[−]	'bad'	[−]
dyad V	good or bad	[+]or[−]	non-entity	[0]
'mixed' (Recip)	good & bad	[+ −]	good & bad	[+ −]
bi-polar	good vs. bad	[+]or[−]	good vs. bad	[+/−]

a woman's view of her partner, her mother and so on). Different reproductive stories may thus be represented in a very simple form (see Table 2), irrespective of the individual content of the fantasy or cultural influences.

The placental paradigm indicates how positive and negative affects, and unconscious valuation of the umbilical connection, underpin the woman's internal representation of the primitive exchange with her baby during pregnancy. This, I suggest, foreshadows her orientation towards parenthood and mothering.

For the Facilitator, placental linkage is experienced as doubly positive – sweet surrender to fusion of baby and mother. In her vision of herself as a good, bountiful, placental mother, she sees herself maintaining her baby's experience of a blissful intra-uterine world by continuously providing perfect conditions, while she herself vicariously re-experiences womb-connectedness, emulating or outdoing her own archaic mother. In cases where the woman feels that she was deprived of this idyllic early experience, she may distance herself from her early mother, idealizing her own resources, compensating herself by proxy for assumed deficits of her own gestation, and feeling vicariously gratified by her own rich provision for the foetus growing inside her. In her mental representations, the baby then features as an embodiment of certain aspects of herself, identified in her mind with a deprived baby-self hidden within her adult self, or a silent unfulfilled aspect of her ideal-self. Mothering, like a post-natal extra-uterine placental provision, is envisaged as exclusive and continuous (dyad I).

For a pregnant Regulator, anxiety often governs the interchange if she feels the woman she has hitherto been is endangered by the inexorable process of pregnancy. Furthermore, she is unable to control the parasitic invader who has appropriated her insides, feeding off her and spewing its waste into her. She may feel the need to erect a 'barrier' of emotional detachment to protect herself from exploitation by the uncontrollable greedy-needy foetus and, following the birth, may continue to experience the infant as dangerous, unconsciously representing a repudiated insatiable, weak or dependent aspect of herself (dyad II).

Yet another woman's inside story may hinge on imagery of herself as empty, or full of 'bad stuff'. Fearing that her vulnerable baby is being exposed to harmful forces inside her (dyad III), she will try to counteract her own deficiencies by eating special foods or thinking good thoughts, and strive vigilantly to protect the foetus from her own bad influences by constantly ensuring the baby's safety. Doubts about her mothering capacity may relate to a sense of herself being flawed by deprivation of early nurturing, and/or through loss of self-esteem arising from complications during the pregnancy, labour or birth. A shift may occur post-natally, as obstacles arise that prevent the Facilitator within her from fulfilling her own standards of perfection. She may become depressed, feeling she has betrayed her own ideals and failed her baby irrevocably. No longer able to see herself as an ideal, generous, good mother, she feels she has become a bad mother to her vulnerable, innocent and trusting baby, impairing the experience of an idyllic infancy, or inflicting long-lasting damage (dyad III). In one mother's words: 'The birth was so bloody awful, I felt a murder had been committed and our relationship was spoilt before it even began.' Such relationships may become 'corrective', with the mother desperately hoping to assuage her own guilt by compensating for imperfections.

A fourth mother may experience the foetus and herself as mutually harmful, threatened by noxious substances if the 'placental barrier' between them becomes permeable. She may feel the only way to protect herself from the inner assault, or the baby from her internal 'poisons', is to get on with her usual life, disengaging from the pregnancy and leaving the foetus to 'sink or swim'. Post-natally, she may contrive to create distance between herself and the baby by emotional withdrawal or geographical separation. A temporary spatial barrier serves a dual purpose – protecting the mother from ascribed infantile criticism or emotional contamination (being sucked back into old dependencies) and allowing her opportunities to go elsewhere to replenish her adult resources. In addition, if she is doubtful about her own maternal qualities, shared care-giving not only shelters the baby from her constant influence, but also gives her an alibi against future blame. Shared-care may seem essential in itself to the Regulator mother intent on mitigating her own 'bad' forces by utilizing a Facilitator care-giver to provide positive ones: 'Work is my sanity [says one depressed mother]. When I'm stuck at home with the screeching baby I feel I'm going crazy and don't know who I am any more, or what he wants from me, or how long I can stand his helpless, clinging dependence without throwing him out of the window' (dyad IV).

Although I have presented these as separate positions, it is unusual for a woman to be completely fixed in one orientation. Most women oscillate between two or three positions at different times within a pregnancy, and even during the course of a day. However, an affective 'climate' of pregnancy prevails, as one coupling position predominates or two alternate. Where a woman holds a determinedly 'fixed' position during pregnancy, post-natal difficulties between mother and baby are foreseeable as disillusionment or paranoia set in.

Sometimes during pregnancy a woman is able to achieve an intermediate balance that holds both herself and her foetus in focus as two separate but interrelated ambivalent people. Neither 'good' nor 'bad', but *mixed*, she is aware of the reciprocal give-and-take of their respective positions, a temporary connectedness during which they commensally share food and space. Usually, this capacity for healthy ambivalence goes hand in hand with a realistic assessment of her own mother (and partner) who is also accepted as a related but separate individual, and a mixture of both 'good' and 'bad'. Although in some ways 'Reciprocators', as I have called this fifth dyad, appear to be in an intermediate position between Facilitators (dyads, I, III) and Regulators (dyads II, IV), and indeed engage in both types of behaviour, they, too, have their own underlying philosophy that guides their baby-care activities. Reciprocators tend from the outset to conceive of the child as a potentially whole and multi-faceted person, with whom they can interact reciprocally through negotiation rather than either facilitating (adapting to the baby) or regulating (expecting the baby to adapt) following birth. In other words, rather than seeing the baby as symbiotically merged with the mother and totally dependent upon her (like the Facilitator), or as separate but as yet pre-sociable or asocial and in need of socialization (like the Regulator), the Reciprocator sees the baby as a separate, outgoing, sociable person capable of forming relationships and making demands. Since the infant is regarded as sharing similar emotions to the parents (although at a different level of sophistication), the Reciprocator parent feels she or he can learn to understand the baby, and can be understood. The mother of a two-week-old baby tells this story: 'Parenthood is a permanent state of self-questioning and transactions – we're learning all the time and getting to know each other; there are some powerful moments of communication and exchange. But my mother, who is quite alarmed by my attitude, wrote me: "Make sure she doesn't get the upper hand while her daddy's away".'

Finally, there are women who refuse to engage with the foetus at all. This may involve psychotic denial of the pregnancy or a conscious disengagement from the baby. Either way, it augurs badly for the future relationship (dyad V).

His story

Similarly, fathers-to-be have a comparable range of positive–negative conceptualizations of self, partner and baby from which they construe their own stories. Feeling enriched and generous, one man may try to make his contribution to the gestation by nurturing his pregnant partner, indirectly helping the baby grow with his attention and stroking, or directly 'feeding' the foetus with his semen. Another may wish he had his woman's positive capacity to be pregnant, yet feels concerned about her exploitation by the foetus, or guilt-ridden about having made her undergo the sufferings of pregnancy on his behalf. Yet another may be so envious of the woman's capacity to form, carry and have the immediate intimate connection with their baby that he feels the need to compete with her, acting as arbiter of childbearing lore or go-between for the foetus. Yet another partner feels separate from the idealized dyad of mother and baby, either because he already seems left out by them or leaves himself out, wishing to protect them from his presence – which he sees as worthless or contaminating. He may react to exclusion by withdrawing into depression or take flight into busy activity. Alternatively, he may feel compelled to fight with his rival over his female partner's body and affection. In this case, he may become very demanding of her attention, or seek another sexual partner, particularly if he feels persecuted by the idea of the baby spying on him or grabbing his penis during intercourse; or, he may try to prevent the woman's closeness to her foetus through verbal prohibitions or even physical violence. Finally, identifying himself with an endangered, imprisoned, vulnerable foetus, an expectant father may insist on controlling his partner, perhaps by attending all ante-natal clinics – not in order to support her, but as birth-advocate for the baby whom he feels to be threatened by the woman. Likewise, he may wish to determine her intake and behaviour, or, seeing himself as the saviour, he may try to intervene between foetus and mother if he feels them to be mutually incompatible.

In general terms, we may identify two ends of a paternal spectrum: a 'Participator' father, who feels elated when, following his excruciatingly helpless and envious experience of watching the exhilarating birth, he can finally participate more fully, greeting directly the baby hitherto experienced only through the mediating mother. If, during pregnancy, identification with the foetus has allowed his vicarious re-entry to the maternal womb, fatherhood now grants him a symbolic repossession of infancy. Drawing on maternal aspects of himself rooted in early identification with his nurturing mother (whom he emulates or surpasses), he cradles and croons, strokes and caresses the newborn, and takes over most of the baby-care if his partner permits it. However, if she has set her heart on exclusive mothering, their respective desires for exclusivity may clash: 'I yearn to be everything to my son, but she has the milk and she was there first', says one such father poignantly.

By contrast, the 'Renouncer' father feels quite clear about the gender division of labour: 'I'm sure I will be close to my son when he's one or two. I know it's old-fashioned, but just now I'm proud to be looking after my family, protecting them and being the breadwinner.' At an unconscious level, the infant may be seen to embody many split-off, weak, needy and dependent parts of the father that he is reluctant to repossess by empathic caring. Renouncing his own infantile experience and feminine identifications with his early mother, he postpones fathering until the baby can talk. Depending on his partner's orientation, he may be let off the hook of primary care, or drawn into it against his will by a mother who feels persecuted by the baby and wishes for relief.

Finally, fathers too may believe in reciprocity. What distinguishes the Reciprocator parent, male or female, seems to be an ability to encompass simultaneity and continuity of various senses of self (physical, social, intra-psychic, pre-verbal and speeched) and of masculine/feminine identifications, without having to repudiate or fear being taken over by them. The capacity to tolerate the ongoing struggle within, without hiving off sections of themselves, enables Reciprocators to conceive of the child, even before birth, as a potentially whole, ambivalent and multi-faceted person with whom they can interact; and, as such, sets the scene for a particular set of familial narratives.

Interactive stories

When both parents are Reciprocators, the household will neither revolve entirely around the child nor be adult-centred. Although the baby's needs are entitled to full consideration, by the same token so are everybody else's in the family, including those of the parents. Special concessions are made to the infant's inability to wait, and to his or her limitations in communicating and understanding language, or in holding on to a memory for very long. However, this does not mean always putting the baby's needs first (as in a Facilitator/ Participator mode) or pressurizing the baby to adapt to the parents' rhythms (as in a Regulator/Renouncer mode). Adjustments have continually to be made, as routines and activities are reassessed at every phase of the baby's growth in accordance with changing needs and the daily fluctuations of the household.

A Regulator espoused to a Participator may instigate a role-reversal of parenting, with him acting as the primary care-giver. Alternatively, parents may share care between them, as many a Facilitator and Participator do. Likewise, a Regulator/Renouncer partnership may reach an agreement to establish a dual-career household with hired care for the baby, treating their adult relationship as the primary unit (in contrast to the Facilitator's emphasis on mother and baby).

Mismatch of the partners' orientations can have a profound effect on family life. For instance, a Facilitator whose vision of mothering entails her own continuous, exclusive care of the baby may become depressed post-natally if her Participator partner competes with her over primary care, or if economic, medical or social circumstances force her to leave her baby. Conversely, when a traditional Renouncer insists (perhaps on the basis of his own internalized model of parenting) that his Regulator spouse be a house-bound mother, she may suffer post-natal distress if full-time motherhood poses a threat. Being exposed without respite to her tiny baby may feel dangerous and depressing, particularly if she experiences the baby as aggressive, wild or judgmental, and is unable to interpose the safeguard of a 'defence barrier' between them (see dyad II of the placental paradigm – Table 2). Similarly, lack of employment and economic dependence may undermine her decision to share care as she tries to resume her previous identity and 'real' life.

In other mothers, *internal conflicts* cause depression. Feeling frustrated by motherhood, but guilt-ridden and reproached for wanting to leave her child, a woman may herself be torn between the orientation she had anticipated pre-natally and the reality of her circumstances as a mother:

> I feel I'm not allowed to be a real Person. I'm supposed to be totally devoted, but when I'm with him I'm always wishing I was somewhere else or that he'd go to sleep and not need me. It's unbearable for me because all the things that I depend on to feel my usual self, like reading and sleeping and keeping myself looking trim and well-dressed, are incompatible with being a full-time mother on-call. I'm trying to do things right, and am afraid that if I deviate at all from our routine all hell with break loose. I feel desperate because I know how very important it is for him to have a good start and give him everything he needs, but ever since his excruciating birth I haven't the space to recuperate and pull myself together and/or feel good about myself as a person, and I'm turning out to be such a terrible mother (dyad III).

Such bi-polar conflicts may also reflect inner contradictions between internalized maternal and paternal demands.

As we have noted, conscious perceptions of affective permutations fluctuate during pregnancy with each expectant parent's psycho-social conditions. Post-natally, they are also influenced by the temperament of the baby. Although most babies prove incredibly adaptable to parental orientations, some will override these, refusing to adjust, or forcing their flexible, doting parents into an unexpected routine. Parents may become disappointed and severely distressed by a baby who fails to live up to their pre-natal symbolic representations or post-natal expectations; an unsoothable, crying baby will not reinforce maternal bountifulness; a high-spirited baby may refuse to become regulated; or an ordinary baby who will not become perfect, or who 'shows up' the parents' badness, will invalidate preformed parental stories.

Similarly, events surrounding labour and birth – such as prematurity, neo-natal illness, or an unexpected caesarean section – can throw parental orientation off course. In addition, as noted earlier, many parents are simply unprepared for the profound impact of close intimate contact and continuous responsibility for a fragile, needy, dependent baby. Inevitably, parenting, with its exposure to the sounds, sights, smells and substances of infancy, evokes memories of other babies. Where there has been no adult experience of infants, pertinent emotional climates from the parents' own infancies and those of their siblings may be powerfully reactivated. Interestingly, parents do not necessarily maintain the same orientation with a subsequent baby. Internal stories change as a result of psycho-social circumstances, developments within psychic reality and, above all, the experience of having parented the previous baby.

In conclusion, at an unconscious level the emotional constellation of each parent's internal world will determine the outlines of the story they begin to enact, depending upon which fantasy aspects of the paradigm are operative. Whether a benign or malevolent image of self, parent, partner and/or baby predominates, who each represents, and how their respective orientations mesh with each other, will all play a part in fashioning the tales to be told. While the specific *content* of individual fantasies varies from couple to couple, sub-culturally, and even in the same woman in different pregnancies, it is nevertheless possible to summarize some general trends in the stories of family interaction, as I have done in Table 3.

'Our tales are spun, but for the most part we don't spin them; they spin us', comments Dennett, with whose quote this chapter began. What I find when reproductive stories are spun is that ante-natal affective representations of the parents' own baby-selves, and of themselves as future parents, set the scene for post-natal patterns of interaction within the family. Family stories are transmitted through parental beliefs, child-care practices and the unique emotional 'climate' of the household to which the baby contributes through his or her own personality. In addition, the gestation and birth of an

Table 3   Family orientations

Mother	Baby	Father	
+	+	+	facilitation/potential competition
+	+	−	mother/baby exclusivity
+	−	+	couple-oriented; 'socialization' of baby
+	−	−	'mother knows best'; regulation
−	+	−	baby-centred compensation
−	+	+	mother excluded/rejected
−	−	+	deference ('. . . because I said so!')
−	−	−	entrappedness
+/−	+/−	+/−	reciprocation-negotiated exchange

infant provokes intense excitation of unconscious mental life, reactivating residues of the adult's own infantile experiences. In turn, the baby responds not only to the manifest behaviour of the care-givers and the overt story of their intertwining lives, but also interacts with their silent desires, unconscious fantasies and emotional preoccupations. These, as we have seen, are legacies not only from each adult's ongoing life-story, but from the parents' own infantile stories, embedded within a specific time and socio-cultural context, and having evolved under the care – and within the narrative of – his or her own mother, father and/or significant others.

Note

[1] Some of these examples appear in Raphael-Leff, 1993.

Joan Raphael-Leff

6
Daughters Becoming Mothers

A developmental perspective

I recently asked a young female solicitor of my acquaintance, who specializes in family law, for her comments on how daughters become mothers. She replied, 'By shagging a soldier or sailor down Union Street while under the influence of drink or drugs or, more usually, both.' She added that she believed very few daughters become mothers deliberately, accident having the greater part to play. She has a lawyer's mind, and showed me how rarefied my psychoanalytic thinking is for many people, with its assumption of intention and wish at an unconscious level. A lawyer approaches things from a quite different angle, and assumes irrationality exists without having to investigate or try to understand it. This was true of my friend – despite her ability to be deeply concerned with some of the disasters that occur, to be compassionate and involved with her clients' pain, and especially to be moved by the distress of the children involved in family disputes.

As a psychoanalyst who came to psychoanalysis through general medical practice as a family doctor, I have a history of being interested in obstetrics and paediatrics, and more and more in development, both physical and psychological, so that psychoanalysis and its developmental aspects are of compelling interest to me. It is therefore the developmental aspect of the process of daughters becoming mothers that I propose to address, and the fact that mothering is basically a very bodily matter. I am, of course, myself a daughter, and I also have a daughter – although she is not yet a mother. I look forward to the day when she may become one but, to begin, I want to tell you a brief story about her.

When my own daughter was small, about 2½ or 3 years old, and was sitting on my knee, talking confidentially, as children will, about life matters and growing up, and the time when she, too, might be a grown-up and would have charge of her own future, she reflected on our conversation and made a statement about her own future that included the phrase 'When I'm grown up, and I'm the mummy, and you are the little girl, we will . . .'

This way of understanding life events happens in children, and also in the unconscious mind of adults. The unconscious mind was Sigmund Freud's arena, and he laid down principles for its operation, including those of timelessness and exemption from mutual contradiction (1915). Ignacio Matte-Blanco (1975) took the concept of unconscious processes further, and used the term *symmetry* to describe the kind of thinking that my daughter exhibited. For her, time was neither important nor even existent, and it could be imaginatively reversed – I would become the little girl and she would become the mother. Adult Aristotelian thought does not allow us such ideas, and calls them irrational. In our time-ridden world there is another truth: all mothers are daughters, but not all daughters become mothers. Those daughters who become mothers *develop* into mothers. The question is about how they do that, and how different sorts of daughters, with different sorts of early experience, do it differently.

Everything begins from something, and it is not only experience that affects us in our development. I have never found it necessary to assume that all human beings are born with the same set of psychological potentials, any more than we have the same physical ones. We differ, and our inherent potentials for development will differ too. There is no standard invention called 'the baby', any more than there is 'the mother' or 'the father'. These terms contain condensations and distortions of many different kinds, they are caricature figures that we use when talking about development – necessary, convenient fictions. Bear with me while I, too, distort perfectly ordinary, decent people into fictional caricatures for the sake of my theme, and take an imaginary journey alongside a daughter who will become a mother. The description will contain some, although not all, of the possibilities.

An imaginary journey

The process by which daughters become mothers is a long and perilous one. One might say it starts with the girl's own birth, and will be affected by her own reception into the world. Is she herself delivered into the arms of a well-prepared, delighted and happy mother, who is supported by a loving, proud man, and surrounded by welcoming and contented grandparents and siblings? This romantic dream of baby's arrival is rarely achieved. Not all babies are wanted, and even the wanted ones are notoriously inconveniencing, even in the best possible circumstances.

So let's give our caricature daughter a mother who is ordinarily pleased with her new baby and who does not get depressed or put her up for adoption. We'll also make it only one baby – twins are complicated. To help the mother be secure, the baby's parents' relationship could be ordinarily mixed and moderately stable, with possibilities of both joy and pain, and neither of them need suffer from more than an average level of neurosis. You might think that she is rather a lucky baby, or at least in a minority. What will the world she is born into do to her?

Entering the cycle

When a new baby is born, three important questions are asked simultaneously: Is it alive? Does it appear normal? Is it a boy or a girl? Take the last question first. Some years ago I gave lectures and seminars to pupil midwives working in a predominantly Asian part of West London, and had to do much work with the distress of the largely Westernized nurses at the humiliation and punishment of young mothers who had been so foolish as to have a girl baby. A maternity ward in England nowadays is supposed to be visited by proud fathers and euphoric grandparents, not angry and depressed men and viragoes of mothers-in-law screeching in contemptuous rage at helpless, cowering women. The problem for us was to understand how such young mothers, ashamed of this failure within their arranged marriages, a failure unwilled by them, might be able to invest the relationship with the shaming baby girl with the pride and joy that we, in our Western culture, might think was the right of every baby.

Gender is still important, even in our Western, supposedly sophisticated, egalitarian society. Today, our preoccupation is with fear of persecution, and there is an anxiety that even noticing difference might indicate preference or prejudice. Ideas of political correctness can persecute us all. Slightly older babies are frequently dressed, or otherwise presented to the world, with subtle or quite distinct gender messages. Many babies are disguised as neuter, and one has to ask rather apologetically whether it is Daniel or Danielle one is admiring. I say one has to *ask*, because I believe most people want to know the gender of those they meet, even babies, and can become quite disturbed by not knowing. Therefore, right from the beginning of life, gender matters in social situations. It is observable, too, that the behaviour of adults varies according to the gender of the baby. There is a tendency for girl babies to be handled and spoken to more gently, stroked more, and held closer to mother's body more of the time than boy babies, who are more likely to be spoken to in a lively and stimulating tone, and held out to face mother.

Through physical handling, when holding, nursing or changing the baby, as well as through tone of voice, frequency and style of interchange, smiles, laughs, games and responses to distress, there are many ways in which a mother can express her inner feelings and basic attitude to her baby and her baby's gender, and many possible ways in which the baby may pick them up. A woman's pleasure in her baby's body, the calmness or otherwise with which she accepts dirty nappies and regurgitation, dribbles and mess, will depend a lot of her feelings about bodies in general, especially her own and that of her partner. The slightest hint of disgust, or any other evidence of inhibition, will be picked up by a baby, sensitive as she is to her mother's muscle tone, breathing rate and facial expression. Anxieties reflected in questions about the baby's survival and her normality are also likely to affect the patterns of physical care.

How does a baby experience differences in the ways that even the most consistent mother may handle her, while at the same time making some sort of sense of the messages from her own physical, emotional and instinctive internal world? She cannot yet know the sources of pleasure or distress, internal or external, and it is not surprising that as soon as she can recognize the existence of another – her mother or mothering person – much of the feeling is attributed externally. Mother can be a rescuing angel, tender, warm, adoring and adorable, devoted above all to her baby, and perceived as the source of all goodness. Or, at painful, frightened moments, she can become a threatening, witch-like, torturing hag who might devour the baby or cast her out into eternal isolation. The ways in which these early polarized feelings are contained – and they will best be contained by consistent and mostly positive loving mothering – are crucial for the infant's internalization of such capacities herself, and eventually to the kind of mother that she will herself become. She will unconsciously either adopt or defend herself against much of her mother's perceived feelings, and these will affect her own capacity to be angelic or witch-like.

Therefore the way a new baby is handled by her mother transmits much of the mother's unconscious attitudes and feelings, and will lay the foundations for the growing girl's pattern of making relation-ships. In the end, this will affect the relationship she has with her own baby years hence. The work of John Bowlby (1969, 1973, 1980) at the Tavistock Clinic initiated longitudinal studies of attachment that are now showing that the ways mothers and babies relate at different stages have a predictive value for subsequent patterns of behaviour and relating. Studies of the social development of the children of mothers who suffered from puerperal depression show long-term effects on their capacities to relate and the ways in which they do (Murray *et al.*, 1991). A psychoanalyst can now theorize with more conviction than ever that the unconscious attitudes and feelings of a mother inevitably affect her child. In the wider world we can reflect on how society's failures to protect the vulnerable, such as insecure young mothers, cost us much in the long run when their children, in turn, grow up insecure and in need of help.

Out of generosity to our imaginary baby, let's give her a mother who likes herself and her baby most of the time, and who can tolerate the baby's distresses without being persecuted by them, so that she can begin to integrate the extremes of feeling and not be painfully subject to them.

Even when they are babies, daughters have fathers as well as mothers. Fathers are important, not just because the relationship between the parents is bound to affect the mother's internal world, and hence the baby's, but also because the baby notices the separate existence of father very early on, even though the realization that these two important people have a separate relationship, existing prior to and apart from the one they each have with the baby, may not be reached immediately. A father's own joy or otherwise in his daughter will also be perceived by means of his attitude, his handling, and the many non-verbal clues that infants are so sensitive to. A cold, distant or distracted father, who fails to respond to a child's welcoming smile or appeal to be picked up, will crush something of the child's belief in herself as lovable and valuable. While this can be survived if it happens occasionally, repeated doses wear away the potential for self-esteem like drips of water on a stone. In order to help our imaginary father, we must believe that he is basically a kind man, perhaps even in love with the baby's mother; that the child is indeed his; that he, too, is pleased to have a daughter; and that the many anxieties of contemporary life do not threaten him too much. We might even give him a job.

The perils and pains of two-person relationships are the source of internal splitting, and the polarization of relationships and qualities into extremes of good and bad, making people into saints and fiends. Three-person relationships hold further problems, including managing feelings of envy, rage, fear, blame, contempt, denigration and jealousy that are characteristic of the 'two-person' state of mind (see Chapter 3). We must hope that our invented parents, all too rare in reality, are able to help the growing little girl through the realization that, sadly, she cannot marry her Daddy, that the Mummy who stands in her way is, after all, quite decent and lovable and can be put up with, and that the Daddy who interrupts the cosy girly times with Mummy by taking Mummy's attention away from her can also be tolerated.

Of course, many children these days are brought up in one-parent families, and the parental relationship may exist only in fantasy. It does seem as if this fantasy always exists. Those working with abandoned children, adopted children and orphans will tell you that an expectation of two parents is universal among children and is almost always quite conscious. It seems that the 'father in mother's mind' can be tremendously important, and that children look to find him there.

Grandparents, too, are important, and provide a sense of continuity in a child's life, and in a particular way for girls. The cycle of reproduction most directly affects girls and women whose bodies are so inevitably involved in the process. To learn that Grandma is Mummy's Mummy, or Daddy's Mummy, and that the powerful adults who are now parents were once themselves little and immature, gives the beginning of a sense of generation that allows the little girl to know that the situation will not merely be reversed, as my daughter thought, but is ongoing. She can begin to imagine consciously that she will, in time, have her own babies, and that Mummy will one day be a Grandma too. The existence of grandparents modifies the power of parents, who take their place in the hierarchy and are not absolute authorities. Now there are so many single mothers, grandparents may have even more importance. A grandfather, for instance, may become the most powerful male influence in a child's life, and provide a model for the masculine identifications necessary for both boys and girls.

But to begin with, the baby girl exists most strongly in relation to her mother. If her mother is pleased with her little girl's body, and this is most likely when she is pleased with her own and she has a partner who is pleased with it too, then we can expect that things are going well.

A developing world

Supposing our little girl more or less survives her infancy and becomes a toddler – how does she see herself in relation to future motherhood? If she gets on well enough with her mother, and recognizes that her mother is pleased with her own role as a mother, she can easily assume that motherhood will happen to her, although she may reverse the position of mother and daughter in fantasy and wish to mother her own mother. She may play with dolls, with soft toys or even hard ones which may have to be cared for by her, put to bed, dressed up, and taken on shopping trips or on visits – including those to Grandma, who must know the name of the toy and at least something of its history. A family will often accept the need for this pretence to be taken seriously, and enter into the game that the toy, or imaginary companion, needs to be included in family life. The little girl's behaviour will be closely modelled on her mother's, and mothers can be chastened to see in a daughter's behaviour a caricature of their own crosser moments when observing her severity. Little girls who are free enough, and have not become too guilty in their Oedipal conflicts, also develop masculine identifications – and these, in turn, support the development of feminine ones and are an enriching element in life.

When a new baby arrives, the girl is put into a difficult position. In the face of this concrete evidence of the parents' love for each other, the little girl may feel desperately displaced. She no longer occupies the powerful position of being special, the most vulnerable and needy in the family, and she may be full of hatred and resentment. There can be two reasons for this. First, she may be envious of the new baby's position and the attention it gains. How can all her own achievements, her motor ability and sphincter control, apparently so valued by her parents up to now, be passed over in favour of a squalling bundle of unco-ordinated messiness and greed? Second, how can she stand the fact that Mummy has a new baby, given to her by Daddy, and she herself has not? Either way, she stands to lose: if she has developed self-esteem, she may feel devalued; if she hasn't, her lowly position is confirmed. What will she do? Denying her resentment and hatred, a girl may become 'mother's little helper', or she may, in disgust with the mother's absorption with the interloper, turn to her father and use the opportunity to develop the more masculine aspect of herself by becoming quite boyish – taking an interest in sport, using tools to mend things, enjoying her body in an athletic way, and learning to cycle and swim. A new baby, an interest for mother, gives the little girl with an appropriate father an opportunity of developing a new relationship, one that can lay the foundations of a knowledge of masculinity that in due course will become part of her choice of partner.

A warning note here. Our little heroine, however unlikely she is in these days of increasingly complicated relationships, has 'normal' parents – so far, indeed, ones that stay together. But while speaking of a daughter's intensifying relationship with her father, we also have to hope that his love for her and his delight in her will not become sexualized and develop into abuse. If that perverse tendency exists, then the arrival of a new baby and mother's intense investment in the new relationship can be an occasion when a man whose boundaries are insecure may become too gratified by the affection of his daughter, and may confuse her infantile seductiveness with the adult version. The little girl whose Oedipal fantasies are realized by a father who does allow her to rival or supplant her mother has her normal psychosexual development badly disrupted, often too badly to recover. The more serious cases are those in which actual physical and sexual intrusion occurs, together with various constellations of guilt and secrecy, denial and cruelty. However, less overtly damaging situations are also dangerous. Parents who idealize openness and informality to the extent of immodesty about their own sexuality, who are devoted to nudity in the home, or to having their children continue to share the parental bed, are running a risk. The internal fantasy world of the child is hidden from them, and they may be exciting or frightening their child beyond the level that is tolerable. Overwhelming a child's capacity to cope with feelings is traumatic, and the result can inhibit or distort normal development. The results of such damage may not be apparent until puberty or later, when girls may retreat from their own sexual development in various ways – eating disorders, idealization of the body through pathological exercising with resulting ill-health, or sexual or relational problems – including promiscuity and sexual frigidity. These retreats affect her abilities to become a mother herself.

However, to return to our 'daughter' whose fate is to become a mother in time. She will, of course, go to school, meet her teachers, her peers and their families, creating new opportunities to observe and relate to maternal elements in these and other situations. Even if she has no brothers, she will discover the existence and significance of boys and the possibility of romantic fantasy. Age 6 to 7 is the age group for fairy tales, and the mending of the Oedipal wound in fantasy. Evil witches are overthrown, wicked queens meet their deserved end, persecuted and deserving princesses and goose girls meet and marry their princes, and everyone lives happily ever after. The maternal aspect of the girl may be acted out in relation to pets, or small children, who are often very fiercely mothered while her interest lasts – although, it has to be said, they may be suddenly dropped when it wanes!

Identification with some of the mother's attributes continues, often in an exaggerated way. Many little girls become severe and rivalrous moralists at this age, and patterns of acceptance by a particular social group may become imbued with moral flavouring. I have heard the daughters of quite reasonable women exclaim, 'My mother would kill me if . . .' How they dress, the language they use, whether they change for games in the sight of boys or younger children, may carry significance unrecognized by the adult world. The good opinion of peers and adults is paramount. Some girls at this age may be 'good', sometimes priggishly so, while others can be flirtatious and provocative; acceptance by the group is important to both sexes, but the paths to it differ markedly. The extremes of gender identification can be stereotypical: the little girl being a caricature of different aspects of femininity, in contrast to the extreme machismo of the little boy.

Burgeoning sexuality

Our girl is now approaching puberty, and the way in which she accepts her changing body will depend on her growing sense of security about becoming a woman. This will depend significantly on her feelings about her mother as a woman, and whether the development into womanhood still seems an attractive proposition. In turn, this will depend on her mother's attitude in the present towards her own femininity, and towards her daughter's impending sexual growth and blooming, something that is also influenced by father's feelings towards both mother and daughter.

There is a resurgence of the possibilities of conflict and rivalry with mother at this time, echoing earlier times, which can be a source of many problems that adolescents pose in families. Parents can find themselves despised and condemned for their old-fashioned attitudes and their stupidity, and they can find themselves provoked into behaving in ways that allow the adolescent to feel justified in those attitudes. Adolescents are often able, quite subtly, to find the areas of disagreement between parents and use them to their own advantage. The presence of a newly sexual girl, full of the anxieties and contradictions normal at that stage of life, can disturb the equilibrium of even stable families, and dangerously upset those families whose balance and stability are precarious. These young people are not easy to have around, although the questions they ask are often salutary.

Conflict is made no easier when the girl has turned away from mother to father, rejecting her model of womanhood for either a tomboy-like association with the male world or a retreat into isolation. Her peer group can be a valuable mediating influence at these times. The urgent need of the teenage girl to communicate constantly with her group, to the extent that she may 'need' to phone a school friend from whom she has parted only ten minutes before, is very recognizable. Female acceptance is gauged by the response of the 'best friend' of the moment, or of the group. Awareness of minute details of appearance, hairdo, lipstick colour, make of jeans or trainers, is exquisite. For my own private classification I have named this the 'Body Shop' phase of development, as it is in this establishment that one sees girls, as it were, in pure culture, experimenting with the lotions and potions that are supposed to make them acceptable – not – as one might think – to the opposite sex, but to their own group and its delicately judged tastes.

Although the position of parents is difficult, it is terribly important that they can be differed from, argued with, and challenged, either openly or in subtle, silent rebellion; and for a girl, it is frequently mother who is most challenged. Mother's attitudes, reflecting her inner beliefs about what being a woman means, may again be crucial, if only to be differed from. She may be dismissed as being completely out of touch, or she may be taken for granted. The reality of mother as a human being with feelings of her own is unwanted. After all, daughters feel quite grown up enough to be able to take charge of their own lives, and an anxious mother is merely a hindrance. Why should she be concerned with what time her daughter gets in at night; doesn't she trust her? On the other hand, a trusting mother may be accusingly asked: 'Why did you let me go on the school trip? Weren't you worried about me? X's mother didn't let her go! She cares!' The implication, then, is that permissiveness means unlovingness and neglect.

Nor are fathers let off the hook. A man who has quite ordinarily loved his little girl suddenly finds that she has metamorphosed into someone who is quite disturbingly sexy, reminiscent of his own adolescent dreams, or even his adult ones. The presence of a bevy of her friends at a weekend or on a holiday, unaware that they might have an effect on the person they see as an 'old man', may be too much for him. He may attempt to restrict her behaviour: 'You are not going out dressed like that!' 'What do you think you look like?' Or he may become over-flirtatious and, in their eyes, laughable.

A mother's response to her partner and her own sexual development is important. She may still be confident of her own sexuality, or she may respond badly to her own ageing and her daughter's flowering. A rivalrous mother may become over-invested in her own attractiveness and pay excessive attention to her own clothing and feminine attributes. Or she may respond to her own rivalry by suppressing it, and her own attractiveness at the same time. Much too often the combination of a beautiful, flowering, adolescent daughter and a wife whose response is to retreat into dowdiness leads to marital tensions. Not a few men find younger colleagues attractive when their daughters bloom. Many mothers with difficulties owning their sexuality, and who may not be too far from the menopause, take what they see as a welcome opportunity to resign from the arena, leaving their daughters to fight the battle for them, with disastrous results for their own lives and those of their partners and daughters. Daughters will observe the effect of their own maturation on their parents and on the relationship between them. If this effect is felt to be damaging, there is more scope for feelings of guilt to emerge and to lay the foundations for future problems when the daughter herself becomes a mother. On the other hand, a mother who is confident in sharing the role of sexual woman, who understands the necessity for her daughter to identify away from her, who can take joy in her own and her daughter's achievement – even when she seems to be excluded from all that interests her daughter – conveys that being a woman is a good and satisfying place to be. It is then that the signs are hopeful.

In later adolescence peer groups are less fluid, tastes and friendships settle down, and awareness of feminine characteristics acquires a sense of needing to relate to the opposite sex. Gradually the awareness of boys, and later on men, prepares the way for the next relationships in which womanhood defines itself. These new actors on the scene change things dramatically, although old attitudes, including the internalizations of parental attitudes, will be brought to bear on the new situation. Many young women unconsciously choose their partners on a maternal model. Ask a girl what characteristics she's looking for in a boy, and you will often hear the answer 'someone to look after me'. The actual attitude of a mother to her daughter will still matter.

When a girl brings her boyfriend home, more unconscious attitudes are revealed in the family, and these will, in turn, affect the girl. One woman who, as a daughter, found her mother's flirtatiousness and her father's rivalry with the young men she brought home excruciating, reacted violently against them and left home early for a rather promiscuous lifestyle, finally settling down with an older man who epitomized Establishment values in being publicly respected, but who repeatedly betrayed her. Her own daughter has echoed and reversed the maternal conflict in espousing 'good causes', thus being apparently ultra-respectable. At the same time, her aggressive political correctness risks damaging her career prospects. The daughter's promiscuity lies not in sexuality, but in promising more than she can deliver to her worthy causes; in contrast, her mother's stance took the more usual one of serial sexual partners, experimentation with drugs, and fringe criminal behaviour.

Our daughter, like most young women exploring their sexuality, will require the assurance that it is accepted at some level, and particularly by her mother. In adolescence there is a reawakening of Oedipal anxieties, not this time because of the desire for father, but as a result of rivalling mother, who may unconsciously be perceived much as the little girl saw her so long ago – witch-like and punishing of her wishes for independence. If the earlier problems were severe, unconscious echoes of those conflicts, including the girl's guilt about rivalling mother (now by actually daring to be like her in seeking a rewarding sexual life and eventually babies), may inhibit the development of her sexual life. Many young women find sexual satisfaction easy to achieve before marriage, when it is forbidden fruit and secret. Once married, or otherwise openly in a relationship, satisfaction may be much more difficult. Mother is being openly rivalled, and the punishment meted out to the girl by her own unconscious belief that her sexuality is resented as much as she once resented that of her mother, may be severe. Enjoyment may be curtailed, sexual life may be experienced as a burden or a duty, and in extreme cases womanhood itself may be experienced as victimhood. Such young women may have difficulties in marriage or its equivalent, in conceiving, in enjoying pregnancy, in labour, and in caring for their own baby if and when one arrives.

So let's give our young woman a late adolescence with enough identification away from her mother, an enjoyable amount of rebellion and licence, but let's protect her magically from extremes of behaviour. She can experiment a little with soft drugs. In time, she can go on the pill to keep her from early pregnancy and its strains, or from a guilt- or remorse-inducing termination (which could affect her relationship with subsequent babies), or from a live baby requiring ultra-rapid maturation on her part – which she might be too resentful or immature to manage. She can be lucky enough to avoid HIV, and she needn't break her heart too often before she finds, say in her mid-twenties, a heterosexual relationship with the potential to mature.

Coming full circle

Having found a partner, the next stage in the journey to motherhood is conception, which does not always go to plan. Having allowed our heroine to avoid unwanted pregnancy, will she conceive easily? Will she, indeed, have a choice? Or will she join the increasing queues at the infertility clinics? And if she does not conceive, what unconscious meaning may that have for her? Sometimes the guilt of daring to rival mother, perhaps increased by the guilt of stealing mother-in-law's precious son, can inhibit sexuality and make conception difficult. I have met a couple who could make love freely and easily – except at the fertile time, when they became quite overcome and inhibited by anxiety. Another couple, married for some years and quite active sexually, were amazed to be told that, in spite of all they believed, they had never achieved penetrative intercourse. But let us allow our couple to conceive.

I have been struck many times with a major potential change in the internal world of my women patients – that is, the change that can occur in a woman's closest relationships during a first pregnancy. It is often said that very early disasters in development are given a second chance during adolescence, that children at this stage of major physical and emotional change re-work many of their very early conflicts with their parents and siblings. I believe that, for many women, there is yet a third chance that is given in their first pregnancy, another stage of enormous physical and emotional change.

Historically, babies have simply been a consequence of sexual intercourse, frequently an unplanned consequence, and not, as the infantile fantasy might lead us to believe, the prime purpose of adult sexuality. Even today, many babies are unwelcome; but pregnancy changes women, and provides an extraordinary opportunity for adjustment in stepping into a new stage of life. Many young women in the after-effects of adolescence, having dismissed their old-fashioned and useless mothers and begun their adult lives with an unconscious counter-identification or a conscious decision to be different from them, begin to experience a warmth and wish to be close to these redundant figures in their lives. They start to ask questions: 'What was I like as a baby? Was I breast fed? For how long were you sick? What does labour feel like?' These are body and feeling questions, and thus questions about what it is actually like to be the sort of woman Mum is or was. It may begin to become apparent that Mum did, after all, bring her up and can't have been all that bad, or that some of the reasons for Mum's behaviour become clearer. Of course, a young mother's feelings about her pregnancy will also be influenced by those of the baby's father, of her own father, of siblings and friends, but very often the internal attitudes, both conscious and unconscious, of a previously dismissed mother emerge into prominence and colour the experience vividly. Once again, it is the unconscious feelings and attitudes of the future grandmother that can make the difference. A woman pleased with her own womanhood will be pleased that her daughter is about to continue the generations, and her attitude will allow and encourage the blossoming of the mother-to-be, while an anxious or depressed mother, who feels that womanhood is a burden, may respond badly to her daughter's news and make things worse.

It is interesting to observe how and when young women tell their mothers about their pregnancy. Mother may be the last to know or, more rarely, the first; but the anxiety about how she will receive the news is very high. It is as if the 6- or 7-year-old's savage and vengeful internalized mother that would 'kill her if . . .' is resurrected. And mother's response matters too. She will be watched for hostility, which can be seen in indifference or overwhelming excitement. Frequently, a split occurs. Mother is seen as patient, helpful and good, and it is the 'mother-in-law' who becomes the bad one, the hostile, envious witch-like demon, whose presence is feared as if she will cast the evil eye on the coming baby. (The evil eye is Envy, and in Mediterranean cultures new babies often wear brooches made like an eye to ward it off.)

Being pregnant is an admission of having been sexual, and the support of the young father-to-be in facing the world matters. How he accepts the changes in her body matters too. He will have to be mature enough to share it with the intruder, and be proud of her, of the proof of his own potency and fertility, and of himself in his future fatherhood. He will have to face his own parents with the admission of maturity, and face whatever that means to them.

In pregnancy, all may not go well. The incidence of miscarriage is high, and there is often no reason other than the fact that the development of an embryo is a miraculously complicated matter and can fail. The young mother, though, may accuse herself of inadequacy, or even, if she has in fact been ambivalent about the pregnancy, of causing the loss through hostility. Guilt can lead to a high level of anxiety in subsequent pregnancies and colour her feelings and attitudes to later babies. There are also other potential problems. The exhaustion that is normal in the early stages of pregnancy may frighten her. Security about her bodily functions and attractiveness may be threatened. The support of her partner will once more be essential.

Professionals may help or hinder. Her doctor can look after minor anxieties, as can a useful midwife – who may sometimes stand in for an absent or failing mother-figure. Ante-natal classes can reassure and inform, and provide a new peer group of those in a similar position with whom to share experiences and doubts. But, above all, the new mother has to accept her own helplessness in the face of this quite new situation. Once pregnant, there is the inevitable outcome of the pregnancy to face and the fact that this, unlike many other physical processes, cannot be controlled but will take its own course. She is sharing her body with a new being, and that new being is out of her control. Her attitude to bodily helplessness and vulnerability will be vital. Like all women (and unlike men) she has had some preparation through the experience of menstruation, a loss of body fluid outside her control, and if she has achieved mature sexuality she will have experienced orgasm, that temporary relinquishing of separateness and control that can be so very threatening to the less confident.

Suppose that she is still lucky and can relax enough to allow labour and delivery to proceed with no more than the normal amount of discomfort or pain. And suppose that her baby is born alive, healthy and vigorous. Will her attendants allow her to meet her child in a gentle way? Or will she be too thoroughly encouraged to 'bond', and the child put to the breast too early before having the reflective time to breathe and look around that some babies need? Or will she be so guilty at her triumph that she tries to give it away? Long ago, when delivering babies, I was greatly struck by how often a newly delivered mother would say to her attendants when they congratulate her: 'Oh, you did it all. You were wonderful. Thank you so much.'

Young mothers are a target for interference. So many people 'know best', and streams of conflicting advice pour at them. Baby-stealing is not just something that happens when some deranged person invades a maternity ward, but occurs in more subtle ways. When a well-meaning midwife gives a baby a bottle in the night – 'I thought I'd let you sleep, you looked so tired' – she may habituate the baby to a rubber teat, making it more difficult, or even impossible, to establish breastfeeding. When the mother comes home uncertain of her feelings towards her baby, she may allow her own mother, or mother-in-law, or friends and neighbours to 'steal' her baby in a similar way.

Difficulties in sharing her body with the baby can occur either on account of unconscious hostility to this being who has invaded her life, or because of guilt at her achievement. Can she allow herself the triumph of breastfeeding her baby and continuing to sustain the new life by herself? Or will she be so overcome with guilt and anxiety that it seems safer to transfer the burden to the bottle and the cow? Much of the answer to these questions has to do with anxiety about changing from being a daughter to becoming a mother.

Our daughter has reached early motherhood, and she will have to carry on alone from now on. She has been allowed to avoid most of the major pitfalls, and she has a chance to learn from her baby – the best teacher she has – about how to become a mother. Her baby will tell her how often to feed, and change, and cuddle, and play. If our young mother is still lucky, her partner and her mother may be proud of her and of the newcomer – she may even be proud of herself. The next generation will then have a chance.

Jennifer Johns

7
The Good-Enough Father of Whatever Sex

'L'être dont l'être est de n'être pas'. (The being whose essence is in not having an essence.)

Simone de Beauvoir

The father in contemporary politics

Much of the material in this chapter was first presented at the 75th anniversary conference of the UK National Council for One Parent Families entitled 'Modern Families: Change or Crisis'. The conference took place in a far more politicized and tense context than usual, generating media interest, demonstrations and counter-demonstrations outside the meeting hall and a good deal of stress and anxiety inside. For once, there really was a coming together of the political and the personal. It was a rare moment when psychoanalytic developmental psychology and a depth psychological perspective on family process were at the heart of political debate (see Samuels, 1993).

This chapter, designated as a psychological depiction of the challenge of fatherhood, is also a political challenge to our received wisdoms about the father himself. It tries to break up the monolith called 'father' by introducing two exciting, fresh and novel figures, whom I call the 'good-enough father' and the 'father of whatever sex'. The idea is to show that there is both more and less to fathers than the moral panic about lone parenthood suggests. Scanning the huge and passionate debate about lone parenthood in most Western countries with a psychologically attuned eye, the following thought comes to mind. We are witnessing a damaging and misleading idealization of fathers and the roles men play in families. It is folly to base policy on this idealization. However, the fact that there is such idealization gives political debate in the 1990s about lone parenthood a very psychological character. The politics are psychological and the psychology has become highly political.

What drives the continuing stigmatization of women who parent alone in many Western countries is our world's total failure to come to terms with the imminent collapse of some of the things that used to support male domination of society – a collective failure that has left many men utterly unsure of their personal roles. Men still have the power, of course, but they lack fixed identity. This unsettles them so much that they find living with it difficult or impossible, as the British suicide figures for the past decade show: male suicide almost doubled; female suicide declined. It cannot simply be unemployment that is responsible for the rise, for we have had recessions before.

It seems that all the government, some academics, sections of the media and many therapists are able to do is to yearn for the return of the father as a source of stability, discipline and order in the family and, by some kind of alchemy, in society as well. This yearning persists in spite of the fact that the so-called 'traditional' family was a very short-lived phenomenon (if it existed at all). The family has always mutated in a duet with economic and industrial organization (see Seccombe, 1993). That is why it is so important not to fall for the temptations of underclass theory (Murray, 1990) and to pillory today's lone parents and their families – never mind the scarcely hidden racism in that tendency. It is supine, ridiculous and nasty to yearn for yesterday's ideal family. That family, source of so much misery, was but one staging post on a long journey. Too much nostalgia makes you go blind; you can't see the truth for the tears.

In this yearning, the father is presented as a sort of public school fagmaster, the older boy who is assigned younger boys as servants and, in return, helps their character formulation. A first leader in *The Times* on 19 November 1993 showed this up very well by bemoaning the absence of fathers as a 'moral presence' in the family. The trouble is that, when faced with thinking like this, there is, in progressive circles, a vacuum where new ideas should exist.

Even in progressive circles there is a denial of the possibility of there being other styles and models of fathering (see Samuels, 1985, pp. 162–5; Samuels, 1989, pp. 66–91). My view is that if we worked out the detail of these fresh approaches we would not end up with a set of views and values that would leave lone-parent, fatherless families in the lurch. These new ideas about fatherhood stress the father's active, direct emotional involvement with his children from the earliest age. The new models of fatherhood support an egalitarian, co-operative, non-hierarchical family, rather than pointlessly seeking to restore father and his authority as the (flawed) source of rules and regulations – not to mention reinstating him as the source of sexual and physical abuse of women and children.

As a clinician who has carried out research into lone-parent families for nearly twenty years, I observe that many of the most disturbed people I see in analysis come from highly conventional backgrounds with two long-married parents. Hence, I simply cannot agree that there are any *inevitable* damaging psychological outcomes from living in a lone-parent family. This point would be even stronger were lone-parent families to be given adequate resources, approval and support from the community. When we talk about resources, we should perhaps think of more than money, housing and so forth – although these are clearly important. We should also think, for example, of what it does to the evolving personality of a child to know that the set-up at home is being attacked out there in the real, adult world as inferior, bad, mad and needing control. My own children certainly picked up quite specific social and political values and assumptions like these from television before they were 3 years old.

Playing the father role

There are two crucial psycho-cultural implications of these new approaches to fathering. The first has to do with the passionate debate that rages over the consequences (or lack of them) of lone parenthood for child development, especially, or even exclusively, when the lone parent is a woman. For convenience, we could call this *the lone mother question*. The second implication has to do with the equally passionate debate over what fathering is these days, even when it is done by men. We could call this *the crisis in fatherhood question*.

The insight I want to share, and around which much of this chapter revolves, is that these two apparently different questions lead us in a surprisingly similar direction. Addressing one question helps us in engaging with the other. Both questions stimulate responses based on the same search, which is to find out what fathers do, or can do, that is life-affirming and related to others – beyond being merely a 'moral presence'.

If we do this, we can begin to create and assemble a psychological information pool, or resource, for women bringing up children on their own, or women bringing up children together with other women. Such women are truly fathers of whatever sex when the father is revisioned as being 'unpatriarchal'. Immediately, we undermine everything that our society assigns or wishes to assign to men. Anatomy ceases to determine parental destiny and the lone mother question is completely reframed.

There is a crucial sequence in which this project has to be carried out. Initially, we have to find out more about fathers, then move on to see if we can depict the father in a less hypermasculine way, and then, finally, address women. To women the questions are: Can you do these things that male fathers do? Do you *want* to do them? The invitation is for women to assert their capacities to be fathers of whatever sex, which would surely make them good-enough fathers, rather then setting them up to fail as phoney, ideal fathers. We should not forget that men fail to be ideal fathers too. I am not anticipating that women would choose to perform all of any list of fatherly functions, nor would they necessarily perform these functions in *precisely* the same way that men might perform them. Would that matter, though? Some would say that might be a pretty good thing! Difference does not always mean deficit.

Gathering enough information about fathering might enable women to decide how much of it they could do by and for themselves. This is why I give a twist to the usual formation and propose that we start to call women who parent alone good-enough fathers. I am sure that many women who parent alone, or parent together with other women, are doing a lot of being a good-enough father of whatever sex without naming it as such. This group of women represents an incalculably valuable resource. They could herald a whole new approach to parenting that plugs into the fluidity in gender roles that has evolved since the Second World War, and that is not going to be wished and/or legislated away by government.

To those who have a negative reaction to the idea that women can be good-enough fathers and play the father's role, I say: Men, too, only *play* the father's role. Fathering does not come 'naturally' to men along with penises and stubble – it has to be learned, and every new father finds there are rules in our society about how to do it; there is a masquerade of fatherhood, a male masquerade, to adapt Joan Riviere's term (Riviere, 1929; and see Butler, 1990). Women who father as good-enough fathers of whatever sex may teach a thing or two to men who father – who knows? I remember my daughter setting up a game with me by saying, 'You be the daddy, Daddy', and then, at some point in our family play, announcing 'Now I'll be the daddy, Daddy'.

This is the bottom line, lived-experience behind the academic work on the cultural construction of gender and its roles (see, for example, Foucault, 1979; Weeks, 1985). Men already play the role of father as much as women will come to play the role. And they play it differently at different times and in different places; parenting is multicultural. It is surely significant how much we all use this word 'role' in relation to parenting. So, for the sake of completeness, I want to reverse what I have been saying. Women who look after very small children are *playing* at being mothers, playing the role of mother. Motherhood, too, is not as 'natural' as some people continue delusively to think it is. Maternity and paternity have evolving histories.

What of the second question, the question of the crisis in

fatherhood, what fatherhood is and means for men? Let's see what happens if we make use of the same words and images, but this time with a focus on fatherhood and men. We certainly need to make the role of the male parent more interesting and meaningful for our younger men who have, quite rightly in my view, started to reject a dictatorial, Jurassic style of fathering – even if their female partners were prepared for them to be like that, which, these days, they mostly are not. This refusal of male dominance by women, coupled with men's beginning search for inspiring ideas about manhood and fatherhood, are crucial social and psychological changes on which the debate about fathers should be focusing. 'Men' has become a category, one of many, and not some sort of privileged vantage point. This huge change in Western consciousness does not mean that men and women now have identical agendas; I have become suspicious of simplistic calls for partnership between the sexes. Men will not give up their power that easily, and there is a lot of making up to be done. But writing as a man, a father, an analyst, I have come to see that it is not the actual maleness of the person from whom we obtain fathering that is the key issue. The main thing is that what happens in the relationship between the father of whatever sex and her or his children be good-enough.

To summarize, this chapter is supposed to work on two levels: as a resource for women who parent alone, and as an agenda for contemporary men who want to father in a new way that is psychologically realistic. To underscore the two levels, and to explain the terms and words I use, let me pose a series of trick questions: When a man takes care of a very small baby, what should we call what he does? Is it *fathering*, part of an enhanced and expanded definition of father? Or is it *mothering*, because looking after the newborn is what mothers traditionally do? Or is it a bit of both? Similarly, if a woman lays down the law in a family, is she *mothering*, part of an enhanced and expanded definition of a mother? Or is she *fathering*, because laying down the law is what fathers traditionally do? Or is it a bit of both?

It can seem very frightening how totally our language for parenting has collapsed; that is why some want so desperately to speak a language that they need to believe once existed. However, I do not see the breakdown of our language for parenting as a disaster. I see it as an opportunity, and as ushering in a quite new kind of politics, fuelled by what people actually experience in their emotional and personal lives.

The politics of parental warmth

In all the justified concern about child sexual abuse, we have, perhaps, forgotten to say enough about the positive aspects of a father's physical warmth. In fact, I would go so far as to say that many conventional families have lacked this kind of experience, which can generate its own particularly pernicious brand of psychic pain. Any woman bringing up children alone, or together with another woman, is bound to be giving some thought already to what the positive outcomes of providing fatherly warmth would be. She will be doing this to decide whether or not to attempt to become the father of whatever sex, providing similar experiences leading to similar outcomes, and she will be thinking about ways to do this.

Fatherly warmth leads to a recognition of daughters as female persons in their own right, not simply as little mothers, and not only as creatures tied into the image and role of mother. The sensitive and empathic break-up of an equation that woman equals mother, as well as being important on a personal level, has enormous socio-political implications. Many feminist writers have shown convincingly that the 'reproduction of mothering' is terribly limiting for women. It ties them into the role of the one who looks after others, who responds and reacts to their needs, who puts her own needs last, and who dares not risk disfavour and disapproval by expressing her assertiveness and demands. Fatherly recognition of the daughter as other than a mother can be seen as one key way in which women break out of the cycle of the reproduction of motherhood. Other pathways then emerge: a spiritual path, a work path, a path that integrates her assertive side, a path of sexual expression (not necessarily heterosexual), maybe a path of celibacy. Crucially, there have to be pathways that are not man-oriented and that involve movement away from the father – for example, a path of solidarity and community with other women.

Women bringing up children alone can, by imagination and thought based on sharing experiences, send similar messages to their daughters. They can do this by understanding their daughter's evolving sexual potential – and everyone has a sexual potential from the earliest age – as the most easily recognizable in a series of moves that takes her away from a mix-up or overlap with the mother. My stress on the sexual daughter is deliberate here. I am not saying mothers are not sexy; of course they are. What I am saying is that a recognition of a daughter's evolving sexuality by a *woman* plays a part in turning that daughter away from a path in life that is completely circumscribed by the maternal role. To function as the father of whatever sex may mean a woman who parents alone actually seeking out and accentuating what goes on in families concerning competition between parent and child of the same sex. If she can communicate to her daughter that the daughter is a potential rival (in many diverse respects, not just Oedipal rivalry) and can go on to communicate that this is not a bad thing, then she will be able to provide the kind of differentiation from the mother that the father's recognition, fuelled by mutual physical warmth between father and daughter, can provide.

Paternal warmth challenges our cultural habit of splitting perceptions of the male body into something horribly abusive and violent or something meekly pretty, hairless and nice. Male bodies have potential to do good as well as harm, and discussion about *both* possibilities will take us far beyond the images of men's bodies idealized in advertising.

Communicating positive physical warmth is pleasant and moving for both participants. The father, as well as the daughter, receives something out of what I call 'erotic playback'. Once the initial 'woman equals mother' equation is broken up, the outcome for a girl is unpredictable. She may want and need to grow away from (as well as towards) her father, away from the world of men in general as well as towards it, to seek out, work with, fall in love with, and raise children with other women.

My point is that fathers do not simply liberate or permit daughters to take up different psychosocial roles from that of maternity, but foster a *plurality* of psycho-social roles, meaning the ways in which they do or do not shake down for women into a workable blend of oneness and manyness. This is a key social issue for women – how to be more than one person while, at the same time, still managing to stay psychologically whole. The many mainstream books about superwoman and her balancing act indicate that these ideas about the father–daughter connection are not just of professional psychological interest.

What about the father's physical warmth and erotic playback in relation to the son? For sons, a good-enough physical connection to the father helps lead to the growth of what might be called homosociality (after Sedgewick, 1985). The political implications of this are truly immense. What I am depicting is a certain kind of intimate father–son relating, prompted by positive physical warmth that is frankly expressed between them. This could inspire the new kinds of social organization that Western societies urgently need just now. The emphasis is on co-operation and non-hierarchical organization, which are just as valid modes of masculinity as the pecking order and the rat race. They are also modes of being that women will find more congenial than aping all the worst features of the male drive for success.

In these new visions of social organization, men learn from other men just as they love them. Homosociality is illustrated by the ways in which the gay community has responded to AIDS, particularly at a time when AIDS was thought to be a problem only for homosexuals. This kind of father–son relating provides practical and inspiring political models: love between men – as between father and son, and even between brothers – as a kind of political practice or praxis. Notice the paradox: the group of men regarded by our society as the least 'manly' have been reframed as pioneers, frontiersmen, and the new leaders in forging a way through a huge and hostile territory.

Perhaps the most difficult obstacle to overcome is the fear that ordinary, devoted, good-enough fathers will somehow be effeminate, the code for 'homosexual'. Our culture has employed a fear and loathing of homosexuality as a weapon to keep men tied into the role of provider in the family, the one who must therefore remain emotionally distant. The pay-off for men has been access to economic and political power. The cost has been in terms of paternal warmth.

This virgin territory is a place in which the female father of whatever sex comes into *her* own and can function as a resource for her male co-fathers. Women know more about community and non-hierarchical organization from the inside, as it were. Women who parent alone will probably already be considering how to make co-operation more attractive to their sons, rather than it being regarded as bland or, worst of all, non-manly. They may use what power they have to reinforce and support an absence of hierarchy and unbendable rules, asking, even challenging, their sons to use their imagination as much as their biceps. And the sons respond to the challenge. They know at some level that being an old-style, oppositional man, testing the limits of authority, is only one way to be male. Not that boundary-testing behaviour is going to vanish overnight; and it has some positive aspects in that rules should be challenged, and gathering new knowledge may involve breaking rules. Yet the father of whatever sex knows quite a lot already about working co-operatively – remember, in the old language that has collapsed, she's a woman.

The politics of paternal aggression

So far, what I have been writing has been more on the erotic side of life – physical warmth and recognition of the daughter as other than mother, father–son togetherness as leading to reforms in how we conceive of society itself. What about aggression, an altogether more problematic theme with our current obsession about violence in society? Surely, some will say, only men can handle their sons' aggression?

Much depends on what we mean by 'handle' aggression. If we mean eliminating aggression from the picture altogether, either by discipline or stoicism in the face of frustration or adversity, these might well be the hopelessly unachievable goals that a typical old-style male parent, destined for a career in politics, might aim at. For me, the question is not how to handle, manage, discipline or eliminate aggression; aggression is a part of life and it is not all bad. Rather, the task is to see how it might be kept moving and prevented from degenerating into destructiveness. Aggression is part of communicating. It is a valid way of securing attention. But who is to say whether an act of aggression is horridly destructive or constructively self-assertive?

I have developed an experiential way of considering this question. We can use the human body as a sort of index for aggression. There is head aggression, which might take the form of a verbal onslaught. There is chest aggression, exemplified by the ambivalence of the bear hug. There is genital aggression – pornography, Don Juanism or the materialistic sexual thrills of the tycoon. There is arm aggression, suggesting a range of images and acts encompassing pressing the button, striking a blow with a weapon, and strangulation with bare hands. Leg aggression is often practised by fathers: it means walking away and ducking confrontation. Anal aggression, coming out of the bottom, means enviously smearing the achievements of others, perhaps by snide comments – what in encounter groups we used to call 'coming out sideways'.

My idea is that the relationship between the child and the father of whatever sex is the place in which movement between these various styles of aggression is worked on and developed. The main aim is to keep aggression fluid and moving through the various styles, so as to avoid one style starting to predominate over the others. When that happens, there is movement from benevolent aggression to pure destructiveness.

But there is more to communicating aggression between father and child than keeping several styles going at once. There is also the possibility of there being an element in fathering that can help to *transform* antisocial, sadistic, unrelated aggression into socially committed, self-assertive, related aggression. I see this transformation as taking place on the social level as well as in families.

Fathers work on these questions without knowing they are doing so. For their sons, the goal seems to be to allow aggression its place in open and emotionally mobile relationship. For their daughters, the goal seems to be to validate and reinforce the capacity to challenge and fight with men. A woman's capacity to confront the patriarchy stems, to a certain extent, from how her father played back her aggressive response to him.

As far as women who parent alone are concerned, the main thing in relation to daughters is the need not to retreat into some spurious all-female, nicey-nicey, sisterly alliance. I know from talking to lone parents how tempting it is for anyone who is isolated or who fears rejection to do this. Equally, many women who parent alone have already simply had to come to terms with aggression in the family. Perhaps lone fathers of whatever sex need to know that it is not only OK, but may often be a good thing, if they and their daughters fight. (They're going to fight sometime anyway.) This would change the terms of debate about lone-parent families and, I dare say, pose a few challenges for two-parent families. For example, I think it is important that fathers of whatever sex encourage their daughters to challenge male authority; it is intelligent, not disloyal, for mothers to approve of this.

There is always going to be tension and frustration in a family that is always going to bear the possibility of aggression. However, this can be reframed from the earliest time as part of a relationship, not as something to be eliminated. In terms of actual parenting behaviour, women who parent alone need to be reassured of what many know already: it cannot be wrong in principle to engage in rough and tumble play with boys, and that such play becomes a bit too real from time to time. It is not always a bad thing when events get a bit out of hand – just look at the psychological damage done to people who grew up in tight, emotionally over-controlled families, where father was certainly – and perhaps simply – a moral presence. What kind of training in 'handling' aggression is that?

Can fathers change?

I have deliberately not taken an easy road in proposing that the father of whatever sex can be a good-enough father. I have not mentioned the fact that many children living in families headed by one parent do have contact with the other parent, or the ways in which women who parent alone can facilitate contact between their children and adult males, or the part male mentors might play in some families. These are obvious points that have often been made. However, the battle of ideas has to be fought without recourse to a more palliative contribution if the stigmatization of lone-parent families by means of idealizing fathers is to be halted.

If some readers cannot agree with me, if the idea of a father of whatever sex being good-enough just goes against everything they believe in, I would ask merely that they note that it is *possible* to say it, it is *possible* to depict the father of whatever sex as a good-enough father, it is *possible* to challenge the assumption that only a male can do some of these things. I would urge such readers not to forget how many men do not or cannot do them before concluding that it is impossible for a woman to do them.

Perhaps some readers have little problem with women doing the fathering, but do not like the idea that fathers, or men in general, can change. In fact, fatherhood shows incredible cross-cultural variation and changes over time; it is not something written in stone. There is one piece of empirical research that fascinates me. Everyone knows that fathers and mothers are said to play with children very differently. If they are videoed, the fathers are seen to be much more active and physical, while the mothers are quieter, more reflective and protective. The picture seems logical and eternal. But if the play of fathers who, for whatever reason, have sole or primary care of children is videoed, *their play resembles that of mothers* (see Raphael-Leff, 1991, pp. 372, 533). Fathers can change. Maybe men can change.

One way in which men are changing is that they are becoming more aware of a deal that they have made with society. In this deal, the male child, at around 4 or 5 years old or even earlier, agrees to repudiate all that is soft, vulnerable, playful, maternal and 'feminine' by hardening himself against these traits. In return, he is given special access to all the desire-fulfilling goodies that Western capitalism seems able to provide. Increasingly, and especially in mid-life, men are becoming aware that the deal was not altogether a good one from their point of view. Among many experiences that are denied them by this deal is the experience of being a hands-on, actively involved father.

I have always urged caution in relation to men changing. The parallel with feminism and the women's movement is fallacious because of the political reality of men already possessing power and resources. The depiction of the sobbing little boy inside every powerful man as 'feminine' is also highly sexist. Empirical social scientists tell us about the unchanging picture in most households, with men not looking after children, not doing their share of the chores, and being responsible for most of the sexual and physical abuse that is perpetrated.

Yet the aspirational atmosphere is changing. This is very hard to measure empirically, and the intuition of a depth psychologist sometimes does not pass muster when compared to 'real' social science. I was in the United States at the time of the Anita Hill–Clarence Thomas Congressional hearings (on the question of his sexual harassment of her, and its impact on his nomination to the Supreme Court), and the implications of those events changed the American political scene. I think the general attack on lone-parent families and its aftermath may have a similar effect in many places. As Bill Clinton found in his 1992 election campaign, and the Republicans found when they made their huge gains in 1994, there are profound electoral spin-offs from paying heed to identity politics (see Butler, 1990). This is almost the key background political and social issue of our times. If men are changing, if we are about to see good-enough fathers in larger numbers, then the very existence of male power takes on a new significance. The existence of male power means that, if changes are taking place in the world of men and fathers, there will be immense political and social effects in the not too distant future.

Gender issues are specially important for politics. They are also important for therapy, because gender is something that sits midway between the outer world and the inner world. On the one hand, women are socio-economically disadvantaged compared with men, and this can be measured. On the other hand, gender is a story of a most intimate and private kind that we tell ourselves about who we are; it is a story whose narrative rules are very few and getting fewer. Thus both our public *and* our subjective lives are riddled with gender issues. Indeed, one way of understanding the unending wave of sex scandals in British politics is to see them as highlighting how shaky and shifting are our present images of masculinity, and how problematic we are finding it to work out what are and are not acceptable modes of behaviour for men.

A word of caution. When discussing male economic power, or the psychological power of the father, we run a risk of lumping all men together. Taken as a whole, men certainly have power; but many black men, gay men, men who are physically challenged, men living in homelessness and poverty, men who have lost custody cases, young men dying in pointless wars, and men whose countries have been invaded or occupied, might well dispute that they really do have power (see Dollimore, 1991). Disadvantage is structured into differences other than those of gender.

Throughout this chapter I have referred to lone parents knowing many things about good-enough fathering and doing them already. That does not remove the need to put ideas like these down on paper and insert them into public debate. People living in lone-parent families have become experts at living with the changes in gender role that are sweeping over the Western world. Could we reframe lone parents and their children as today's experts at coping with changes that threaten to drive everyone crazy by their depth and rapidity? There's an opportunity here as well as a crisis. The attack on lone parents has presented us with an opportunity to inject psychological realism and sensitivity into our politics, acknowledging that the old politics, which sought to leave out personal experience, are falling to pieces. People living in lone-parent families may be the expert practitioners of this new kind of psychological politics. Can we learn from them?

The father in contemporary psychoanalysis

When D. W. Winnicott coined the phrase 'the good-enough *mother*' in 1949, he had a number of aims in mind. Undoubtedly, he wanted to highlight the undesirability of either idealizing or denigrating the mother. He wanted to make sure that his ideas about mother–baby relating did not become a persecuting ideal for mothers. He also sought to introduce the notion that a kind of graduated failure of mothering, leading to the possibility of there being hating feelings between mother and baby, was a good thing. Mutual hate was a vital step on the road to achieving what Winnicott (1968) called 'unit status'. To be good enough, a mother had to be able to fail, indeed to become a very bad mother and to hate her baby as much and as thoroughly as her baby fantasized that she did.

The good-enough *father* has not been written about very much. Re-theorizing the father is necessary for psychoanalysis because it has introjected an image of the father that is politically biased, reflecting a specific historical and social period in Western culture. When Winnicott (1968) disputes the seriousness for a small baby of having a psychotic *father* (as opposed to a psychotic mother) or when he speaks of the father showing his gun to his children as a way of explaining what the outer world is like (Winnicott, 1944), it reeks of cultural and historical contingency. Yet psychoanalysis worldwide continues to offer what I call the 'insertion metaphor' as the penetrative, unwavering root image of the father's psychological role in early life. The pre-Oedipal father is supposed to insert himself, like a giant depriving and separating penis, between mother and baby – who would otherwise stay locked in a psychosis-inducing and phase-inappropriate symbiosis. In fact, the distinction between Oedipal and pre-Oedipal begin to look increasingly artificial and defensive. In Margaret Mahler's amazing language, the father awakens a 2-year-old from sleep and turns that child towards the (or is it his?) world (Mahler, 1971). This comforting but reactionary story about fathers –

father holding mother who holds baby (with its third-term denial of the detail of a more direct relationship with children) – is one that urgently requires critique, not least because of the appalling insult to mothers and babies contained in the notion that they have no commitment and capacities in themselves to becoming separate. Do mothers and babies really want to be psychotic? Moreover, what's so wonderful about the rapture of psychoanalytic separateness, rapture over the strong ego, a question well posed by feminist theorists on both sides of the Atlantic? (See, for example, Jordan *et al.*, 1991.)

In Jacques Lacan's work we find a dematerialization of the father, so that he crops up in accounts of development solely as a metaphor, just a name or Name in a complicated psycho-social theorem; a third term. This approach, particularly in Lacan's own writings (see, for example, 1977), lacks a sustained recognition of the interplay between father's concrete, literal presence and his metaphorical function. For Lacan, as John Forrester says:

> the father's function is *strictly metaphorical* – he functions neither as real father (flesh and blood) nor as imaginary father (though he later figures in fantasy as an ideal or punitive agency) but as the Name of the Father, with his name assigning the child a place in the social world and allowing the child to become a sexed being through the phallic function (i.e. sign of sexual difference) to which the Name of the Father refers (Forrester, 1990, p. 110).

I do not think it is really possible to divorce the literal and the metaphorical as Lacan does, neither for purposes of description nor as a mode of understanding. Hence, references by Lacan to the phallus cannot dismiss the fleshy actuality of the father's penis as the raw material from which the metaphor has fashioned itself.

According to Forrester's authoritative account, Lacan 'affirms the centrality for the subject's history of the triadic Oedipus complex' and gives us a 'revised version of Freud's Oedipus complex' (pp. 110–11). While this is certainly so, we should not overlook the way in which the Lacanian Oedipus complex, and Lacan's account of the father's role, rest utterly on a simplistic and highly arguable narrative of mother–infant relations. Lacan is a prisoner of psychic determinism; if the Oedipus complex follows earlier stages of development, then it cannot avoid having been conditioned by them. Lacan is not totally in thrall to chronology, for the unconscious is not structured like a clock. However, the Lacanian Oedipus complex requires the pre-existence in the theory of a state of symbiosis or fusion between mother and infant. That symbiosis would not, or could not, dissolve or rupture without the father's insertion of himself between mother and infant. Lacan is no more than a crude Mahlerian here: the mother–infant relation is assumed not to contain any capacity *within itself* for the separating out and subsequent psychological development of the infant. The father–infant relation is assumed not to exist – or is not mentioned – until the mother–infant relationship – taking place within a fantasy of non-differentiation – is firmly established. Paradoxically, the centrally important symbolic father–child relationship is only constellated and brought into being by its imaginary target: the fused, 'dual unity' of mother and infant.

There is a suspiciously neat symmetry in Lacan's theory, and he falls victim to the seduction of morphological analogy. Mother and infant enjoy an imaginary fusion. This fusion is broken up by (a) the father as the third term on an inexorable road to the Oedipus complex, and (b) language, bringing with it a plethora of social and cultural imperatives. Because (a) and (b) seem to fulfil the same function, language and the father are claimed to be more or less the same. Language certainly operates in the closest possible concert with the social and political status quo. This means that language is both creator *and* creature of the social system. It follows that the father, too, is both representative and builder of a repressive and static social reality, and constrained and limited by social reality that has power over him. However, Lacan fails to notice the lack of power of the individual father in the face of social reality and consequently fails to notice that society's repressive 'father' is not the only father there is. That is why, for Lacan, *le nom du père* is generally *le non du père*. Hence, there is no possible place for a subversive and radical account of the father.

The claim that infants fuse with their mothers in early development does not stand up as an objective account of what goes on at that time. If fusionary states do *not* exist in the way Lacan presupposes them to, then the father *cannot* have the functions that Lacan ascribes to him, portrayed in a contra-distinctive and even complementary manner to the functions of the mother. And they do not. Observational work on mother–infant interaction has seriously undermined theories that postulate some kind of 'normal autism' or 'primary narcissism' as the earliest mental state of the infant (Stern, 1985). Instead, what is nowadays being noted is the existence of an intense conversation or proto-conversation between mother and infant, and, where this can be observed, between father and infant as well. The extent of mutual communication is massive. *Even the small baby is not necessarily operating in a world of fantasy.* Babies may well fantasize that they are 'at one' with their mothers and fathers, but these fusionary fantasies exist in an interplay with more communicative and interactive styles of functioning. That is, the presence and healing function of 'at oneness' is guaranteed by the implicit knowledge of mother and baby that this is phase-appropriate fantasy. In short, there is nothing that needs breaking up by the father. Separation from mother need not be a bloody business.

This last point requires underlining. The claim by Lacan (not to mention Mahler and Winnicott) that there is a mother–infant fusionary relationship that the father must rupture for mental health to result simply does not recognize that babies *themselves* desire to grow and separate from the mother as well as to rest in permanent oceanic bliss. Mothers, too, may sense that they have other things to do with their time than remain immersed in primary maternal preoccupation, characterized by devotion to their baby, and with the goal of achieving a good-enough fit between environment and inner world. Where would Lacan's theory be if the capacity of the early fusionary fantasy state to overcome itself were acknowledged? There is an in-built capacity of symbiosis to self-destruct. *Babies and mothers have an investment in separation.*

Crucially, where is there in Lacan an account of the pre-Oedipal father–infant relationship? I suggest that Lacan was as culture-bound as anyone else. Could a conscious recognition of the positive, direct, physical, affirming father–infant relationship, dating from the earliest moment, have been possible in the bourgeois France either of Lacan's childhood (born in 1901) or during his adult life of psychoanalytic theory-making?

Although Lacan's position seems anti-essentialist, and this is one reason why there has been enthusiasm for his ideas in feminist and other political circles, there is also an element of eternalism in the theory. Lacan confuses what is the case now with what has always been the case, and with what will always be the case. If this were not so, then Lacan would have no difficulty with the idea of a more positive image of and role for the father in the psychological development of the individual. There is a lack of reference to social and political factors as these impact on psychic reality, and a lack of reference to historical mutability. For Lacan, power often seems to be a purely symbolic factor. This omission undermines the contribution he can make to debates about gender relations, as does the omission to address the ways in which fathering is affected by class or ethnic factors. As Page du Bois comments:

To continue to consider the phallus as the transcendental signifier, to accept the inevitability of the 'idea' of transcendence, ... to believe that the phallus and language control us ... all this seems to me only to perpetuate a metaphysics of wholeness, presence, deism, and worship of the symbolic father. On the other hand, to see how such an ideology supports relations of male dominance, class and racial hierarchy, and the humility of the universally castrated might perhaps allow us to imagine democracy (du Bois, 1988, p. 188).

What of C. G. Jung and the post-Jungians? Because of the absence of a coherent developmental psychology in Jung's own writings, the post-Jungians have had to be in close attendance on psychoanalysis (see Samuels, 1985, pp. 133–72), and most of today's psychoanalysis is *mother* centred. Crucially, Jung overlooked the way in which father–child relationships are built in culture as he sought to identify the essential and invariant features of such relationships – the so-called father archetype or archetypal father. However, if we do explore the father–child relation, we see that, in most cultures, it is made up from the interaction of two other relationships: that between mother and child, and between woman and man. A man does not become a father in any formal sense unless something happens within the space created by these two other relationships. What that 'something' is, and what the father does, varies from culture to culture and across time. Nevertheless, to be a father, in a full emotional sense, a man needs a connection to the woman and for her to have a connection to the child. It is still a direct, primary relationship, still passionate and intense, but it is a constructed, discovered relationship. Actually, the way that the father–child relationship is constructed makes it no different from the mother–child relationship which, as many writers have shown, is not as natural, biological, innate, ahistorical, universal and given as we used to think (see Badinger, 1981).

Realizing that the father himself is a culturally constructed creature of relationship leads to all kinds of rather exciting possibilities. If the father relation is always a product of two other relationships, and hence of culture, then it cannot be approached via absolute definition; it is a situational and relative matter. If we can face this, we will sense that a new judgement is required on what probably seem to many like hopelessly idealistic and Utopian attempts to change the norms of father's role. Father's role *can* change, because written into it is the refusal of absolute definition. This refusal is made possible because of male power and freedom *and* because of the historical and cultural mutability of the father relation. Hence, in one sense of the word, the only 'archetypal' element is that there is no archetypal element. In full paradoxical form: the archetypal thing about the father is that he is culturally constructed.

If fathers can change in principle as well as in life, if there is no archetype of the kind that would hold us back here, what can *we* do to help the process along? For bringing the good-enough father into existence would truly mean the dismantling of the patriarchy that many say they want – practically, politically, theoretically. Researching the psychoanalytic literature, it is still hard to find texts of paternal sexuality that depict its benevolent aspects as opposed to seizing on its undeniably malevolent aspects. Yet very little has been said about the father's potential to carry a positive attitude towards the mobility, enfranchisement and emancipation of others. Here are some ways in which that potential might be realized:

- Changing the social pattern in which only women look after small babies.
- Fostering a culture in which parenthood and work may coexist.
- Working towards more co-operative and less hierarchical forms of political and social organization.
- Getting a clearer understanding of male sexuality in general, and paternal sexuality in particular, so as to work better with problems such as child sexual abuse.
- Changing how we define and what we expect from good-enough families to include lone-parent families and other transgressive modes of family life.

And for therapists:

- Expanding the clinical repertoire of practitioners as fathers in the transference, especially *female* practitioners.

Andrew Samuels

8
Becoming Parents: What Has to Change for Couples?

Derek and Enid are shocked by the intensity of their fight. It is just one week since they brought their new baby Samantha home from the hospital in a haze of fatigue and excitement. Enid's parents, who live a four-hour journey away, arrived almost immediately to help with the new baby. Now, though, Derek is barely speaking to them since Enid's mother laughed at the mess he made when he changed Samantha's nappy. Even though he has been given a week off, Derek stomped off to work this morning. Enid resents his time away and feels jealous of the fact that he gets to leave while she is not scheduled to be back at work for another three months. She points out in an irritated tone of voice that Derek forgot to put out the rubbish today. Derek responds defensively by saying that this has never bothered her before. She snaps back that they have never had a daughter to take care of before, and soiled nappies simply can't be left around. After putting Samantha to bed and listening to her cry for fifteen minutes, Enid goes in to pick her up. Derek objects, saying that giving in to her cries just prolongs the agony. Enid accuses Derek of trying to make life for Samantha just like it was when he was growing up. Derek says that he is tired of her constant criticism of his family and asks Enid to pay attention to the merits of his argument. Enid has just stomped off to bed, leaving Derek feeling confused, frightened and lonely. In separate rooms, each is brooding about what happened to the picture of an idyllic family that they have been constructing together since they learned that Enid was pregnant.

In 1974, more than ten years after we had started our own family, Philip Cowan and I began working with couples about to become first-time parents. The idea of looking closely at this major life transition was stimulated by a collision of events in our own personal and professional lives. We are the parents of two daughters and one son, who are now in their early thirties, each trying to carve out a satisfying way to balance family relationships and work. However, many years ago, when they were barely out of nappies, we realized that we were losing touch with our relationship as a couple. Although we entered parenthood enthusiastically, we were totally unprepared for the stress we had begun to experience in our marriage. It was the late 1960s, and in addition to the turmoil in the larger world at that time, we found ourselves surrounded by families coming apart at the seams, with separations and divorces everywhere we turned. As we tried to make sense of what had happened to us and to the relationships we were hearing about from friends, colleagues and families seeking therapy, we began to think of the period in which partners are becoming parents as a particularly vulnerable time for a marriage.

We were concerned about the impact of becoming a family on the couple's relationship and on parents' earliest relationships with their children. It was common knowledge that parents' styles of working and playing with their children were central ingredients of their children's development. At the same time, it was becoming clear from clinical psychologists, social workers and psychiatrists who worked with families in distress that when there were problems in the relationship *between* the parents, the children might also begin to have difficulty at home or at school. This suggested to us that mental health professionals with expertise in family relationships might offer expectant couples a safe setting in which they could work on difficulties in their relationships as partners, so that they could cope more successfully with the expectable strains and challenges of the family-making period. We hoped that this intervention would help keep the unexpected stress of this major transition from spilling over into all the relationships in the family. If we could be effective in helping fairly well-functioning couples strengthen their resources as *partners* – while they were becoming parents and before their stress affected the quality of their relationships with their babies – we might be able to modify unsatisfying or destructive patterns and keep them from cycling through another generation.

We explored the research literature at that time to see what was known about couples making the transition to parenthood. Our search revealed that psychology and psychiatry had not been interested in the challenge for partners making the transition to parenthood – unless the women had suffered serious post-partum depression or psychosis. We also found several case studies of men who were patients in therapy and had recently become new fathers, with suggestive titles like 'Fatherhood as a precipitant of mental illness'. The only published studies we found of couples who were not already patients in the mental health system had been conducted by family sociologists. The studies were all retrospective, asking parents *after* they had become parents how their lives had changed from their pre-baby days. They also focused almost exclusively on mothers, as if to suggest that only women were expected to change with parenthood.

One paper (LeMasters, 1957) described fifty-seven couples interviewed after they had been parents for several months or several years. In collaboration with the couples themselves, LeMasters concluded that the transition to parenthood constituted a crisis for a marriage. Sociologists must have found this conclusion quite surprising judging from the raft of studies that followed, all claiming that *crisis* was an overstatement of what happens to marriage when partners become parents. Although different researchers marshalled evidence for one side of the debate or the other, the general conclusion from the sociologists' point of view was that the transition to parenthood could be expected to be stressful for a significant number of parents. Although this idea is more widely accepted in the 1990s, it has been surprising to both family researchers and new parents themselves, who picture the arrival of a first child as a time of growth and fulfilment.

Despite evidence that partners becoming parents might be at risk from distress as a couple, there was not one study that followed couples systematically from before to after having a first baby, or evaluated preventive interventions for men, women or couples becoming parents. Long after we had launched our own 'Becoming a Family Project', we discovered that Pauline Shereshefsky and Leon Yarrow and their colleagues (1973) had offered *expectant mothers* in Bethesda, Maryland, a counselling intervention before their babies were born, and Christopher Clulow (1982) and his colleagues at the Tavistock Marital Studies Institute in London, England, had offered expectant *couples* six once-a-month groups from before to after having a baby. But because the publication process is slow and laborious, we did not discover each other's work until some years later. In retrospect, it is remarkable how similar our ideas were – about using the opportunity of the transition to parenthood to provide interventions that might facilitate the development of parents and babies, and about the importance of a strong marriage in the development of young families.

The 'Becoming a Family Project'

In 1974, we designed a small pilot study to evaluate the effectiveness of working with expectant couples in small groups with trained mental health professional staff as co-leaders. Our overall goal was to help couples face the disruptive aspects of the early family-making period instead of sweeping them under the carpet for years – as we felt we, and so many couples we knew, had done. We followed twelve couples from late pregnancy until their babies were 18 months old, talking with each couple at regular intervals, beginning in the seventh month of pregnancy and ending in their second year of parenthood. We worked with some couples more intensively during this period, meeting with them every week for six months – that is, throughout the last three months of pregnancy and the first three months of parenthood. Based on the findings of that pilot study, the United States National Institute of Mental Health agreed to fund a larger longitudinal intervention study of first-time parents, beginning in 1979.

Once again, we invited expectant couples into our 'Becoming a Family Project' as they approached their seventh month of pregnancy, and followed them regularly with visits, personal interviews and questionnaires until their babies were 18 months old. Because one of our central questions was 'What happens to marriage when partners become parents?', we included couples expecting a first baby and a comparable set of couples who had not yet decided whether to become parents. This allowed us to compare the shifts in couple relationships with and without babies over the same period of time.

Our second major goal was the systematic evaluation of our couples group intervention designed to strengthen couple relationships *during* the transition to parenthood, and to make the transition a more satisfying and less stressful experience. In this chapter, I concentrate on what we learned about the changes experienced by most new parents and on the impact of our couples groups during the first two years of parenthood. In Chapter 9, Philip Cowan describes what emerged as we followed the couples and their children through the pre-school and early elementary school periods.

The design of the study

We recruited childless couples, and couples expecting a first baby, in 1980 and 1981, and offered a randomly chosen one-third of the expectant couples an opportunity to work with us in one of our couples groups. Each group had a staff couple and four couples expecting a baby at about the same time. We met with these men and women weekly for six months, starting in the seventh month of pregnancy and continuing until the babies were 3 months old, with the babies attending the group meetings as soon as they were born.

The couples

We recruited couples from both clinic and private obstetric gynaecology practices, and through public service announcements in local newspapers and radio stations. These efforts attracted ninety-six couples who lived in twenty-eight cities and towns in northern California; seventy-two of them were expecting a first baby, and twenty-four had not decided whether to become parents.

The expectant parents ranged in age from their early twenties to their early forties on entering the study in late pregnancy: the average age of the expectant mothers was 29; of the fathers, 30 years. The childless partners were, on average, one year younger – the women 28, the men 29 years. The expectant couples had been together for an average of four years, some as few as eight months and several as many as ten or twelve years. Most of the couples were married, and all were living together and considered themselves to be in a long-term relationship when they entered the study. Fifteen per cent of the participants were African–American, Asian–American or Latino, and 85 per cent were Caucasian. All of the men and women had completed at least Grade 12 in High School, and many had completed additional vocational training or college degrees. Their family incomes spanned a range from working-class to upper-middle-class levels.

How do we assess family members' well-being or distress?

Our ideas about family adaptation suggest that we need information about five key aspects of family life in order to have a sense of how the parents and children are managing:

- At regular intervals, we ask about each family member's sense of self *as an individual*. We ask about parents' views of themselves, their self-esteem, their feelings of vulnerability and their symptoms of distress.
- We ask about many aspects of *the parents' relationship as a couple*. We are looking for his and her view of the tone of their relationship – the ways they show caring and experience intimacy, their division of family labour, the issues on which they experience conflict or disagreement, their style of solving the problems that confront them, and their satisfaction and disappointments with their overall relationship as a couple.
- We ask about *the relationships between the partners and their parents*, to get a sense of the legacies that each new parent brings from the past generation.
- During their visits to our project playroom, we observe *the relationship between each parent and their child* – how warm, responsive, strict or permissive they are, how often they set limits for their child, how much anger or humour we see when they work

and play together in our project playroom. We ask about each parent's perceptions of their child and ideas about parenting.

● We assess the *balance between the stresses and supports* reported by each parent. We know that having jobs outside the family, and relationships with extended family, friends and co-workers, can offer extra support or added stress for both men and women. At each point in the study, we calculate the balance between stress and support, using parents' descriptions of stressful life events and the availability of people who can offer support.

We evaluate these five aspects of family life systematically at five time periods: in pregnancy, six and eighteen months after the baby is born, and again when the children are $3\frac{1}{2}$ and $5\frac{1}{2}$ years old. All our interviews, questionnaires, observations and discussions in our couples groups focus on these aspects of the family, on how they are intertwined, and on how they are affecting each family member.

Great beginnings

When does the transition begin?

The men and women in our study describe almost as many starting points for their transition to the parenthood journey as there are travellers. Some trace the beginning back to their own childhoods when they played with dolls or pretended to be parents. At the other end of the spectrum are men and women who are still not thinking of themselves as parents late in pregnancy, even though much of their day-to-day behaviour is beginning to be governed by the needs of the ever-present foetus. We begin our study of couples in the seventh month of pregnancy, when the pregnancy is likely to be viable and parenthood experienced as more of a reality. We start by asking partners to tell us about their process of deciding to have a baby.

The fateful decision

It seems to us that the decision to have a baby is a complex one these days. How did the two of you come to be having a baby at this time?

Couples' responses to this question in our initial interview suggest that they adopted four general decision-making styles. Approximately half of the couples were quite deliberate in becoming pregnant. The other half were distributed among three groups characterized by less planning or no planning at all.

- About 50 per cent of the couples were *Planners*. They talked about their feelings over time, eventually came to the decision that they felt ready, and – in time – initiated a pregnancy that both partners welcomed.

- In this age of commonly understood birth control technology, we were a little surprised to learn that some couples either failed to discuss the issue or stopped using birth control, as if they were leaving to fate the decision about becoming a family. We characterize about 15 per cent of the couples as *Accepting Fate* because they describe themselves as becoming pregnant 'accidentally', but they accept willingly what fate has determined.

- Another 17 per cent of the couples we characterize as *Ambivalent* – not just at the beginning, as most partners are for a time, but still going back and forth about what they want to do near the end of the pregnancy.

- A final 17 per cent of the couples had serious disagreements about going ahead with the pregnancy. One partner was very enthusiastic or determined to have the baby, while the other did not feel ready but was going along in order to maintain their relationship. Of nine couples in this *Yes–No* category, seven husbands were saying 'No' while their wives were saying 'Yes'.

The *Planners* managed the transition very well, with relatively stable marital satisfaction throughout the first two years of parenthood. By contrast, the marital satisfaction of the *Yes–No* couples plummeted from late pregnancy to eighteen months after the birth of their babies. Perhaps the most dramatic finding emerged when we had followed all of the couples through their first child's entrance to elementary school. All seven couples in which the husbands were initially resistant to parenthood had divorced by the time their first child was 5 years old. This suggests that couples can learn a great deal about how their relationship as a couple will fare after the transition to parenthood by paying attention to the tone and the content of their discussions about whether or when to have a baby.

Having a baby changes your life

It seems as if everyone 'knows' that when partners become parents their lives change dramatically; but it is clear that knowing and being prepared for significant shifts are different matters. The couples in our study who stay together but do not have babies show remarkable stability over the course of our study in all five aspects of life that we investigate. By contrast, the couples who become parents describe significant and often unexpected shifts in every domain.

What's happened to me?

We examine change in partners' sense of themselves by having them complete an exercise we call 'The Pie' before, and a number of times after, having a baby. On a circle 3 inches in diameter, partners include 'pieces' that represent various aspects of themselves, such as son, daughter, parent, lover, worker, electrician, teacher, salesperson, friend and so on. The size of each piece represents how large each major aspect of life feels, not how much time is spent 'being it'.

The differences between men's and women's changing sense of self are evident immediately. For example, from pregnancy to eighteen months after birth, the size of the *worker* or *student* piece increases for new fathers and decreases for new mothers. The *parent* piece increases dramatically for both – but twice as much for women as for men. What gets squeezed as the parent piece expands? The *partner* or *lover* aspect of new mothers' and fathers' self-descriptions declines – or, in a few cases, disappears altogether – in the first two years of parenthood. As we shall see, these differences between partners are central contributors to their satisfaction with their overall relationship as a couple.

An intense new relationship

After giving birth, each parent begins to establish a new and intense relationship with the baby. Many men and women describe the intensity of this relationship as unlike any other they have experienced. They soon discover that newborns do not come with 'owner's manuals'. Every time they think they have figured out the 'basics', the ever-developing child changes in ways that send parents 'back to the drawing board'. Virtually all parents describe this new relationship as one of the most exciting, fulfilling and complex they have experienced. At the same time, they are exhausted from the almost constant state of excitement, fatigue and disequilibrium that comes with struggling to solve unexpected puzzles, juggle competing responsibilities, and find their way into the fascinating but mysterious mind and heart of this newest member of the family.

Shifting relationships with parents and in-laws

Most couples having a first child experience shifts in their relationships with their parents and in-laws. For some, the birth of a baby brings up sadness if one or more of the parents' parents has died. A new closeness often develops between the existing generations, but this can be a mixed blessing. She wants her parents to come as soon as she gives birth. He wants the three of them to be a private, cosy threesome. It is common for some of the grandparents to visit, most with the intention of being helpful, but new parents are often startled to find that their parents seem to require looking after too. Old knots in the family ties can suddenly reappear.

Shifting relationships with friends and work

All the new mothers in our study took some time off work, and about half stayed home full time for the first two years or so of their child's life. This shift not only alters women's work identities, but limits their opportunities for daily contact with co-workers and friends. Friendship networks begin to shift for both men and women. Close friends who have no children may feel like they are drifting away, partly because they don't know how to respond to the new parents' preoccupation with their baby, and partly because the new parents baulk at their invitations for spontaneous get-togethers or outings where babies are not entirely welcome.

Men begin to work longer hours to make up for the income their wives have given up to stay at home with the baby, and to establish themselves as the major breadwinners now that family expenses are increasing. New fathers often feel that there is nothing substantial they can do for their babies when they are nursing and sleeping much of the time. New mothers can feel abandoned during this period, which confuses their husbands who think of their increased work outside the family as a major contribution to caring for the security of their growing family.

What's happened to us?

Given all the changes we have described, it should not be surprising that men and women experience significant shifts in their relationship as a couple in the early years of becoming a family. Here we focus on two central and interrelated changes: the division of 'Who does what?' and parents' overall feelings about the quality of their marriage.

'*Who Does What?*' Before the birth of the baby, expectant parents describe their current division of household tasks and decision-making on our 'Who Does What?' questionnaire. We ask them to predict how they will share a number of tasks related to the daily care of their baby, such as feeding, changing nappies, putting the baby to bed and arranging for babysitters. Modern couples are convinced that there is a new egalitarian family in which men take an active role in caring for babies and young children. The fact is that women in most industrialized societies still take most of the responsibility for childcare and housework, even when both partners work outside the home. We find that the division of household and family tasks becomes much more salient and traditional after the baby is born; women do significantly more, and men significantly less, of the housework and baby-care than either partner predicted they would.

Given the pervasive belief that egalitarian families are now the norm, both men and women find this reality unexpected and disturbing. Couples say that arguments about 'who does what?' top the list of issues they tend to fight about. The greater the discrepancy between men's and women's pregnancy predictions of how they will care for the baby and father's actual involvement in baby-care later, the more symptoms of depression mothers report when the babies are eighteen months old. Furthermore, the less husbands are involved in household and childcare tasks, the more unhappy their wives are with their overall relationship as a couple. Of course, this story can be told the other way around: when husbands are more involved in the day-to-day family tasks, their wives are less depressed and much happier with the overall state of their marriage.

Marital disenchantment   In the changes we have described so far, partners with a new baby are shifting as individuals, as couples, and in their relationships with the older generations. The women are becoming isolated from work and friends. Partners' mutual role arrangements at home are becoming more traditional, the partner--lover aspect of self is getting squeezed, and relationships with parents and in-laws are undergoing complex rearrangements. Not surprisingly, the amount of marital conflict and disagreement goes up in nine out of ten couples. At first glance it does not seem difficult to explain why we and many other researchers find that satisfaction with marriage goes down during the couple's transition to parenthood.

Yet the explanation for why some couples change more and some less is not quite so straightforward. We find that change *in itself* does not predict decline in marital quality over this time. Work and family role changes propel men and women into different and separate worlds. Compared with couples who remain childless over the same period of time, partners having babies become more different from one another, not only in their roles but in their views of themselves, in their ideas about child-rearing, and in their perceptions of what is happening in their new family. When we measure these differences *between the spouses*, we see that it is those couples whose differences become greater *and* whose fighting increases that become more disenchanted and less satisfied with their marriage. As Christopher Clulow (1982, 1991) of the Tavistock Marital Studies Institute points out from his experience in the First Baby Project, differences in roles are not the only differences new parents face. As they form a new family, parents have difficulty distinguishing between the real baby and the imagined or constructed baby, as did Derek and Enid in our opening example, and this adds to the stress of couples' attempts to adapt to their new roles and responsibilities.

Who is doing well?

The story I have been telling about stress on new parents' marriages focuses on group trends or averages. In fact, there are significant differences in how couples fare during the transition to parenthood. Overall, *the couples who make the best adjustments, in terms of fewer symptoms, less stress and more satisfaction after having a baby, are those who were doing best before the baby was born.* In other words, children do not come along to disrupt idyllic marriages, but, as we see in the case of the *Yes–No* couples who disagreed about whether to begin the family journey, neither do they bring warring couples together. These conclusions are now supported by a number of studies: Jay Belsky's in Pennsylvania (Belsky and Kelly, 1994), Martha Cox's and Jerry Lewis's in Texas and North Carolina (Cox *et al.*, 1989), Frances Grossman's in Massachusetts (Grossman *et al.*, 1980), Joy and Howard Osofsky's in Kansas (Osofsky and Osofsky, 1984), and Christoph Heinicke's in southern California (Heinicke, 1984).

Risks and distress associated with this normal transition

Although on the face of it the couples entering our study appeared to be starting fairly low-risk families, we have been surprised by the level of stress and distress in these well-educated, two-parent, above-the-poverty-line families during the early years of parenthood. Our results leave us concerned that the difficulties encountered by ordinary couples with young children may become lost in the attention given to 'families at risk', who are usually described as those with the least financial, social and psychological resources. Researchers and clinicians who focus on problems of poverty, alcoholism and emotional disorders like depression, antisocial behaviour and schizophrenia, tend not to come in contact with normative family distress and what follows from it. They tend to minimize or dismiss the idea that a substantial proportion of 'normal' families are at risk of developing mental health problems. Let me illustrate from the families we have studied:

Post-partum depression

Although the research literature would lead us to expect only one or two women in 1,000 to suffer from clinical post-partum depression, in our study, 1 in 100 women *and 1 in 100 men* suffered an episode of clinical depression that required hospitalization and medication in the months after their babies were born.

Depression

We ask parents to complete a short list of symptoms of depression. From the time their babies are 1½–5½ years old, between 25 per cent and 33 per cent of the new mothers and fathers report enough symptoms of depression to place their scores in the clinical cut-off range, which suggests that they may be seriously enough depressed to need professional help.

Risks that span generations

In talking to us about their growing-up years, 20 per cent of the new mothers and fathers spontaneously describe themselves as 'adult children of alcoholics'. Although none of the parents in our study appear to be abusing alcohol or drugs themselves, those whose parents had suffered from serious alcohol problems describe their 3½-year-olds as doing less well developmentally than parents with no alcohol problems in their backgrounds. This is troubling to us, because our research staff's observations of all of the children in the study reveal no significant differences between these two groups of pre-schoolers. Two years later, when all the children are 5–5½ years old and in kindergarten, the grandchildren of alcoholics are described by their kindergarten teachers as more withdrawn or shy, or as having more aggressive behaviour problems than the other children in our study. This is a clear demonstration of the kinds of family problems that can cycle through several generations unless they are better understood and attended to.

Marital distress

When we look at parents' descriptions of their overall marriage on a questionnaire to assess marital adjustment, between 9 per cent and 35 per cent of the fathers and mothers have scores in the clinical distress range at different points between pregnancy and six years later. If we count the maritally distressed *and divorced* couples six years into the study, about half of the husbands and wives indicate that they are experiencing marital disenchantment or distress by the time their first child enters kindergarten.

Academic and behaviour problems in the children

By the end of kindergarten, at age 5–5½, approximately 10 per cent of the children are showing problems serious enough for their parents to have sought professional help – for learning or behaviour problems like aggression with siblings or peers, attention deficit disorder, or emotional problems like seriously low self-esteem or depression. As Philip Cowan shows in Chapter 9, these problems often affect the children's ability to concentrate on their school work.

The fact that a small but meaningful proportion of these parents and children are experiencing serious strain or distress in the first years of family life highlights the need to develop preventive services for families who will take advantage of them if they are available. Despite the fact that couples are changing in fairly predictable ways during this major adult transition, men and women experience many of these shifts as unexpected and negative. The vulnerability that they feel in their relationships as couples is particularly disconcerting, especially if they do not realize that their disappointment may be an expectable part of the transition to parenthood. Clearly, these feelings can affect the stability of the marriage and their children's early development.

The couples group intervention

We find that parents' individual and marital distress after they become parents is foreshadowed by how they manage these aspects of life before they have babies. We know that half of the couples who may be expected to separate and divorce eventually do so in the first few years of parenthood. It seems clear to us that the family-making period is an ideal time to provide help for couples embarking on their family journey. We developed groups to ease their transition to parenthood by working with stressors as they occur, to enhance the satisfying aspects of their relationships as couples, and to facilitate the development of more nurturing relationships between them and their babies.

Each couples group, with four couples expecting a baby at about the same time and one staff couple as co-leaders, meets every week for six months throughout the last three months of pregnancy and the first three months of parenthood. Our discussions in these groups focus on central aspects of family life that family researchers and mental health professionals have shown are key ingredients in satisfying marriages and in the development of young children's competence *or* early emotional and behaviour problems.

There were three staff couples in our 'Becoming a Family Project':

Philip Cowan and I trained two other 'real life' couples, Ellen Garrett and William Coysh, and Harriet Curtis Boles and Abner Boles; three of the partners were graduate students working on their doctorates in clinical psychology. The staff couples met twice weekly, once with the participating couples, and once at a staff training meeting in which we monitored and tried to be systematic about our work with the expectant couples. For the first three months of the groups, before the babies begin to arrive, we set the stage by talking about how the couples are managing the different aspects of their lives that we are assessing and we encourage them to spell out their pictures of life as a family.

All parents in the study have personal interviews with their staff couple and complete questionnaires before the groups begin, which encourages them to focus on each of the aspects of life I have been describing: How do they see themselves as individuals and as couples? How do they describe their division of family labour? How do they go about working on differences between them, and how successful are their problem-solving strategies? What are their ideas about parenting, and how are these connected to the parenting they experienced in their families of origin? These questions provide an opportunity for discovering that partners in most couples have different experiences and ideas about family issues.

As the babies are born, they become part of the groups. Now our discussions mirror the couples' lives at home. We can hardly complete a thought or sentence, we are so preoccupied with the babies' movements, cries and fascinating developments. We get a vivid picture of what each couple is contending with and why finishing any task or discussion is a challenge. In the last three months, couples bring pressing problems. We help them experiment with solutions that make sense for them, and all of us follow eagerly as each couple takes steps to settle into life as a family. It is unusual for couples to have this kind of safe haven for sharing their vulnerabilities and successes, and the closeness that develops among the group members during such a critical period makes the endings of the groups particularly poignant.

What the group meetings do

We include this cartoon as a shorthand way of describing our general attitude about our couples group intervention. We are trying to help couples by 'doing a bit of the work' on their relationship *with them* during a challenging and potentially stressful family transition period. We hope to help them do some of the future relationship work on their own, or to know when they are hurting or floundering enough

'The work being done on your marriage – are you having it done, or are you doing it yourselves?'

that they could use some professional help. We think of the groups as doing preventative work because we begin by exploring these important issues with couples as their families are forming. We try to capitalize on the normal, moderate level of confusion, anxiety or distress that many men and women experience as they embark on one of life's major, joyous – but stressful – transitions. In the groups, we encourage couples to explore their ideas, their dreams and the places that they get stuck in their relationship with one another or their children – before they feel overwhelmed and discouraged by unexpected shifts in their lives as couples, before their discouragement spills over into the tone of their relationships with their children, and before the children and parents develop unrewarding patterns that may require longer-term help in the mental health system.

The discussions in the couples groups are semi-structured in the sense that our staff couples provide part of the 'agenda' for each evening, and the participants supply the rest by bringing questions or problems for the group to consider. Over the months of meetings, we talk with the couples about their reactions to the questionnaires they have already completed and about their experiences of being parents of newborns. We work with them on the kinds of challenging marital, parenting and three-generational issues and problems that most of us confront at some time in our development as partners and parents.

The problems that couples raise for discussion are about both practical and psychological matters, and often feel urgent. *She* wants him to tell his mother that it is up to *them* which family name to give their baby. *He* argues that that will put distance between him and his mother at a time when they have just reconnected around the news of the pregnancy. *She* begins to consider returning to her job outside the family and *he* wants her to be a full-time mother.

Expectant and new parents often need help to find more satisfying ways of balancing their own and their children's needs. *He* 'knows' that their son should be left to cry so he won't get spoiled, but *she* 'knows' that babies must be picked up and soothed in order to feel secure.

Our attitude is that *it is not a problem* that couples have such differences, for every couple has some. The secret of having more satisfying relationships is in what couples *do* about them once they emerge. We encourage husbands and wives not to let these disagreements stop them. We help them explore what is important to each of them, and ask more about the origins of the issues that each one feels passionate about. Some parents are determined never to let their baby feel frightened. Others are equally impassioned about talking to one another in a way that is respectful of the other's feelings. Some couples need help hearing each other out, or knowing when to put a problem discussion on hold because one or both of them are too angry to feel safe working together. Spouses who get a sympathetic hearing in the groups learn that they are not the only ones with unresolved problems, and that other couples too have embarrassingly ineffective ways of arguing. Learning more about the human condition seems to be reassuring or consoling, and allows some spouses to move beyond their fights to find more productive solutions.

In all of these groups, we work with partners as far as they wish to go. Some are reticent about such intimate matters, others more outspoken. We help them monitor their own level of comfort with talking in the group and urge spouses to expand on their expectations, their dreams and the impasses they find difficult. We do not function as 'experts' in the sense of offering ideal solutions. Based on our training, we encourage each partner to express previously unexplored feelings, to suggest an experimental next step, or to get far enough beyond his or her distress to begin moving in the direction of their desired goals as parents and partners. One of the benefits of having both parents in the room is that we can work with both spouses' ideas, objections, fears and styles to find solutions that satisfy both of them. In these days when so many mothers and fathers must work outside of the home, couples tell us that the two hours with us each week is often the only time they have for a complete conversation or to think a problem through.

One mother comes to a group in tears because her husband is suggesting that their daughter begins to sleep in her own bed; she makes a case for needing to nurse at night and is clearly not ready to move the baby into another room. He is agitated about feeling characterized as not being understanding; he feels vulnerable about his desirability, and is reacting as if this situation will never be resolved. As we explore further, we hear more about his earlier insecurity, about his sexual experience, and about her history of feeling rejected by her mother. This has left her committed to nurture her daughter in what may be an overdetermined way, and him feeling particularly sensitive about rejection. Until both partners have a better understanding of where her fierce opposition and his desperate need originate, they will continue to feel strain in their marriage and their sexual relationship. She has been feeling as if she must make a choice between her husband and her daughter, and he is fearful about her decision.

In another group, a wife wants to know what to do when her husband becomes frightened and says they must stop arguing because the argument is too heated. She feels unfairly characterized by him as a threatening person, which leads her to shout that if he would just agree to go on, they can get the problem 'solved'.

While these are common problems in couple relationships, it is not commonly understood that partners' powerful reactions to each of these issues are coloured by years of personal history, traumas from their own lives as children, and passionate feelings about not repeating painful patterns from their pasts. Most couples need help to see that these critical aspects of their histories play a role in their day-to-day impasses. If they are typical, the couple will have difficulty completing a satisfying conversation about these issues in the sleepless, vulnerable months with a new baby, because on the way someone will get hurt, insulted, furious or frightened. Backing away to protect themselves, one of them will shut the conversation down before they have reached a satisfying resolution.

We find that in almost every group, some couples are surprisingly amenable to authoritative and sympathetic help from leaders who do not get frightened by their intense reactions and impasses. As we work with them, the partners in difficulty learn they can each receive a fair hearing, which leaves them readier to work towards more satisfying, less destructive ways of struggling with one another. At the same time, other couples in the room take note and talk all the way home about how their own style of working out problems measures up. When husbands and wives are tense at home, they tend to talk less so as not to make matters worse between them, but, paradoxically, talking more could bring them closer together. According to the participants, the group discussions give them a fuller picture of what goes on behind families' closed doors. For some this provides a measuring stick of how they are doing, and for others it offers examples of more productive ways to manage their lives as parents and partners.

When there is a crisis in a group couple

In several of the groups we have led since 1975, we have seen a couple through a major life crisis. In one group, it became clear to us that a mother was beginning to suffer from a post-partum depression with psychotic symptoms when their baby was barely 3 months old. She and her partner had recently moved to our part of the country and they needed our assistance to find the appropriate help for her. In another group, a mother was unexpectedly arrested for a crime she was accused of having committed months earlier during her pregnancy. In both groups, the bewildered and frightened fathers came to the group with a frantic infant who had only been breastfed and never taken a bottle. The other couples in each of these groups, frightened as they were by the intensity of the problems, were extraordinarily supportive to the couple in crisis. Some offered practical assistance, others psychological support, and both groups urged that we continue to meet until the mother in trouble was able to return home. Although such dramatic events are rare, some couples in every group that we have led or supervised over the past twenty years have been grappling with compelling and painful issues – with their parents, with their children, or with one another in their marriages.

The impact of participating in a couples group

What kinds of effects can we document as we follow the couples over time? First, most of the participants *say* that the work in the groups is invaluable and unique in their lives. For half a year, the group provides husbands and wives with a regular, safe forum for talking about some of the impasses they face. At least some of the participants explore their frustration and distress more fully than they say they have been able to do on their own. Even in these 'low-risk' families, we hear stories from the past of parents who were physically or emotionally absent, of emotional deprivation, of physical or sexual abuse, and of the kinds of emotional roller-coasters that accompany alcohol abuse for parents and children. New parents need help to break these patterns, and they say that their experiences in the group provide support, a better understanding of their own emotional reactions, and examples of other ways of reacting to their confusion and stress.

When we look at all the information men and women have provided almost two years after the 'Becoming a Family Project' groups end, we see different patterns in couples who did and did not participate in one of our couples groups. The new fathers who participated in a group describe themselves as more psychologically involved with their babies than fathers with no intervention; their 'father' pieces of 'The Pie' are significantly larger than those of fathers without a group. The new mothers from the groups feel more satisfied with the 'who does what?' of their lives. Although their husbands are not significantly more involved, the wives from the groups seem to feel that their husbands are working with them on the important family issues, even if their roles in the hands-on work of caring for their babies are not equal. The group couples report less marital disenchantment between pregnancy and six months after giving birth, and their level of satisfaction remains stable in the second year of parenthood, whereas parents with no group experience show an even steeper drop in marital satisfaction in the second year of the study than they had in the first year.

What is happening in the groups to account for these effects? Partners find that their own experiences are mirrored in some form by others in the group. They say that this allows them to see their unexpected shifts in a more sympathetic perspective. In fact, their answers to our questionnaires show that the views of spouses who participated in a group diverge less from one another's – about themselves, their marriage and their family. It is as if working with us in the groups keeps both husbands and wives from slipping into more separate and traditional ways of thinking and being, and staves off the marital disenchantment reported in almost every study of modern parents. The groups give both men and women a chance to hear others' experiences and views, which expands their views of what takes place in 'normal' families.

Our separation and divorce data are consistent with the finding of more stable satisfaction in the intervention couples *for the first three years of parenthood*. By the time their children are 3 years old, 15 per cent of the parents with no intervention have separated or divorced, whereas *all* of the parents from the couples groups are still in intact marriages.

While we wish we could end our story on that optimistic note, the positive effects of the groups on the parents' feelings about their marriages, as you might expect with a time-limited group, begin to wane by the time the children are 4 years old. By the time the children in the study are 5 years old and entering kindergarten, the separation and divorce rate is 20 per cent in couples with and without the intervention. While this may at first sound discouraging, reports from the couples who remained childless help to put this figure in perspective: *compared to the 20 per cent divorce rate for the new parents, the rate for couples who remained childless over the seven years of our longitudinal study is 50 per cent.* That is, having a baby helps keep couples together, at least for a time. Because we were able to keep them together in a more positive state of mind for three years, we believe that 'booster shots' – additional groups that meet periodically during the early child-rearing years – might have averted the pile-up of additional stresses (second and third children, illness, financial stress, job loss) that accumulate over time and wear down even the most resourceful of couples.

We should note that, although we believe them to have distinct advantages, couples groups are not the only ways of helping new mothers and fathers adapt to becoming a family. Christopher Clulow and his associates, who mounted the 'First Baby Project' in London, years ago coached health visitors to pay more attention to *family issues* as they made regular home visits after each child was born. That work has spawned a recent, similar project directed by Mel Parr at Parent Infant Partnership in London.

What has to change for partners becoming parents?

It seems clear that when couples embark on their family journey, they open the gates to potential stress and distress in their relationships. Those who work on getting their relationship house in order, so to speak, are more likely to make the adjustment to becoming a family more easily. Couples who are able to begin the process of making the decision to have a baby with an honest discussion of their pictures of ideal life as a family, taking the time to respond to each spouse's degree of readiness, will create a buffer against emotions that can threaten their stability as a couple after they become parents.

Once the baby arrives, both he and she will experience shifts in their sense of themselves as individuals and as couples, just as Derek and Enid did at the beginning. Couples who find ways to stay in touch during this process will be better able to stave off the negative effects of the vulnerability they feel in the early sleepless weeks with a newborn. Couples who do not have productive ways of working out their problems and differences would benefit from getting some help if, at any point in the process, one or both of them feel overwhelmed or discouraged. Parents who themselves feel understood and nurtured are naturally more able to be nurturant and responsive to their children. When parents do not feel cared for, as Philip Cowan shows in Chapter 9, their children are at risk of developing behaviour, academic and emotional problems as they take on the demands of their transition to school. Particularly in these days of an increasingly demanding economy and hurried family lives, in which both parents must work *and* juggle the needs of their children, it is not uncommon for their marriage to be put on the 'back burner' for the first few years of parenthood.

Our results (Cowan and Cowan, 1992) suggest that professionals can offer a preventative step by creating opportunities for parents to make their lives as partners and parents less stressful and more satisfying. Some people wonder why ordinary families need these kinds of services. Our answer is based on the strain in many modern families, which increases in the first years of parenthood as parents' skills and emotional resources are severely challenged. Helping expectant parents to sort out some of their priorities and dreams before they feel overwhelmed with the care of a baby may keep them from feeling at odds with one another and encourage them to try to make their relationship more satisfying. Our experience makes it clear that early intervention offers potential benefits for everyone involved in the complex and rewarding enterprise of becoming a family.

Carolyn Pape Cowan

9
Being Partners: Effects on Parenting and Child Development

If parents of young children find time to browse in a bookshop with a section on family life, they will find hundreds of titles in two major sections. The larger section will contain a myriad of books written by current experts on parenting – each with different (and often conflicting) messages about 'how best to raise your child'. A smaller but still substantial section is filled with books on 'how to maintain your couple relationship, how to revive flagging sexual interest, or how to choose a more compatible partner the second time around'.

It is rare for the books on parenting to venture into the privacy of the marriage, except to warn readers that in the early days of becoming a family, the relationship may be subject to some stresses and strains (see Chapter 8). Conversely, books on marriage appear to be written for couples who live by themselves, without children, relatives, friends or others who might interfere with experts' recommendations to set aside quiet evenings for intimacy and romance. Since nine in ten couples who marry have children, and since quality of the parents' marriage has important implications for children's development, it would seem to be important to address issues of how couples juggle their responsibilities as parents, workers, friends *and* lovers, in ways that help to keep their relationships alive and well.

My goal in this chapter is to bring the topics of marriage and parent–child relationships together. Beyond the task of identifying specific parenting techniques, we need to develop a positive emotional climate in the family. In two-parent families, this climate is largely determined by the way parents relate to each other. I will argue that if we want to provide conditions that allow for children's optimal development, researchers, mental health professionals and parents themselves are going to have to pay more attention to improving the quality of the parents' marriage.

After presenting some statistics to support the argument that families these days need more support and help, I describe some new ideas about how couple relationships affect both mothers' and fathers' relationships with their children. I briefly present some results from two studies, done in collaboration with Carolyn Pape Cowan, that illustrate how the quality of the marriage, as it 'spills over' into parent–child relationships, plays an important role in shaping children's ability to adapt to the challenges of primary school. Finally, I report on some new, encouraging findings from one of these studies, showing that working with mental health professionals in a couples group during the year before children enter kindergarten has positive effects on both parents and on their children's development.

Some background

Why families with young children need help

American and British researchers have shown that by the time children enter primary school at age 5 or 6, one in ten will be diagnosed with an emotional disorder or severe behaviour problems. Another one in ten will develop a diagnosable disorder sometime during his or her school career. Untold others will suffer troubling bouts of anxiety, depression, learning difficulties, attention problems, social rejection, out-of-control aggression, sexual acting-out, or delinquency.

At the same time that substantial numbers of children are having difficulties in learning the skills they need to make it through life, an appreciable number of their parents are struggling too. In the United States, about one in five couples with a first child entering kinder-garten will be divorced by the time that child makes the transition to school, with half of those divorces occurring before the child's second birthday. There seems to be clear evidence that, in addition to the daily challenge of earning enough money to take care of their families, parents are suffering their share of mild to severe distress.

This picture of late-twentieth-century family life is not meant as a prologue to a diatribe about the death of the family or the decay of modern marriage. In both Chapters 8 and 9 in this book, Carolyn Cowan and I are trying to convey a realistic rather than an idealized picture of contemporary family life. The idea that difficulties coping with life, serious emotional problems or mental illness are reserved for only a small and unfortunate segment of the population is far from current realities. Hidden behind the headlines of 'high-risk', single-parent, poor families is the reality that many middle-class two-parent families with young children are also experiencing a significant amount of distress. Most readers will readily recognize this portrait of contemporary life by considering their own families or those of neighbours, friends or colleagues. The odds are that among the people you know, one or more family members are coping with some of the common signs of dysfunction or distress that I have just described.

When any family member is in difficulty, tensions reverberate throughout the family system. Although there are some excellent sources of help available for those in need, there are never enough resources to go around. Given the high incidence of mental health and adjustment problems in contemporary society and the immense effort required to take care of them, it seems reasonable to consider the possibility of trying to prevent at least some family problems from occurring in the first place. There is an apocryphal story told in American community mental health circles about a fly-fisherman wading in a river. He becomes distracted from his peaceful pursuits by human bodies floating past him in the river's currents. He struggles diligently to pull each body to safety on the shore, only to find another floating by. The next day, he complains bitterly to his friend about all the work he's doing to rescue the unfortunate people coming downstream. His friend scratches his head and says, 'Well, I guess I'd try going upstream to find out who's pushing all those people in.' While it is necessary to be as helpful as we can to families who are already 'floating downstream', it seems more practical to devote a substantial effort to help them manage the shallower, calmer waters before they get in over their heads.

If your goal is helping young children, why focus on their parents' marriage?

It seems obvious that if you want to help young children to develop more effective intellectual resources and to engage in more satisfying relationships with their peers, you should try to instruct children directly, and/or help their mothers and fathers to become more effective parents. The first strategy can be observed in public and private school classrooms and playing fields for five or six hours each weekday. The second can be observed in books on parenting, and in parenting classes offered in the evenings and at weekends in schools, churches and community centres. Attempts to improve the skills of parents of young children can also be seen in England and other countries by home visiting nurses who provide child development information, and work with mothers to help them become more effective parents.

Most approaches to helping families with young children are missing two central ingredients. First, almost all of the family-based interventions are directed towards mothers. At the same time that mothers, teachers, family therapists and social scientists decry fathers' lack of involvement in family life, men are left out in the cold when it comes to services and research designed to improve the quality of parent–child relationships. Second, even when there are two parents, as there still are in a majority of families, very little attention has been paid to the quality of the relationship between the partners. It is ironic that during the last several decades, many systematic studies have demonstrated that divorce has negative effects on children, but almost no one was looking at the impact on children of hostile or distant couples who resolutely stay together 'for the sake of the child'.

The importance of family transitions

Karl Alexander and Doris Entwistle (1988), who study the role of the family in children's transition to school, have suggested a useful metaphor that illustrates why it can be helpful to learn more about families who are in the process of making a major life transition. Families approaching the challenges of a transition, they say, are like bicycle racers approaching a steep hill: some begin to have difficulty because the skills that served them well on flat terrain are not adequate for the challenges posed by steep grades. These difficulties tend to spread the cyclists apart, highlighting those with and without the skills or stamina to get to their destination. By studying families as they are making important life transitions, we are in a better position to find out what helps some to meet new challenges, while others fall farther and farther behind the pack.

In Chapter 8, Carolyn Cowan described some of the findings from the 'Becoming a Family Project' – our study of how couples manage the transition to parenthood and how their marriages are affected. Our second longitudinal study, the 'Schoolchildren and their Families Project', shows how the quality of the couple relationship during the early family-making years affects children's adaptation as they make the transition to kindergarten and first grade. We focus on how well children do in their transition to elementary school because problems evident in kindergarten and Grade 1 have been the best predictors of later educational, social and mental health problems during adolescence in studies of both low-risk and high-risk populations. In other words, the trajectories that children follow in their academic careers are laid down in their first years of formal schooling. It is terribly important, then, to 'get in' early, to help children cope as well as possible before their academic and social problems become debilitating and intractable.

Five aspects of family life

One of the couples in our transition to parenthood study, Derek and Enid, was described by Carolyn Cowan (Chapter 8), in the week after having their first baby, Samantha. In contrast with their hopes and dreams about an idyllic time at home as a new family, they ended up in separate bedrooms after an upsetting fight. The fight, ostensibly caused by a disagreement over taking out the rubbish, occurred after a tense week during Enid's parents' visit to 'help out' after Samantha's birth. Let us now look in on their family four years later:

> Enid is irritated. She has just explained to Derek for the third time in the past two months that she is concerned about where Samantha will go to kindergarten next year. The local school has a very bad reputation, but the money for a private school seems out of their reach. Derek seems preoccupied. Enid raises her voice a little, pointing out what Derek already knows, that Samantha is his daughter too. Derek, who has had a very trying day at work, pleads to have this discussion at another time. Enid recognizes that this has been a difficult day for him, but her work day was difficult too, and she has already postponed this discussion for several weeks because things have been tense between them. Samantha comes into the room wanting to 'play with daddy'. Derek begs off politely, but Samantha persists until Derek suddenly grabs her by the hand, puts his face right up against hers, and tells her through gritted teeth to go to the other room or she'll get a spanking.
>
> Enid's anger erupts full force now, not on the topic of schools but on Derek's harshness with Samantha. In an attempt to defend himself, Derek accuses Enid of being overprotective. Enid counterattacks, accusing Derek of continuing the abusive pattern from his family. Derek, angered after many years of Enid's negative characterizations of his family, stomps out of the house, brushing Samantha roughly as he goes out of the door. The couple spend another night in separate rooms, wondering what has gone wrong. Samantha plays alone quietly in her room, wondering what she has done to make her parents so upset.

There are four major themes we can extract from this single vignette. First, Derek and Enid's fighting, which increased early in their transition to parenthood, has continued unabated over time. It has not occurred to them to get help to change this disturbing pattern. Second, when parents are at odds with each other, it is likely that the conflict will spill over into the relationship between at least one of the parents and their child. Third, children's explanations to themselves of why their parents are fighting play an important role in determining how conflict between their parents affects them. Finally, relationships among mothers, fathers and children do not exist in a vacuum. Parents behave the way they do at least partly as a carry-over from their own childhoods, especially in response to stressors from outside the family.

The patterns shown by Derek, Enid and Samantha illustrate what

Carolyn Cowan and I have described as a 'five-domain model' of how the family affects children's development and adaptation. This means that if we want to understand family factors affecting children's transitions to elementary school, or how the family copes with any other developmental transition, we will do best if we consider information from five aspects of family life:

- *Each family member's sense of self and adaptation level.* Whether or not Derek and Enid fight a great deal, and the impact of this specific fight on the family, depends in part on whether each family member is relatively well-adjusted and whether any of the family members are in a state of mental or emotional distress.
- *The intergenerational relationships among grandparents, parents and children.* Is Enid correct in her assertion that Derek has experienced years of abuse? What about Enid's family? Are they contending with a clash of family cultures in which a tradition of harsh discipline styles (from Derek's lineage) is colliding with a tradition in which warmth is valued far more than control (from Enid's lineage)?
- *The balance between stressful events and social supports outside the family.* We tend to focus in our example on work stress because it seems to be an ever-present spectre, especially when both parents work, but stresses can come from economic hardship, violence in the neighbourhood, loss of support from friends, and other external sources. As we can see, what happens outside the family has an effect on all the family relationships.
- *The quality of the marriage.* We view the marriage as a lynch-pin in family life. When it is going well, the partners are happier and the children feel the benefits. It can also function as a protective shield, buffering family members from external and internal adversities. Conversely, as we will see, the marital atmosphere can function as an amplifier, turning up the volume on difficulties in one part of the family so that everyone is adversely affected by the 'noise'.
- *Parent–child relationships.* By focusing on the marriage, we do not mean to minimize the importance of what parents do with their children. The main emphasis in this chapter, though, is how the quality of the couple relationships affects what happens between parent and child.

How we study families

Our detailed study of the connections between marital and parenting relationships began when parents were in their early to mid-thirties and their children were pre-schoolers; in one study, the children were

$3\frac{1}{2}$ and in another they were approximately $4\frac{1}{2}$. In both studies, the families lived in about thirty cities and towns in northern California. About 15 per cent of the participants were African–American, Asian–American or Latino, and 85 per cent were Caucasian. All of the men and women had completed at least Grade 12 in High School, and many had completed additional vocational training or college degrees. Their family incomes spanned a range from working-class to upper-middle-class.

We invite the families to visit a laboratory/playroom at the university for about two hours and ask them to engage in a number of tasks. First, the child meets alone with two members of our research team who learn about the child's developmental level and problem-solving styles. This is followed by a period in which the mother works and plays with the child, and another in which the father does a similar set of tasks and games with the child. Finally, we ask the whole family to come together to interact around tasks that are both challenging and fun.

Of course, there is no way that we can come to know a family intimately in one two-hour period, but we have designed a range of situations that give us a good idea about how each family works together and gets along. In one task, an experimenter takes the child out of the room, tells him or her a short story, and tests to see that the child remembers it. When the child comes back into the playroom, the parent, who has not heard the story, asks the child to repeat it. This is analogous to the situation in which a parent asks a child what he or she did that day at nursery school or day care. We find that about half the children do not want to tell their parents the story. Some parents laugh and go on, others ask questions that help the child to tell it, while still others interrogate their child relentlessly until the parents give up in frustration or disgust.

In other tasks, the parent presents the child with difficult puzzles or games. We tell the parents that we are not interested in how well the child performs, but rather in how the two of them usually work and play together. We end the session by opening a small sandbox along with hundreds of miniature figures, and inviting the parent and child to 'build a world together in the sand'. Each parent works with the child on a similar set of activities, and then the whole family works and plays together in a third set of tasks. Some of the family tasks are difficult and have correct answers, and some are designed to be enjoyable, with no set outcome. All the sessions are videotaped with the family's permission. Throughout these visits, some parents are warm and supportive, some are warm and demanding, and others are controlling and critical. The videotapes support our vivid impression that families react to these visits in many and varied ways.

In our observations and coding of the videotaped visits, we focus on various aspects of the parent–child relationship in each separate visit, and on how the parents behave towards each other when the whole family is together. In the parent–child sessions, we are particularly interested in two dimensions of behaviour: first, whether the parents tend to be warm and responsive or cold and critical; and second, whether the parents tend to set limits and structure the situation to help the child, or whether they tend to be distanced and disengaged. Diana Baumrind (1979), a researcher at the University of California at Berkeley who has followed children longitudinally from age 3 to young adulthood, has shown that children develop best when parents are *authoritative* – warm and responsive *and* set age-appropriate limits with the children. These children develop more adaptive academic and social skills than children whose parents are *authoritarian* (cold and limit-setting), *permissive* (warm and responsive without setting limits), or *disengaged* (neither warm nor limit-setting). In the whole-family session, we are interested in the level of warmth and co-operation the parents show towards each other, or the level of anger and competition between them as they attempt to help their child with difficult tasks.

Finally, a year or two later, when the children enter kindergarten, we give each child an individual academic achievement test in a home visit. Even though the children are now scattered in many dozens of classrooms, we are able to enlist teachers' help by asking them to fill out a 106-item checklist to describe *every child in the class.* Fortunately for us, teachers have agreed to do this not knowing which child from our study is enrolled in the classroom. This allows us to see how the child in our study fares in a number of different aspects of classroom life compared with all the other students in the class. We are especially interested in whether teachers see the children as socially accepted, as shy and withdrawn, or as expressing their problems in hostile and aggressive behaviours or in tension, anxiety or depression.

The role of the marriage in parent–child relationships

When we analyse the information from each family at different points in the study, we see that the role of the marriage in family life is quite complex. Let me describe four different patterns: simple spillover effects; complex spillover effects; marriage as an amplifier of negative effects; and marriage as a buffer, protecting children from stressors in other parts of family life.

Simple spillover

Parents who are hostile and angry with each other when they are working and playing together with their child in the whole-family visit are less warm, less responsive, less limit-setting and less structuring in the separate parent–child sessions. It is as if the anger generated *between* the parents overflows its container and spills over into at least one of the relationships between parent and child.

Complex spillover

In a study with Pat Kerig (Kerig *et al.*, 1993), we found that the story about spillover is more complicated than the notion that marital distress is associated with strain between parents and children. We noticed that mothers and fathers appeared to be treating sons more positively than daughters. Comparing fathers' and mothers' work and play sessions with sons and with daughters showed that both parents, but especially fathers, were more authoritative (warm, responsive, structuring) and less authoritarian (cold, angry, not responsive, disengaged), with sons.

Looking at this finding in more detail, we could see that it wasn't that parents were treating sons more positively, but that they were treating daughters more negatively. However, *this occurred only in families in which the parents were unhappy about their relationship as a couple.* Mothers who indicated on a questionnaire that they were not very satisfied with their marriage tended to respond negatively to their daughters when the daughters asserted themselves. Fathers who were maritally dissatisfied treated their daughters more negatively regardless of what their daughters were doing. It looked as if maritally dissatisfied fathers reacted to their daughters the way they reacted to their wives. That is, the negative spillover from marital distress to difficulties in parent–child relationships was most pronounced in father–daughter pairs. This finding raises a question currently intriguing us and other family researchers: under what conditions does marital conflict affect children negatively? The answers will eventually provide a much more differentiated picture of complex spillover effects.

Marriage as an amplifier of negative effects

So far it seems as if problems for the child begin with the parents' marriage, but we also find that the marriage is 'in the middle', functioning as an amplifier of difficulties arising in other aspects of family life. For example, with Nancy Miller, Mavis Hetherington and Glen Clingempeel (Miller *et al.*, 1993), we found that in the families in our study, mothers' and fathers' symptoms of depression were not related to aggressive behaviour shown by their 3½-year-olds in our laboratory/playroom. We believe that if we were studying a group of families already in therapy, parents' depression would be associated with problematic behaviour in the child.

We also found, however, that when mothers and fathers endorsed more symptoms of depression on a questionnaire, they were more likely to be in a distressing couple relationship. When the parents were depressed *and* their marriages were in trouble, their parenting was less effective and their children showed more aggressive behaviour. We found this pattern in our sample of 3½-year-olds, and again in another sample of families in which the first child was entering adolescence. In both samples, conflict and competition in the marriage amplified the impact of parents' depression so that it had negative effects on parent–child relationships and, ultimately, on the child's behaviour.

Marriage as a buffer

I do not want to leave the impression that the quality of parents' marriage has only negative effects on parenting. The example I just described could be stated another way around. Rather than emphasizing the negative impact of marital conflict as an amplifier of depression, we could focus on the positive impact of a good marriage in preventing parents' depression from spreading into other aspects of family life.

Here I want to describe an example in which a positive marital relationship can buffer the child by interfering with the repetition of negative parent–child relationships across the generations. Both developmental and family researchers have shown a growing interest in the ways that maladaptive behaviour is passed on from one generation to another. An intriguing new body of research has emerged in which adults are asked about their memories of early relationships with *their* parents using the Adult Attachment Interview developed by Carol George, Nancy Kaplan and Mary Main at the University of California, Berkeley (see Main and Goldwyn, in press). Coders analyse both the content of the interview (descriptions of childhood) and formal aspects of the interview (especially the coherence of the narrative) to create categories representing adults' 'working models' (conscious and unconscious mental and emotional pictures) of their early attachments. Men and women who describe relatively happy childhoods in a vivid, convincing and coherent fashion are described as having a *secure* state of mind with reference to early attachment relationships. What is most important, individuals who describe relatively unhappy childhoods, but do so in a vivid, convincing and coherent manner, are also described as having a secure state of mind about their early attachment relationships.

Insecure states of mind, found in about one-third of most samples, are coded when a person asserts that his or her early relationships were happy, but can't remember them well, or is still preoccupied, angry and not coherent in talking about past and present relationships with parents. Of course, we do not know what *really* happened in the past. We assume, however, that one's state of mind about past family relationships will influence one's current attitudes and behaviour.

Indeed, in a study with Deborah Cohn and Jane Pearson (Cohn *et al.*, 1992), we found that parents' insecure states of mind concerning their early attachments, as we understand them from their detailed interviews, are correlated with our observations of parents' behaviour with their child. When *both parents* are classified as having secure states of mind, their parenting in separate sessions with their child has warmth and appropriate limit setting.

When *both parents* are classified as having insecure working models, their parenting shows little warmth or limit-setting. The unique finding from our work is that when mothers classified as insecure are married to fathers classified as secure, the mothers' parenting quality is as effective as that of mothers classified as securely attached.[1] Furthermore, the quality of their marital interaction is more positive and less negative than that of couples in which both wife and husband are classified as insecure. The findings are consistent with the hypothesis that a nurturant marriage can buffer the negative impact of one partner's impoverished early experiences and provide a family context in which effective parenting is possible in the next generation. It seems to us that a good marriage can provide an opportunity for a parent who is still negatively affected by his or her early experiences to develop a new and more positive state of mind about intimate relationships – a more optimistic outlook and set of expectations that spills over positively into the parent–child relationship.

The role of marriage and parenting in children's adaptation to school

Let me describe the central role of marriage in the child's adaptation to school with the help of two schematic diagrams that summarize the main features of the results of our transition to parenthood study, in which we followed the families from late pregnancy until their first child entered kindergarten (Cowan and Cowan, 1992). The information in Figure 1 comes from a paper written in collaboration with

Figure 1

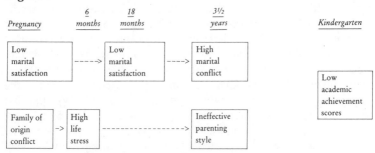

Marc Schulz and Trudie Heming (Cowan *et al.*, 1994).

As we move from left to right in Figure 1, we follow couples as they begin the transition to parenthood, cope with the first six months of becoming a family, settle into the issues raised by toddlerhood, and show us how they work and play with their 3½-year-olds separately, and then together as a family. Before we look at what happens to their school achievement in kindergarten, let us examine how the parents' descriptions of the family environment are linked with what we see when we watch the parents working and playing with their pre-schoolers in our project playroom. We tell this story by focusing on the paths to family difficulty, but we can use the same findings to follow the development of family strengths.

We find two family 'pathways' that lead to strained relationships between parents and their pre-school children. First, when parents report a fair amount of conflict and dissatisfaction in their marriage during the late stages of pregnancy, they tend to be similarly unhappy with their marriage almost two years later. When their children are 3½, those unhappily married parents are observed by our staff teams as more angry, cold and competitive, and less warm, responsive and co-operative *with each other*. These couples in observably conflictful marital relationships tend to be less authoritative – less warm, responsive and structuring – during the parent–child visits than parents whose marriages are more harmonious.

A second pathway to children's difficulty begins with parents who recall more conflict in *their* families of origin. Those parents report more stressful life events and more symptoms of depression during their pregnancy-to-after-birth transition, and show more conflict as a couple and less effective parenting with their pre-schoolers two years later.

Family contributions to the child's academic achievement

How well does all of this early family information predict the children's academic achievement in kindergarten? We measure the accuracy of prediction by determining how much of the variation in the children's academic achievement we can predict from the family information we gathered earlier. Perfect prediction would be 100 per cent. In studies such as ours, the ability to predict 20 per cent of the variation, though it sounds low, is doing pretty well. We find that using the family information we gathered, we can predict 52 per cent of the variation in children's academic achievement test scores at the end of kindergarten. That is, if we take into account parents' general perceptions of conflict in their families of origin, their stress during their transition to parenthood, their marital quality before and after the birth of their first child, and the level of warmth and structure they provide for their pre-schoolers, we can account for a great deal – though not everything – about how the children are faring academically at the end of their first year of formal schooling.

Family contributions to children's relationships with their peers

The same family variables that predict half of the variation in children's academic competence, predict only one-fifth to one-quarter of the variance in the teachers' ratings of how well the children managed in their peer relationships at school, depending on which aspect of relationships with peers we are examining. However, in a new study done in collaboration with Deborah Cohn and Jane Pearson (Cowan *et al.*, in press), we were able to add more detailed information from the Adult Attachment Interview with each parent about the mothers' and fathers' growing-up years and about the quality of their relationships with their parents now. With this richer information about parents' early experiences with *their* parents, we can explain much more precisely children's social adaptation with their peers at school (Figure 2).

Here we see that mothers' and fathers' attachment histories are associated with different outcomes in their children. When fathers' descriptions of their growing-up years are not coherent, either because they talk of idyllic relationships with no supporting examples to illustrate, or because they seem angry or preoccupied with their parents' lack of loving behaviour, they tend to be in marriages that have a great deal of conflict. As we described earlier, this marital conflict seems to spill over into the parent–child relationship in the harsher, less responsive reactions that we see when the fathers are observed with their children during the pre-school period. Two years later, the kindergarten teachers see these children, both boys and girls, as much more aggressive towards their peers than children whose

Figure 2

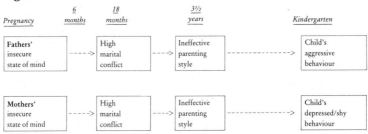

parents have less conflict. This set of family relationship predictors accounts for 60 per cent of the variation in the teachers' ratings of the children's aggression.

Mothers who describe their growing-up years as harsh or rejecting, or without some kind of coherent integration of their narrative, tend to be in marriages that are high in conflict. These women are more angry and less structuring with their children during the pre-school visits; and two years later, their children tend to be more depressed, shy and socially rejected at school. These predictors account for a high degree of the variation in the teachers' descriptions of the children. Although we cannot jump to very general conclusions from just one study, we can speculate that, even though fathers and mothers who are insecurely attached tend to be in more conflictful marital relationships, the spillover creates different kinds of problems in the children's adjustment.

We have known for some time that when parents' marital conflict leads to divorce, their children have more academic problems and difficulties with peers at school. Our study suggests that when *married* parents fail to regulate their conflicts successfully as a couple, their children are also at risk of social and academic problems as they embark on their school careers.

I need to make clear what these results signify and what they do not. The fact that we can predict a substantial proportion of children's academic and social competence from pre-school family assessments reflects, in part, the fact that parents and children share a set of partially overlapping genes. Even if all the predictive power comes from the quality of family relationships, we need to remember that we cannot predict children's competence perfectly. Some children do much better and some do much worse than we would expect from our knowledge of the family environment. Nevertheless, if our goal is to make life better for young children we should pay attention to the quality of the parents' marriage because of its power to colour the child's everyday life in the family and in the outside world.

Intervention effects

All the results I have just described are based on correlations, which means that if the scores on one measure go up, so do scores on the other. We do not really know from these kinds of studies whether there is any *causal* relationship between the quality of the marriage and the quality of parenting shown by the parents participating in these studies. And, if there is a causal relationship, we don't know how it works.

Carolyn Cowan and I designed an intervention study to test our ideas about the marriage–parenting connection more directly. About 110 families with a first child about to enter kindergarten were recruited from pre-schools, childcare centres and public service announcements in northern California. Based on both parents' scores on marital adjustment and symptoms of depression, couples were randomly offered one of three interventions:

- *A maritally focused couples group.* These couples participate in a group meeting weekly for sixteen weeks prior to their children's entrance to kindergarten. In addition to helping them discuss a variety of family topics specified in our theoretical model, leaders engage the couples in discussions about their marital issues and problems. Sometimes one or both partners ask directly for help in communicating better with each other. More often, the discussions begin with a description of tensions or disagreements about child-rearing, or about dealing with parents and in-laws. The group leaders help partners explore implications of these tensions for their relationship as a couple.

- *A co-parenting-focused couples group.* These couples participate in a couples group meeting weekly for sixteen weeks prior to their children's entrance to kindergarten. In addition to helping participants discuss family topics specified in our theoretical model, leaders engage the participants in examining how strains in various aspects of family life affect the ways partners work together in parenting their children. One husband complains that he is always depleted when he comes home from work, but his wife makes extraordinary demands on him to look after the children from the moment he walks in the door. In contrast with the leaders of the marital groups, who try to help partners resolve their marital conflict, the leaders of the co-parenting groups help them explore more satisfying ways of co-operating to look after the children during stressful work-to-home transition times.

● *Short-term consultation.* These couples are offered an opportunity to consult with a staff couple once a year to discuss any troubling family issues or problems in the years before, during and after the child's entrance to kindergarten. The issues raised by the couples who use the consultation are often similar to those raised by the group participants, but they have much less time with our staff to resolve them, and they do not have the opportunity to listen to couples struggling with similar problems in different ways.

The couples groups in this study resembled the ones that Carolyn Cowan described for couples making the transition to parenthood. All were semi-structured, and focused on many of the individual and relationship issues in the five domains of family life we have described in our model. A male–female staff team of mental health professionals worked with couples to shift some of their negative attributions of one another, to regulate their strong emotional reactions more effectively, and to find more adaptive and satisfying problem-solving strategies as partners and parents. The groups met weekly for four months before the children entered kindergarten. We gathered family information prior to the child's entrance to kindergarten (at approximately $4\frac{1}{2}$ years of age), at the end of kindergarten ($5\frac{1}{2}$), and at the end of Grade 1 ($6\frac{1}{2}$).

In comparison with parents in the consultation intervention, mothers and fathers in both marital *and* co-parenting groups reported fewer symptoms of depression after the intervention groups, especially between the kindergarten and Grade 1 follow-ups. On average, couples who participated in the maritally focused groups showed less conflict in front of their children after the intervention.

Couples who had participated in the co-parenting groups showed more positive results. Like our earlier transition to parenthood intervention, the co-parenting groups helped fathers work and play with their children more effectively. The men from the groups that emphasized parent–child relationships showed more effective (authoritative) parenting in the two years after the groups ended. Both mothers and fathers from these groups reported an increase in satisfaction with their marriage. Most exciting of all were the effects we found on the children's adaptation to school. When parents participated in one of the co-parenting groups, their children showed significant improvement from kindergarten to Grade 1 in their reading and spelling achievement scores. Furthermore, the children described themselves as more accepted and less socially rejected by their peers, and their teachers reported fewer shy/withdrawn, depressed behaviours for these children compared to the other children in the study.

Throughout this chapter, I have been emphasizing the importance of the marriage in affecting parent–child relationships. Why didn't the maritally focused group work best? We found that when couples who were already experiencing a lot of marital conflict entered the groups, their conflict tended to *increase* over time, whereas high-conflict couples in the co-parenting groups tended to improve. When the marriage is in difficulty, helping parents work together on issues about rearing their children seems to have positive effects on their parenting *and* on the marital conflict. Our results suggest that if Derek and Enid had participated in one of these groups, they might have been able to settle their differences about dealing with Samantha in ways that ultimately reduced their irritability and tension with each other, at least when Samantha was present.

We want to emphasize that the unique aspect of these co-parenting groups is that they include both fathers and mothers. An intervention that puts the spotlight on marital difficulties may create more than ideal disequilibrium for already warring couples. By contrast, a couples group in which mental health professionals help both parents work together on what is important to each of them in parenting their children appears to increase their satisfaction as a couple, reduce their conflict in front of their children, *and* facilitate the children's academic and social adaptation early in their school careers.

I have argued that when normal families go through normal life transitions, they tend to experience a great deal of disequilibrium and some distress. The data showing that we can predict children's academic and social adaptation to school from family information obtained during the early years of child-rearing means that we know enough to identify which parents and children are at risk for difficulty *before* that difficulty comes to the attention of teachers and mental health professionals.

I have also shown, through both correlational studies and an intervention study, that the quality of the couple's relationship is central in the dynamics of family life. If the relationship feels positive to the partners, it increases the probability that they will relate warmly and effectively to their children; in turn, the children tend to relate well to their teachers and peers in the classroom and do better in their academic work. If the tone of the marriage is negative and full of unresolved conflict, there are risks for the child unless the parents do something to alter the tone and process of their interactions.

Although I have been focusing exclusively on two-parent families at the lower-risk end of the spectrum, our work shows that low risk does not necessarily mean *no distress* or *low distress*. Some of the children who will be identified as having academic and behaviour problems in their early years of schooling come from relatively well-off middle-class families. It is becoming clearer that divorce, single parenthood and poverty are not the only risks for today's children. When parents cannot regulate their exchanges of hostile or negative feelings and do not work together to solve the problems that disturb them, their children are at risk for problems at the beginning of their school careers. Unless something is done to interrupt these negative patterns, children are likely to follow a trajectory that ends in negative outcomes as they make their way through adolescence into adulthood.

What about single-parent families (usually single mothers)? We know that despite added stress, fewer financial resources and only one parent to juggle all the tasks of making a living and raising a family, many children from single-parent families are doing well. When they have difficulties, the reasons appear to be similar to the ones we have described in our studies of families with two parents in the home. Many single mothers are in intimate relationships with partners, and when these relationships work well, their children are more likely to be advancing academically and socially. We also know that the transmission of positive and negative relationships across the generations affects the current relationship between mother and child. Poverty and other stresses in life tend to affect children by disrupting the quality of mother–child relationships. We intend to examine these ideas more closely in a new study of single mothers with children in transition to school. We expect that many of the aspects of family life that we have been describing apply to the success or difficulty of children in single-parent families as well.

The focus of parent educators and mental health professionals concerned with the well-being of children has been on improving the quality of the parenting they receive. I certainly support any programme that helps mothers and fathers to establish more satisfying relationships with their children. What is necessary in addition, I believe, is a focus on the conditions that make better parenting possible. In order for parents to be nurturant and responsive to their children, they must be in adult relationships in which they feel responded to, nurtured and valued. We know that relationships with friends and family often fulfil some of that function, and that an ongoing satisfying relationship with an intimate partner has the potential to provide the nourishment that parents need in order to pass it on to the children they love.

Note

1 We had only two couples in which husbands with insecure states of
mind were married to wives with secure states of mind, so we could
not examine the outcome of this marital pairing.

Philip Cowan

10
Parents Becoming Partners

From the seventeenth century to the early twentieth century, marriages were less based on the idea of romantic love than they are today. The majority of remarriages (and possibly repartnerships) took place following the death of the first spouse. Nowadays, the situation is very different. This century has seen the emergence of the *companionate* marriage (see, for example, Richards, 1995). It has also seen the phenomenon of widespread divorce. After the Second World War, the divorce rate rose considerably, doubling in 1971, and thereafter growing steadily. In 1993, there were 165,000 divorces in England and Wales. Latest predictions indicate that two in five marriages are likely to end in divorce. More than one-third of marriages are remarriages for one of the partners, and these remarriages are statistically more vulnerable than first marriages.

In a recent lecture, Carol Smart presented a sociological view of marriage that stands in contrast with the family law view – a 'pure relationship' or 'confluent love' which is entered into 'for its own sake and for what can be derived by each person from a sustained relationship; which continues only so far as it is thought by both parties to deliver enough satisfactions for each individual to stay within it' (Smart, 1995). This perception of confluent love as something that can be ended by either partner is in sharp contrast with the ideas enshrined in the Children Act 1989 and the Child Support Act 1991, both of which endorse the principle that parenthood is for ever. It is also at odds with the 'for ever', 'one and only', ideals of romantic love.

In the early 1970s, the sharp rise in divorce was blamed on the introduction of the 1969 Divorce Reform Act, which was consolidated in the Matrimonial Proceedings Act of 1973. This laid down that divorce could be granted by establishing that a marriage had broken down irretrievably, which, in turn, required proof of one or more 'facts' (most of which retained the pre-existing concept of matrimonial 'fault'). Although a couple who have been separated for two years or more can now obtain a divorce by agreement (five years is required without agreement), they are more likely to use other 'grounds' (especially behaviour and adultery) that require proof of fault by one or even both partners. The government White Paper (Lord Chancellor's Department, 1995) allowing divorce after a year-long period for reflection will, if adopted by Parliament, change the fault-based approach to divorce by substituting concern about the consequences of divorce in place of establishing the grounds.

As things are at present, more than 200,000 children each year experience their parents' divorce and perhaps remarriage (possibly more than once), and these children are getting younger. That is not the end of the story, either. We know that births outside marriage accounted for 32 per cent of all births in 1992; and that more than half were to parents living at the same address (and therefore, presumably, committed to each other). Another fifth were registered by both parents, but from different addresses (Utting, 1995). It is likely that a proportion of these relationships also break down, swelling the number of children affected by parental separation. The late Jackie Burgoyne wrote about cohabiting partnerships: 'it is the relationship, not its legal status that counts [and that] once this is defined as less than satisfactory by one or both partners it is threatened ... Relationships that "die" cannot be perpetuated by legal ties and should be offered a "decent burial" ' (Burgoyne, 1991, p. 247).

But does this apply to parenting relationships as well as partnerships? It is often only when relationships break down that parents are explicitly confronted with the law, and this becomes an important contextual factor for many stepfamilies as they develop. It is therefore useful and often helpful to know something about current law in relation to children when parents divorce.

When a married couple become parents, both partners are assumed to have parental responsibility under the Children Act 1989. This means that in the event of divorce there is a legal presumption that children should have contact with their non-residential parent (save in exceptional cases). For cohabiting partners who separate, the situation is different. Irrespective of whether the birth is jointly registered, unmarried fathers can only acquire parental responsibility by the couple signing a joint responsibility order or by obtaining a court order. Despite his obligation to maintain the child, there is no automatic assumption of joint parental responsibility. There is no requirement for the resident parent to consult about co-parenting, except for major changes such as taking a child to live abroad.

The courts, from their position, are required to consider the welfare of the child as the first and paramount consideration. The law assumes that delay in decision-making is bad for children, and that courts should not make orders unless doing so would be better for a child than no order at all. The following check-list is provided to help the *courts* in their decision-making:

- the ascertainable wishes and feelings of the child according to age

and understanding;
- the child's physical, emotional and educational needs;
- the likely effect of a change of circumstances on the child;
- age, sex, background and any characteristics that the court considers relevant;
- any harm that s/he has suffered or is at risk of suffering;
- the capabilities of each parent or any other person the court considers relevant;
- the range of powers available to the court under the Act in the proceedings under consideration.

Problems most often arise when there are conflicts over residence and contact for the children. These, as I have indicated, are particularly poignant for unmarried fathers. Dissatisfaction with current divorce law procedures, together with the spiralling costs of legal aid, have played their part in the search for a new context in which marriages can end and new relationships begin. The prospect of 'process divorce' and the extension of mediation procedures provides a change in the context within which stepfamilies are formed.

Because the media make much of the failure of 50 per cent of remarriages, I will give some examples of couples who are trying hard to build 'good enough' stepfamilies, drawn from my own practice as a mediator and marital and family therapist. I use the words 'remarriage' and 'repartnering' interchangeably. Because of the negative mythology related to stepfamilies, words need to be chosen carefully so as to try and avoid colluding with the folklore that lies deep within us and is regularly expressed by the tabloid media. Apart from the legal differentiation between cohabiting and remarried stepfamilies, I will not differentiate further between the two. But what is a stepfamily? Let's take this in two stages.

What is a step-parent?

A step-parent is someone who marries or lives with a partner whose children by someone else join them in some measure because of that previous relationship. As we have seen, separation and divorce are today the usual precursors to making new partnerships, and it is apparent that many are very cautious in making what they intend as a permanent commitment when a former relationship has ended in failure. We do know that men are more likely than women to repartner quickly, that younger women also usually repartner (although more slowly than men), and that older women are less likely to remarry than both. We also know that, after divorce, it is more likely that children will reside primarily with their mothers (more than 90 per cent), so that for young children of young women, step-parents are most likely to be stepfathers. I have described these as 'stepfather households' (Robinson, 1991) and will return to them when considering stepfamilies.

Many of these men may have had to give up day-to-day relationships with their own children, either by the terms of the divorce agreement or because they have chosen to live with their new partner and her children. Trying to build a relationship with someone else's children when still mourning the loss of this special intimate relationship with one's own is a painful and often precarious process. These are the words of John, who has moved into Kate's house with her teenage childen, while his 8-year-old son, Bob – whom he sees regularly – lives with his mother:

> Alongside this love and enjoyment of each other, there were also many painful areas. I missed Bob terribly. I had always spent a lot of time with him and been very involved with him. I had had a very poor relationship with my own father who had been absent for most of my childhood and who died when I was in my early twenties. It had therefore been extremely important to me to be a good father to Bob and to give him the paternal love that I had missed so much . . . I was lucky in the sense that Bob made it very clear that he wants to see me regularly and spend time with me. However, he was also very angry with me and expressed this very openly. He frequently used to ask me whether I loved Kate more than him, and wouldn't accept it when I told him that the love was different.

Stepfathers, while not having the same roots in mythology as stepmothers, nevertheless have modern myths to cope with. For instance, in research that I conducted some twenty years ago, all the stepfathers of young, and especially teenage, stepdaughters made direct or oblique reference to their sexual anxiety about being alone with their stepdaughter.

Stepmothers, particularly those who marry divorced men, are less likely to be full-time stepmothers than their counterparts, although many have their stepchildren living with them at weekends and for holidays. The role of stepmother is a particularly difficult one, not only because of the age-old myths of the wicked stepmother, but also because of the expectation that women are responsible for the emotional life of families and family connectedness (Smith, 1990). Indeed, many stepmothers expect this of themselves; just as many stepfathers expect to be the disciplinarian in the family – as well as to be the primary wage-earner and manager of the family's finances. It makes little difference that in this day and age it is less likely that their wives will expect this, particularly if they have been on their own with their children for some while prior to the remarriage.

Stepmothers may play an important role in validating non-residential fathers' relationships in their children's lives (Walker, 1993), but they can face difficulties as non-residential parents themselves:

> Ruth is divorced and with two children of her own. She is planning to marry Charles, whose wife died three years ago and has two older children. One of these, Lucy, is a teenager who does not want her father to marry again as this would necessitate selling their family home so they can all move in together. Charles has weathered standing firm about this, including Lucy's proprieties about him having a sexual relationship with Ruth – 'you don't have sex at your age' [incidentally, 45 years old]. Although Lucy has met Ruth and her younger children, apparently uneventfully, there is uncertainty about how Ruth can build a relationship with her teenage stepdaughter – who will live with them full time when they buy a house together – without indicating that she is trying to take the place of Lucy's dead mother.

Despite the difficulties, there are of course advantages that step-parents can bring to their stepfamily: new ideas and skills, objectivity, friendship, and often a freedom from the 'contamination' of past family history. To summarize thus far:

> a stepparent is the partner or spouse of the birth parent who intends to make a long term commitment to that parent and thereby comes into some kind of relationship with his/her children by a previous partner. This requires careful negotiation and reflection between the remarried parent and stepparent. While perhaps most of them seem to have the phantasy that they can be just like an ordinary nuclear family, as the research into the non clinical population of the callers the Stepfamily Telephone Counselling Service shows, nearly as many stepfathers as mothers and stepmothers seek advice before entering into stepfamilies (Batchelor et al., 1994).

What is a stepfamily?

Stepfamilies are complex and confusing partly because there are multiple variations and arrangements for living. All stepfamilies are born out of loss, whether formed after a death of a birth parent or following divorce. This necessitates mourning the loss of previous relationships – whether at individual, couple or family levels. Typically, each parent and the children are at different stages of the grieving process. If repartnering takes place too soon in this process, then problems are likely to arise as a result of truncated mourning.

Stepfamilies are unique in their own history, social context, interactional patterns and family identity, and there are several different bases for categorizing them. Cockett and Tripp (1994) distinguish three kinds of reordered families: lone-parent families, stepfamilies and redisrupted families. Demographic distinctions are drawn by the household in which parents and children primarily live. Burgoyne and Clark (1984) distinguish between different types on the basis of family goals. I prefer a combination of household and legal factors. Because over 90 per cent of children reside with their mother after divorce, the majority of subsequently formed stepfamilies will be *stepfather households*, where the children and their mother live with the stepfather. Another distinction is between full-time and part-time stepfamilies; children who primarily live with their mother and are in regular contact with their father and stepmother (typically every other weekend and Christmas as well as holidays) might be described as part-time or *stepmother households*.

Fifteen years ago I listed four types based on legal standing (Robinson, 1980). There were *legitimizing stepfamilies*, in which one parent (usually the mother) who already has a child marries someone who is not already a parent. This terminology was never strictly accurate and, with the abolition of illegitimacy in law, has become redundant. Nevertheless, it is one way of recognizing the fact that the incoming spouse of the birth parent (usually the father) does not share the same biological or family history of the child, and that the child does not have a previous live-in relationship with his or her birth parent. These are the true single parents, so perhaps *single-parent stepfamilies* would be a better way of describing them.

Rose is a lone parent with two children (named Stephen, who has had no direct relationship with his father, and Jade), whose Asian father encouraged Rose, sexually abused by her own father in childhood, to 'go on the game'. Later, Rose became friendly with Andy, who moved in with the family, retrieved her from 'the game', and effectively became Jade's psychological father. There were problems. Stephen resented giving up his role as 'man of the house' and his place in mother's bed. This resulted in Andy losing his temper after an argument and hitting Stephen which, in turn, led to a court appearance, the involvement of social services, and later, at the request of the Guardian ad Litem, myself. At that time, Andy was excluded from the home and Stephen was anxiously triumphant. I worked with them in exploring what being a stepfamily might mean. Andy didn't like the word 'stepfather' and wanted to be more involved, whereas Stephen retained an idealized picture of his real father whom he would look for when he was older. Gradually they became friends, and Stephen allowed Andy to set some limits for him, something Rose had always found difficult.

Revitalized stepfamilies are a second category, created by the remarriage of the natural parent to a step-parent following the death of a previous partner. While revitalized stepfamilies have usually had the opportunity to go through a recognized mourning ritual, unlike those created following divorce, there are some particularly difficult issues to be faced by them. For instance, many revitalized stepfamilies continue to live in the bereaved family's previous home, and the idealization of the dead parent can put particular pressures on the step-parent. If the mourning for the lost parent has not been addressed or completed, it is possible that there will be unmentionable secrets in the stepfamily that impede the integration of the new step-parent.

Reassembled stepfamilies are a third group created following divorce from a birth parent, and where the step-parent, although perhaps previously married, has not yet been a birth parent. Entering into an established, ongoing family, particularly when new partner and (usually) her children have been together for some while and have long-established family, domestic, behavioural and psychological rules, can be an estranging, overwhelming, sometimes traumatic, and usually noisy experience.

Combination stepfamilies comprise the fourth group, and are those in which both parents have children from previous partnerships. As I have already indicated, such stepfamilies are likely to be in stepfather or stepmother households, the latter usually being part time. These families may also include children, one of whose parents has died, as well as the children of the other step-parent who continue to have contact with their non-residential parent. Because combination families are usually larger than the conventional nuclear family of today (with two birth parents and their 1.8 children), they frequently have accommodation and overcrowding problems. When children have been used to their ordinal or unique gender position in the family, the arrival of a step-parent and his or her children may mean an unsettling disturbance from being the youngest child to becoming an older step-sibling. Of course, any of these families may then have a child from the new relationship, creating another full-time or part-time half-sibling to the children and stepchildren. Here is John again:

> I felt it was much more difficult for Kate than for me. How does a woman end her marriage without either abandoning her children or throwing her husband out of his house? . . . Kate came in for more severe criticisms than I did . . . I felt totally unprepared to live with teenagers . . . At present I keep out of any conflicts between Kate and her children; frequently this feels very difficult, as it is very tempting to jump in and take sides . . . I know stepfamilies in which the 'stepfather' has very quickly taken on an authority and disciplinary role: this feels very inappropriate for me, although at times understandable.

To summarize:

> A stepfamily is created when someone who is already a parent forms a relationship with a new partner who then becomes a stepparent to the children. In some stepfamilies both partners have children who then become stepbrothers and sisters. They may not all live in the same household, but some with their other birth parent, creating both a full-time and a part-time stepfamily household. All the children who have connections with a parent and stepparent belong to a stepfamily, and the structure may include two stepparents if both birth parents have formed new partnerships. A stepfamily also exists when the children are adults, even if they were adults when the stepfamily was created by a parent's new marriage or partnership (Batchelor *et al.*, 1994, p. 10).

Preparing for stepfamily life

As a family therapist, I find it helpful to think in terms of family life cycles – that is, individual, couple and family transition points that require family members to resolve certain basic dilemmas, many of which, like adolescence, have biological connections, while others, like marriage, have public and legal status (Carter and McGoldrick, 1989). What is common is that a family having reached and begun to resolve these transitions will never be the same again. The changes are irreversible.

I have described elsewhere (Robinson, 1991) the stages of the 'divorce life cycle': including the grieving, the physical separation, telling the children, and negotiating the legal process in which couples

Figure 3 *'Stepfamily life cycle'*

Divorce of birth parents – decisions about residence and contact
Death of birth parent – resolution of grief and mourning

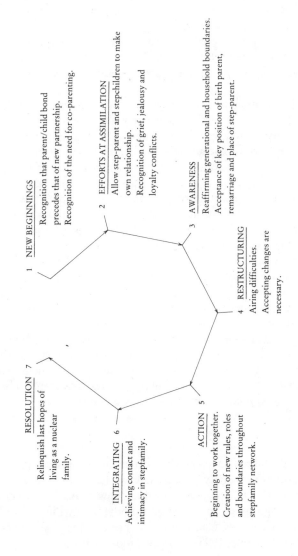

1 NEW BEGINNINGS
Recognition that parent/child bond
precedes that of new partnership.
Recognition of the need for co-parenting.

2 EFFORTS AT ASSIMILATION
Allow step-parent and stepchildren to make
own relationship.
Recognition of grief, jealousy and
loyalty conflicts.

3 AWARENESS
Reaffirming generational and household boundaries.
Acceptance of key position of birth parent,
remarriage and place of step-parent.

4 RESTRUCTURING
Airing difficulties.
Accepting changes are
necessary.

5 ACTION
Beginning to work together.
Creation of new rules, roles
and boundaries throughout
stepfamily network.

6 INTEGRATING
Achieving contact and
intimacy in stepfamily.

7 RESOLUTION
Relinquish last hopes of
living as a nuclear
family.

Source: Margaret Robinson, February 1995 (developed from Papernow, 1984).

necessarily become involved, whether or not they recognize and take charge of it themselves. I will close with the 'stepfamily life cycle' that often follows (adapted from the work of Papernow, 1984, and Robinson and Smith, 1993). Some of the processes in becoming a stepfamily are depicted in Figure 3.

In summary, I refer again to the excellent Stepfamily Telephone Counselling Service research. This identifies some key factors in understanding the stepfamilies who consulted them, including:

> The beliefs, experience and expectations about 'family life' brought to the new situation, particularly about gender roles and family loyalty, including cultural beliefs and religious practices related to repartnering. The attitude of 'significant others' to the separation and new relationship and its consequences, particularly key relatives such as grandparents, or close friends. Beliefs about the purpose of repartnering, whether it is focused on 'love', economic security, procreation, respectability, companionship or to find a 'mother' or 'father' for a child, socio-economic status and education. The quality of family life prior to separation (whether stable or violent), and the history of each household prior to the stepfamily household formation ... including time spent in lone parent households. The cause of the end of the previous relationship, whether by death, divorce or a combination of both, and the nature of the separation process. The stage of the separation process at which the new stepfamily household was formed and the age and stage of life cycle of the new partners and the relative knowledge about child care they bring with them. Finally, the disruption caused to the life style of the new stepfamily members (such as changes of school, home housing and health) and the financial consequences of such changes (Batchelor *et al.*, 1994, pp. 67–8).

I will end as I have already written: 'We cannot turn the clock back – rightly or wrongly, as a society we have now moved beyond the nuclear family and we must find new ways of recognizing and providing support at crisis points in the family life cycle' (Robinson, 1991). This conclusion has also been drawn by others (see, for example, Utting, 1995); it is never more true than during divorce and when parents repartner.

Margaret Robinson

11
Love is Lovelier
the Second Time Round

Bad governments damage many things – they can even damage the intelligence of their opponents. A government may be so bad that it seems necessary to remove it; anything else would be an improvement. This is good rhetoric but bad intelligence. Even under closed tyranny, opponents must think very hard about how to overthrow a regime and how to prevent it coming back . . . Equally, no new government can do much with the assembly of negative forces generated by a previous bad government: the central activity by which a new government stands or falls is the very difficult process of converting enough of these negations into positive ones for practical construction.

This quote is from a paper by Raymond Williams (1981, p. 141) about the Labour movement, which was trying to analyse what happens to governments and their oppositions during a period where contest is derided and uniformity is upheld. I believe that the ideas, which relate to the effect governments can have on their opponents, are helpful in trying to think about second marriages. I would like to offer the same passage in a transformed state:

Bad marriages damage many things – they can even damage the intelligence of the partners. A marriage may be so bad that it seems necessary to remove it; anything else would be an improvement. This is good rhetoric but bad intelligence. Even under closed tyranny, partners must think very hard about how to overthrow a regime, and how to prevent it coming back . . . Equally, no new marriage can do much with the assembly of negative forces generated by a previous bad marriage: the central activity by which a new marriage stands or falls is the very difficult process of converting enough of these negations into positive ones for practical construction.

These are classic points, but in practice they are so often forgotten or excitedly overridden. I think for governments and marriages they apply equally well! The main point of interest for this chapter is related to the situation where a marriage has not worked. Many people remarry or repartner with enormous hope and optimism. They want to put the past behind them and start afresh. This often overlooks the reality that there is something so important about what partners brought to the first marriage, and their actual experience within it, which remains important, that unless it can be digested in some way the old problems may be repeated.

Although the nature of stepfamilies is such that the couples always have to contend with children, and as a result children tend to play an important part in the adult partnership, I am going to focus largely on the couple and their experience in forming second relationships.

There seem to be two prevailing attitudes to stepfamilies. The first we are all familiar with from childhood, having heard many of the classic fairy tales that tell a story in no uncertain terms. Snow White's stepmother attempted cold-blooded murder; Hansel and Gretel's was cruel and calculating in the face of scarce resources, saving herself and her husband, but abandoning the children knowing they would probably not survive; Cinderella's was equally cruel, treating her like a slave and denying her a place in her father's family. In these stories, the stepmothers hate their stepchildren, and we are invited to hate the stepmothers on the children's behalf. The modern-day equivalent of this seems to be stories we frequently read in the popular press about stepfathers who are violent, sexually abusive or simply neglectful of the stepchildren in their care. The word 'stepmother' itself carries powerfully negative connotations.

The second view can be found in much of the modern stepfamily literature that challenges 'the old negative stigma and myths embedded in so many fairy tales where the stepparent is "wicked" or at fault in some way'. Instead, we hear 'that many of the difficulties experienced by stepchildren arise not from actually living in a stepfamily, but from the stress and conflict experienced within the first marriage before the new stepfamily was formed'. The stepfamily is portrayed as something of a victim, dealing not only with a 'legacy from the past', but also 'continuing tensions between the parents', which can 'be very difficult for the incoming stepparent and stepchildren' (Batchelor et al., 1994, p. xvi). While I support this caring approach, I do not believe it sufficiently manages to address the frequent existence of huge emotional problems in the wake of marital breakdown and the formation of a new family.

Having seen several couples attempting to build a new stepfamily, and helped them to grapple with the extremity of emotions that ensue, I have come to feel that we need to reclaim the fairy tales. At this point I also have to admit to being a stepmother myself, and to having been so for the last sixteen years. I have many memories of those early years, but one in particular stands out and became something of a tale in itself.

We were on holiday – my husband, myself and the two sons from his first marriage. At this time, the boys must have been about 7 and 3. We were on a canal barge, and halfway through the morning I was being awfully jolly, encouraging everyone with the promise of a hot drink and a piece of lovely chocolate cake that I had made. Quick as a flash, my 7-year-old stepson announced, 'Ooh yes, we'll all have that delicious chocolate cake,' then looking down at the water of the murky canal he continued, 'but Jo can have a soggy biscuit.' It took years for this to become a funny story. At the time, I felt like I had just taken a bite of the poisoned apple. In his direct and simple way, my stepson had just demolished my marriage and my sense of belonging to a new family, and reinstated the original family in which he felt he should have a rightful place, while I, clearly, should not.

It does not take much imagination to realize that my stepson must have been feeling displaced, insecure, rejected – in effect, put outside his own family. At that moment, he managed to turn the tables, and give me, the adult, the experience that he himself was finding so unbearable. While much of the popular literature attempts to deny this level of hatred and negativity, and says that it need not be like that, it often is. The feelings are extreme because they are related to threats to survival. I believe we need to face and understand the level of hatred and difficulty that is so frequently brought to light, either in the press or the consulting room.

Paradoxically, the main idea that has helped me think about the extremes of hatred and cruelty is that of idealization. For any couple there is usually a significant period at the start of the relationship that is characterized by idealization. Freud himself described falling in love as temporary insanity. In this chapter, I argue that there is a significant period at the start of a stepfamily when there is likely to be more than the usual level of idealization. When the imperfections of reality encroach, this frame of mind is punctured and tends to flip over into its reverse – that is, hatred and denigration. Stepfamilies tend to come to the notice of therapists long after the idealization is over, when it can be hard to know about or remember, lost or buried as it often is under the weight of the more recent negativity. There is one couple I have in mind where the relationship had become so hate-filled that it was only after two years of therapy that it was possible to tell their therapists that there had been any loving feelings at all. Another couple had a huge shock when watching a video of a family celebration that had not been seen for several years: they saw the wife and her stepdaughter exchanging looks with warmth and love. The husband and wife had both 'forgotten' entirely that these feelings had ever existed.

I believe that the initial period of idealization needs to be recovered, even if only in the mind, to understand fully the subsequent hatred and to maximize the chances of forming a stepfamily more success-fully. Let me give you two illustrations to develop my argument. They are based on composite experiences in therapy and do not describe real couples.

The problem of triangular space

Mr and Mrs Furie met each other during the period when both of their first marriages were breaking down. Mr Furie's first wife had taken little or no responsibility for the children, and there seems to have been a conflict-free agreement between them that he would have custody of the children, who were then young teenagers. Mrs Furie also brought two children from her first marriage to the new family home.

Mr Furie was working outside the home and Mrs Furie was a housewife caring for their four shared children. They lived as a stepfamily for eighteen months with relationships gradually deterio-rating, until their situation reached such a pitch that they separated. She lived with her children and he with his. Living apart, they found themselves to be extremely attached to each other as a couple, and yet unable to live together.

Both Mr and Mrs Furie felt deeply wronged and blaming of the other. She looked exhausted and worn out, and seemed near the end of her tether. She launched into a tirade against her husband. Only by listening to her story in its entirety, and without interruption, did Mrs Furie believe her therapist stood any chance at all of understanding what an appalling man her husband was, and what an innocent victim she had been. Mr Furie, on the other hand, sat calm and smiling. He spoke clearly and rationally when there was space for him to do so and took the role of explaining the events his wife was referring to.

Both partners initially tried to establish the 'facts' of what had occurred prior to their separation when things escalated to a dramatic crisis. Many stories tumbled over each other, involving them, their children, grandparents and ex-spouses. The content was often difficult to follow, but what was clear was that overwhelming feelings had arisen for them, their four children and extended family members around the issue of living together as a stepfamily. There were accusations of lies and violence, and a powerful sense that one partner would be found culpable and the other innocent.

There were two main stories. The first was about Mr Furie's oldest child, Julie. She was rebellious and rude. She never did what she was told, and was felt by Mrs Furie to wield a witch-like power over the other children, leading them astray so that all the children were experienced as challenging her authority as mother. The situation between Mrs Furie and Julie had come to a head one evening when, according to Mrs Furie, she had been trying to encourage Julie to do her homework. Julie had refused and started to leave the house. Mrs Furie obstructed her and Julie lashed out with kicks and punches. Mrs Furie felt that with no provocation she had been violently attacked, and demanded her husband's support and immediate action. Mr Furie found himself sitting on the fence. On the one hand, he was unable to support his wife openly, secretly feeling that her treatment of the children was too harsh, and on the other, although he felt Julie must have behaved badly, he felt unable to reprimand her, fearing a confrontation would lead to an unbreachable gulf between them. As a result, his parenting was weak and ineffectual; he would talk to his children behind his wife's back, trying to persuade them to be tolerant of her over-zealous discipline.

Not surprisingly, Mrs Furie's relationship with Julie continued to deteriorate. Julie became totally unco-operative, and Mrs Furie demanded greater allegiance to her way of running the house and raising the children. Mr Furie's underhand way of managing this tremendous pressure of conflicting loyalties became open family knowledge, which had a major impact on the new marriage. Eventually, their inability to tolerate and understand each other's different feelings about Julie became unbearable to both Mr and Mrs Furie. Mr Furie felt he was being asked to choose between his daughter and his wife, whereas Mrs Furie felt each time Mr Furie had an opportunity to support her, he chose to side with Julie against her. They experienced each other's unwillingness to change their position as a major rejection. The levels of hurt and rage escalated with each family row.

The second 'story' that preoccupied the couple was about Mrs Furie's mother. She was described by Mr Furie as an outspoken, intrusive woman, who saw it as her duty, when her daughter's first marriage failed, to step in and play a parental role with her grandchildren. When Mr Furie and his children moved into the house she continued to be extremely involved with the family, giving special treatment to her own grandchildren in such a way as to lay claim to her continued right to be a surrogate parent in the family. Mr Furie experienced her as interfering with his new relationships with his stepchildren and felt extremely angry with her, blaming her almost entirely for the lack of success he had had in forming relationships with them. At the same time, he was unable to express any of his feelings directly. He would tend to retreat in a conflict, and make jokes, so that it was hard for those around him to know how he was feeling. On one occasion he came home to discover his mother-in-law planning a special birthday treat for his wife's youngest daughter, while his own children appeared dejected and excluded. He exploded, forbidding his wife's mother to come round to the house at all. This enraged Mrs Furie further. In her mind, her new husband was putting his daughter before her, and excluding and offending her main ally, her mother. There was a hate-filled deadlock and, soon after this incident, the couple separated.

One issue seemed to be a consistent part of each story, and that was the intrusion of a third person between the couple. While there is not enough room in this chapter to take a serious look at Oedipal issues, I want to spend a little time thinking about them because they do have a special importance for second marriages, especially those with children. The reason for this is that, right from the very beginning, there is always a third party in stepfamily marriages. Very often, before the couple have had much of a chance to become a cosy twosome, they have also to manage being a troublesome threesome. The Oedipal issues are not theoretical in stepfamilies, nor are they historical. They are alive and kicking in the present.

In 1926, the child psychoanalyst Melanie Klein wrote: 'The fundamental thing, however, and the criterion of all later capacity for adaptation to reality is the degree to which they (that is, children) are able to tolerate the deprivations that result from the Oedipal situation' (Klein, 1975, p. 129). Ronald Britton (1989) develops this idea when he writes: 'The initial recognition of the parental sexual relationship involves [for the child] relinquishing the idea of sole and permanent possession of mother and leads to a profound sense of loss which, if not tolerated, may become a sense of persecution' (p. 34).

Psychoanalytical theory has long posited that it is crucial to a boy's subsequent ability to form satisfying relationships that he is able to share his mother with his father, and also to recognize that it is father and not himself who has the adult, lasting partnership with her. Because of the passionate attachment a child usually has with his mother, this is a desperately painful process, and one that extends through childhood and adolescence.

Children living with both their natural parents will usually work and rework these conflicts, eventually coming to a reasonably satisfactory resolution if all goes well, accepting that they cannot create a partnership with the parent of the opposite sex. Relinquishing this illusion, they can go on to make their own adult partnerships later in life. Painful Oedipal longings are most easily resolved in families where the couple is able to provide firm boundaries and a clear sense that there exists a different kind of relationship between the partners than between parent and child. It is easy to see that if a mother is giving her child ambiguous messages, leading him, for example, to believe that he is more important to her than anyone or anything else, then this is seductive to the child, matching, as it does, his own unconscious longings to have his mother for himself, and satisfy her as if he were an adult. A child caught in this type of relationship is less likely to achieve a satisfactory working through of Oedipal conflicts.

Children living in stepfamilies will often be successful in this part of their maturational process, although they have to contend with a more complex and often less secure situation. When parents separate, there may well be a period when their closest relationships are with the children, or with one child in particular. This may encourage the child to fantasize that perhaps mother or father is, after all, available, or saving themselves for their primary relationship to be with the child. This is exactly what the child unconsciously longs for, so that even when in reality the parent is unavailable, there can continue to be fostered a substantial element of doubt for the child that may hinder resolution of Oedipal conflicts. It goes without saying that while there may be an unconscious experience of Oedipal triumph, it is a Pyrrhic victory; not only do most children suffer extreme grief at the loss of one of their parents, but they may be seriously hindered in later life in forming well-balanced adult partnerships.

If and when the parent does form an adult relationship, the roles in the new stepfamily are often loose, and feel less safe to both parent and child. Step-parents are often unclear about their relationships with stepchildren. Are they parents, aunties, adult friends? Natural parents also have to adjust their relationship with children who have been depended upon during a lonely period.

An example of the kinds of confusion of boundaries and roles that seem to be common in stepfamilies appeared in a newspaper article. The child's confusion about his mother's 'availability' was intended to be understood as touching rather than troubling. This is how a 40-year-old woman described the feelings of her children about to meet the new man in her life:

'It's him!' they cry, unnecessarily. In an agony of trepidation, I head for the door, acutely aware that, like my parents before me all those years ago, my children have infinite power to embarrass and show me up. In the morning my son has some astute and reassuring advice. 'It'll do you good to have a boyfriend, Mum', he says sagely. 'You'll be able to have some fun' (Rowan, 1992).

In this situation, the child is in an ambiguous position; he can either be a jealous partner or a pseudo-wise parent. What he cannot be is a child.

For children whose parents have separated, there is more scope than usual for an experience of a parent being available as a potential partner. This may well hinder the more usual and healthy process of a child gradually recognizing the link between the parents, within which he does not play an equal part and which provides him with a prototype for a relationship 'of a third kind, in which he is a witness and not a participant' (Britton, 1989, p. 36). During the early years, this process helps to develop a capacity for seeing ourselves in interaction with others, and for entertaining another point of view while retaining our own. It is therefore one of the most important areas of development contributing to the ability to form relationships in adult life.

The dilemma of negotiating the threesome is much more problematic for people who have not established a secure link with the main caretaker, usually the mother. These people already feel fragile, and the chances are they will feel even more insecure at the realization that there is a father out there – yet another person competing for mother, and who might take her away altogether. 'In some personalities, the full recognition of parental sexuality is felt as a danger to life.' In some people, the pain of the Oedipal situation is so great that in order not to know about it, 'the psychotic mutilates his mind' (Britton, 1989, p. 37). The individual is then left apparently ignorant of anything other than the two extremes of an ideal, fully satisfied state, and a state of withholding persecution. Violent attacks can ensue at any time when the ideal state appears to be threatened – for example, by another opinion, or anything less than total agreement.

Mr and Mrs Furie experienced any intimate relationship that the other was having that excluded them as a threat to their own. Mrs Furie found the existence of Mr Furie's first family unbearably painful, while he wanted to banish her mother from visiting their home. Because exploring feelings and differing opinions were experienced as threats to survival, they had evolved an effective collusion that meant that they never took place. By the time they came for help, Mrs Furie's attacks would be so scathing and violent that Mr Furie felt inhibited from even mentioning his daughter's name. At the same time, Mrs Furie's allegiance with her mother, and any mention of this relationship, left Mr Furie feeling taunted and humiliated. Their shared fear of intimacy and intercourse was then so great that the constant rowing protected them from coming anywhere near it.

Idealization and the loss of mourning

Another couple, Mr and Mrs Young, were in a different position to the Furies. Mrs Young had not been married before, whereas her husband had three children with his first wife to whom he had been married for nineteen years. The first marriage had been full of longing on his part, especially as he had come from a family where there had been no emotional warmth. His first wife had failed to fulfil his emotional needs, and eventually his anger and disappointment had exhausted her and she had forced him to leave. His two eldest sons, 15 and 16, came to stay with their father and stepmother every weekend and most of the holidays; the younger daughter visited less frequently.

Mr Young left his first wife and immediately moved in with his new wife-to-be. Like many couples in this situation, their passion felt so strong that they assumed their love would infuse the children too. They were thrilled to have found each other. For him to be having a second chance seemed so fortunate, so unlike what he had so far come to expect of life. They did not give themselves any time to experience the loss of what had just ended.

Mr Young perceived his first wife in a totally negative way. She had been unable to love him or respond warmly to such a degree that he could see no good in her at all. His new wife was younger than him and unconfident, but seemed willing to share her new husband's perception of what he had endured. Quite unconsciously she was putting herself in an impossible position. Given her and her husband's perception of his first wife as all bad, she could only place herself as the opposite: a perfect mother substitute and wife; in short, a sort of 'fairy stepmother'.

The new Mrs Young had been raised with firm and 'old-fashioned' values. Cleanliness and personal hygiene played an important part in her family, and there was a strict regime of household chores that were stuck to firmly. When she became a stepmother, it did not occur to her that any discussion or reference to previous family ways was needed. She was trying to be a perfect mother, as she saw it, saving the children from previous deprivation, and providing them with the right way to live.

Mrs Young tried to annihilate Mr Young's former wife and her influence by setting up a regime that he and his children were entirely unused to. By telling them, 'This is the only decent way to live', she was by implication saying, 'The way you were living with your previous wife/real mother was no good.' This kind of enforced idealization, which both partners helped to create, touched every member of the family, destroying the space there might otherwise have been for mourning what had been good in the previous family, and had just been lost.

Idealization is a defence against acknowledging some aspect of reality. When couples fall in love, they seem unconsciously to choose partners who share similar problems and preoccupations to their own. At the same time, there is such anxiety about this that it is unbearable for them to know about it. She does not want to know that he is not a knight in shining armour, nor does he want to know that she is not an all-giving, all-loving princess. Usually, as the couple matures, they are gradually able to let go of these rigid, idealized pictures and replace them with something nearer to reality. So there are moments in everybody's lives when idealization helps us deal with unbearable anxiety. When a stepfamily forms, there is even more at stake. Couples who already have a failed marriage and are bringing children to a new one, might find it especially painful to allow either positive thoughts about what has just been lost, or negative ones about what is being embarked upon. Ambivalence feels too dangerous.

We need to understand why. If ambivalent feelings are allowed and there is a recognition of what was good, maybe very good, in the previous relationship, then there is also a profound sense of loss about what was good in that relationship and is now lost. It is that profound experience of loss that feels unbearable. As a defence against this sense of loss, only the negative aspects are allowed recognition; an aura of badness falls over the past relationship and a picture is sustained that there was nothing worthwhile in that relationship at all. If the past experience is 'set in concrete' in this way, the process of mourning is prevented. There is too much anxiety about grieving, which inevitably involves pain about what was good and is now lost, or what was hoped for and now will never be.

Equally, there is a tendency only to allow the good to be known about in the new relationship, put into words: 'Thank God I have found the right person at last.' At the moment of forming the new family, doubt is disallowed. There is a common fantasy at work in this situation which says that allowing any negative feelings at all would swamp the experience so that it would then become all negative.

Of course, it is not always like this, nor for all stepfamilies. Some people are able to tolerate ambivalence about previous relationships better than others. In those families, there is also a likelihood of tolerating negative aspects in the new one, or at least of having an awareness that problems are likely to arise. If ambivalence can be tolerated, there is no need for idealization. If, for example, Mr Young could have acknowledged how much he had loved his first wife, perhaps treasuring some of the precious times he had had with her, then he might have been left with some space to recognize the sadness and loss about the end of his first marriage, as well as the anxieties about his second.

Unusual amounts of hate tend to arise in situations where there was an enormous amount of love, followed by a betrayal or major disappointment. This is not a difficult or unusual idea, and yet in situations where there are vicious recriminations, cruel exposures and pure hatred it can be enormously difficult to recognize and establish quite how powerful and loving the original feelings have been.

When Mr and Mrs Young came into therapy, Mr Young was in a state of shock. His marriage had ended and his new relationship had started with no space in between. Mrs Young had become a step-parent overnight. Very quickly she found the boys, especially, were hard work and unrewarding, and she resented their intrusion into what she felt should have been a honeymoon period. She became quarrelsome and resentful. When Mr Young felt unable to agree with her negative comments about his sons, her sense of abandonment and resentment deepened, and she began to refuse sex. This reality was in stark contrast to Mr Young's picture of the perfect loving wife he thought he had found.

The defensive idealization I have described is experienced by the new couple as the most amazing kind of falling in love. In fact, it is an experience where any negative in the other is absolutely intolerable. Mr Young held an awesome amount of fear and anger at the mere possibility that his new wife might have negative feelings towards him about anything. This is a very different kind of 'falling in love' to that which would involve an amused, gentle, loving tolerance. In the latter, there is an awareness of negative aspects, but they are drawn into the general rosy glow and sense of well-being. Mr and Mrs Young's interaction had a very different flavour. There was a powerful attempt to keep each other perfect, and there would be an instant unleashing of rage if there was any imputation that reality might be otherwise.

Initially, Mr Young would express to his therapist a torrent of anger and disappointment about his new marriage, while his wife seethed silently. Then there would be a session that had an entirely different atmosphere. For example, the couple would walk down the corridor to their therapy session in a very light mood, laughing and talking to each other. They would sit down and throw each other sidelong glances as if there were some reluctance to get down to 'serious business'. After a while, the session would start with one of them outlining the story of the latest row. Instead of the usual deadly silences and rages, there would be a lot of excited giggling, as if they were two children keeping a naughty secret from the adults.

Eventually, they might share the 'secret'. An unexpectedly child-free weekend had meant they had spent this time in a state of such closeness that it was impossible for them to describe it to anyone else. It was like Nirvana. There was almost no need for words between them, they felt so in tune and able to understand one another. Sex was wonderful, as if they were truly joined. As they would describe these events and feelings, their heads would turn to each other and their eyes lock in a loving embrace.

The therapist would experience embarrassment and pain. On the one hand, she was being asked to witness their private intercourse, but at the same time she was being shown how extremely damaged the relationship was. The other side of denigration and hatred was revealed as sentimental and insubstantial: a state of oneness that could only be reached without the impingement of reality and difference; a fantasy that involved a belief in, and longing for, an unattainable distress-free experience of oneness with another, which might keep them going through all the awfulness and hatred of their rows.

Stepchildren

Where, you might ask, are the children in this formulation? Second marriages are simply second marriages unless there are children. Only then do they become stepfamilies. Because our focus at the Tavistock Marital Studies Institute is couples, most of my comments have been from the point of view of the couple relationship. That is not to deny that the place of children in this scenario is crucial to the whole picture. Therefore I will conclude with some brief observations about how children may be implicated in second marriages.

A new couple often find their 'honeymoon' period is prematurely challenged by the existence of children who are the product of a previous relationship. They have often not had the chance to establish their own sense of shared trust and intimacy before they are catapulted into parenting their own and each other's children, as well as dealing with ex-spouses and unwelcoming in-laws. In this period there is likely to be a deep-seated anxiety about acknowledging conflicts in the new relationship, and losses attached to the old ones. The couple's ability to deal with third parties, such as children and grandparents, will be firmly related to how far they themselves have resolved the Oedipal scenario.

Children are in a special position because they are within the home; they are part of the new family as well as the old. When the couple start to face the conflicts that are to be expected in this complex family situation, not only are the children likely to be involved, but they are perfect receptacles for unwanted projections, idealized as well as negative.

Very often there is an initial attempt to manage conflicts in the new family by placing them between the parents and the children, rather than holding them within the couple relationship. It may feel safer to the couple to threaten the step-parent/child relationships than their own relationship; the prospect of everything breaking apart again at the core can feel intolerable. For the child, of course, the strategy may work in the opposite direction, fuelling the dynamic.

If adults are vulnerable to the projections of children, children in stepfamilies are especially vulnerable to adult projections, lacking the protection often afforded by the affection, love and identification a parent often feels for their biological child. A parent's ability to contain feelings is dependent on their own relative mastery of the Oedipal dynamic. If the adults' development has been delayed in this area, much of the conflict elicited for the couple by the existence of the children is likely to be projected onto the children, exacerbating their Oedipal crises. The children are already vulnerable in this area. Usually one of their parents has rejected the other; in addition, one or both their parents have actually become 'available' again in reality, even if temporarily. This emotional mixture – the children's turmoil alongside the new couple's attempt to hold on to an idealized picture – can easily turn into a melting pot of intense emotions.

Three-person relationships may already have been causing problems in the previous family. If so, the new stepfamily couple is asking even more of itself in this area. The partners need to manage the inclusion of a third person who has not been produced by the two of them. The Oedipal issues are now further enlarged. If the adults are in a state of idealization about the new partner and therefore heavily involved in keeping good and bad separate, or located in separate people, they are unlikely to be able to manage a third. The children tend to represent the third for the couple. They really are the product of another relationship that involved an other, the previous spouse, who now becomes a threat to the new relationship. This may even be experienced as if there were a threat from (or actual) infidelity within the relationship.

So the children are like a constant reminder that there was another relationship, but in a paranoid frame of mind they can easily be experienced as preventing something new from developing. The constant raising of this other relationship, which consisted of an exclusive couple, may well set off an echo of the parental relationship that the person, now adult, was excluded from as a child. There is no doubt that Mrs Furie perceived Julie as coming between herself and her new husband. And, indeed, in my own example, my stepson was making a valiant attempt to destroy the present and re-establish the first family of which he was a part and I was not. Because the children exist in the present, the old relationship is felt to exist in the present, as, indeed, at the parenting level it might well do. The 'third' is often experienced as coming in the way of the new intercourse.

It is not uncommon for couples to form stepfamilies in such a way that members survive as individuals with a past, by sacrificing the new family. The strategy is self-defeating, and because the stakes are so high the ensuing breakdowns tend to be accompanied by enormous bitterness.

It does not have to be like that. The project of the stepfamily is to live and love in the present and to remember and respect the past. Many achieve it. I would like to end with a quote from Edgar Reitz who, when interviewed in 1993 in the *Observer* about his film entitled *Heimat*, said: 'Remembering is a creative act. Our past is a pile of broken pieces. When we remember we take these little mosaic pieces and build a new life with them. When we write down memories or make a film about them, we rescue a bit of life from death and put it on a level where it can exist. In that there is a kind of love.'

Joanna Rosenthall

12
Are Two Parents Necessary?

I opened this book with some of the often quoted statistics suggesting that parenting is becoming increasingly disconnected from partnering, asking whether this was something to be concerned about and how we might understand the dislocations that affect couples as they become parents. In this chapter, I want to propose that the links between partnering and parenting are important because they have the potential both to spur on and to inhibit development for children and adults alike. The links then become important in terms of the future well-being of individuals and the wider community.

Children make a difference to the partnerships between their parents that can strengthen both the partnerships and the adults within it. The parental couple introduces a difference into the lives of children that can encourage their growth as secure and autonomous social beings. However, none of this is guaranteed. There are intrinsic difficulties in holding together partnering and parenting relationships in some kind of creative juxtaposition. This is because the intrusion – for that is how it may at first be experienced – of a third party has destructive as well as creative potential. Third parties challenge assumptions of exclusivity and proprietorship in relationships, they may threaten isolation, and evoke powerful feelings of envy, jealousy and rage. The differences they introduce generate conflict. If, however, the anxieties and passions associated with these conflicts can be contained, they encourage what cannot be perpetuated to be given up, they foster the growth of a healthy psychological 'skin', they allow differences to become enjoyable, and they introduce new possibilities into people's lives.

Structures and process

Assertions of this kind are liable to be misunderstood. They can be read as a wish to resolve some of the problems associated with the diversity of contemporary family life by invoking the two-parent, two-generational model as a remedy for all ills. Worse, they can be identified with the scapegoating of lone parents, which I alluded to in the Introduction. The language of discrimination can take the form of a balance sheet, where people are reduced to cost incurrers and benefit recipients. Prevailing values encourage the language of the marketplace to be used in the debate about relationships, and the language used can mould the nature of the relationships themselves. In the full knowledge of the dangers of this (see, for example, Dunstan, 1994) it is, perhaps, as well to make a start in a language that will be understood.

Economic considerations, while they cannot be the only arbiter of what is good for people, do embody realities that have to be taken into account in assessing psychological as well as economic health. Nobody wants to promote the kind of dependency that enervates individuals and the communities of which they are a part. However, while it is true that stable, conventional families are more likely than lone-parent families to be net contributors to the public purse and less likely to claim state benefits – and, in this sense, are 'necessary' for the financial health of society – it is not always the fact of family structure that results in this outcome. We know, for example, that unstable conventional families generate significant costs through absence from work, increased claims on health and social services, and so on. We also know that stable unconventional families are working at the cutting edge of searching for new solutions to the old problem of balancing caring and providing responsibilities in a society where the gendered division of labour is no longer a tenable solution.

Yet lone-parent families tend to attract a bad press, at least in some quarters. Single mothers have been represented as exploiting parenthood to secure housing. Absent fathers are criticized for being errant providers. Children are depicted as the casualties of fringe families, both in terms of their behaviour and educational performance. When lone parents raise public concern, explanations tend to conflate distinct entities like material disadvantage, social circumstance and family structure as if they are one and the same. Sometimes it is as if the turbulence introduced by the socio-economic and sexual changes of recent years is located in one group that is labelled as problematic and then pilloried for all that we feel most uneasy about. The use of projective mechanisms to manage anxiety induced by disturbing differences has a sound, if worrying, psychological pedigree.

Research offers checks and balances to scapegoating processes, and introduces another kind of discourse whose language accentuates concern about children. A comprehensive survey of studies of the impact of family disruption and lone parenthood on children (Burghes, 1994) demonstrates just how difficult it is to draw unequivocal conclusions. The results make clear that there is no inevitable path down which children will travel as a result of the kind of family they come from, and while there are disparities between children from intact two-parent families and families of different structures (lone parent or reconstituted), 'these seem to stem less from the family structure or disruption *per se* and more from the nature of the disruption' (p. 23). How people come to be lone parents is clearly important. While hedged with qualifications, the report suggests a declining degree of vulnerability for children depending on the route taken into lone parenthood. In descending order of vulnerability the routes are: separation and divorce, lone parents taking on step-parent roles, never-married mothers who stay single and, with an outcome very little different from two-parent families in many cases, those who have been widowed.

Within these different groups there is a variety of outcome. There are many factors that combine to influence how children fare, and the interplay between them is a complex and dynamic one. For example, as well as asking about the effects of divorce on children, one might turn the question round and ask if 'difficult' children who are already performing badly create the kinds of pressures that increase the risk of separation and divorce for their parents. There is evidence of children performing badly before their parents separate, but this may be because their parents are forever quarrelling. The old and still unresolved question about whether parental conflict is more damaging than divorce, and so whether couples should stay together 'for the sake of the children', continues to haunt us. Studies about co-parenting after divorce support the view that what is most damaging for children is being caught up in conflicts between their parents. But those who work with families in distress point out that being triangulated into parental conflicts can happen as easily within intact families as with those that break up.

All the evidence about outcomes points towards the form of family life being of less importance than what goes on between family members. Process predominates over structure. However, structure cannot be discounted; it influences the process of human relationships. For example, in Chapter 1 Penny Mansfield suggested that the formal and externally validated structure of a partnership can act as an anchor for a stressed relationship, without which the partners might drift apart. Margaret Robinson, in Chapter 10, describes the importance of legal context and family constitution when trying to understand particular challenges facing stepfamilies. The traffic goes in both directions. Structures influence the process of relationships; processes constantly seek expression in the ways relationships are structured. It is no accident that many couples choose to marry once a baby is on the way, or that they remarry to encourage the recognition by others of their new partnership.

Most psychoanalytical writing about human development assumes that *two loving parents* are the ideal family environment for bringing up children. *Loving* is one of the key words in this phrase, describing, as it does, the process of what goes on between the parents and between them and their children. D. H. Lawrence (1915), in his image of the rainbow, captures the sense of freedom that can follow for the child:

> She looked from one to the other, and she saw them established to her safety and she was free. She played between the pillar of fire and the pillar of cloud in confidence, having the assurance on her right hand and the assurance on her left. She was no longer called upon to uphold with her childish might the broken end of the arch. Her father and mother now met to span the heavens and she, the child, was free to play in the space beneath, between (p. 134).

The word *two*, though, is also important. As Jennifer Johns indicated in Chapter 6, children who grow up without one of their parents will be curious and have fantasies about the one who is absent. This implies that biological genesis (what the child knows about how babies are conceived) and social form (the knowledge that other children have two parents) contribute to the child's fantasy of having two parents, or the fantasy of his or her self as being made up of two separate but interdependent parts. The fantasy does not depend on having any specific knowledge about the absent parent.

Clifford Yorke (1995) recently reviewed a lifetime's experience as a child psychoanalyst in a series of radio talks entitled 'Childhood and Social Truth'. In these he looked at some connections between social ideologies shaping family life today and the unconscious phantasies of childhood. For example, he described how plural family lifestyles are often presented as the outcome of free and rational choice exercised by emancipated adults. Within this equation, every choice is equally acceptable. The ideology of individualism emphasizes the right of choice over the responsibilities that follow from choosing. One operational consequence is to confuse equality with identity. This, he argues, has resulted in a denial of the difference between men and women, and, most centrally, of the rights and needs of children. He equates this denial with the primitive thinking of childhood that is motivated by the wish for pleasure, has a limited capacity for concern, and promotes the fantasy that the world can be whatever one chooses it to be. He argues that the perpetuation of such thinking depends on amnesia. The inability of adults to remember their early childhood disconnects them from their past and restricts their ability to identify with the needs of their own children. Because unremembered histories have a tendency to be relived, childhood wishes re-enter the social world dressed up as adult rationalizations, moulding it in ways that will maximize the gratification of adults. Make-believe then becomes reality.

The attempt to replace equality of opportunity with the abolition of difference, and the degree of intolerance with which this enterprise is pursued, is, he suggests, the mark of an omnipotent infantile state of mind. It is present in the extremes of political correctness, where the belief persists that reality can be changed simply by declaring it so. In its worst forms it translates into the totalitarian state of mind in which thought is policed and difference becomes deviance. These processes can operate on either side of the family debate, and very powerfully. As Yorke observes, 'There is nothing more dangerously impervious to argument than a strong conviction of unknown origins' (Yorke, 1995, p. 59).

Sexual politics and sexual confusions are principally concerned with identity. How are children to grapple with these fundamental issues if the adults in their world are unable to do so? What happens when the sexual and aggressive energies of childhood coincide with parental divorce? What happens to boys who grow up in an environment where men are perceived as redundant or are hated? How is the intensity of the parent–child relationship mediated if there is no partner to provide respite? How is the illusion of 'exclusive possessiveness', described by Marcus Johns in Chapter 3, to give way to mature relating if there are no third persons? Inner conflicts and personal difficulties can be blamed on social structures, but these questions are essentially ones of relational process that, as Penelope Leach argued in Chapter 2, are reflections of our states of mind.

Fusion and differentiation

I want to look at two processes operating during family formation and to consider the significance of partnership to them, and to the states of mind they induce. The first of these is the fusion that operates in many couple relationships during pregnancy; the second is the differentiation within partnerships precipitated by the arrival of children.

The fantasy of fusion

Imagined in prospect, children bind couples together. As we have seen, the reason for marrying may be firmly linked to the intention to have children or the realization of that intent. Lynne Cudmore described in Chapter 4 how the failure of children to arrive on schedule can shock couples out of a comfortable companionability and even raise questions about the future viability of a marriage. In trying to remedy the situation, a protectiveness can envelop the couple and suppress expression of the very powerful feelings associated with the challenge to sexual identity and thwarting of future hopes that infertility represents. A successful pregnancy, when planned by both partners, gives a partnership added meaning and purpose. Children constitute a joint enterprise that harnesses the energies of the couple together.

Joan Raphael-Leff's narratives of pregnancy, in Chapter 5, illustrate the powerful biological, psychological and social pressures acting to dissolve relational boundaries. The relationship between a mother and her unborn child is, of course, essentially symbiotic. The confusion about what is inside and what is outside, what is me and what is not me, what is fact and what is fantasy, is understandably high. This serves a purpose; it enables the mother to become appropriately preoccupied with her baby, with herself in relation to her baby, and her baby in relation to herself. Space is created to engage with something that has profound social and psychological implications for the mother's sense of herself; time is made to attend to the changes taking place within and around her – that is, providing she creates the time and space to enjoy the experience.

The pressure to fuse in the adult partnership comes chiefly from men acting in response to the growing absorption of their partners with the new life growing inside them. Potentially uncomfortable differences or envious feelings can be managed by denial, idealization and identification, unconscious processes that have the effect of imposing tranquillity on potential turbulence, or of syphoning off feelings through compensating activities. Fraser Harrison (1987) graphically depicts the now well-chronicled identificatory processes operating during pregnancy from personal experience:

> Just before Tilly was born, I embarked on a . . . doomed scheme. Overcome by an unprecedented burst of gardening enthusiasm, I built a rockery beneath a sycamore tree that stood sentinel at the far end of our lawn. With manic energy, I laid waste a jungle of weeds, hauled tons of rock, dug in bag after bag of peat and, at fabulous expense, planted out every variety of heather known to our local nursery. Then Tilly was born. The sycamore shed its leaves, burying the tender heathers in an acid shroud, and I forgot the whole project. By the following spring the heathers were all dead, and the rockery had come to resemble an inexplicable Neolithic monument, a mere riddle of scattered stones.
>
> While waiting for Jack, I developed a longer lasting and

altogether more rewarding mode of creativity. Under the tuition of a true maestro I had already become interested in making wine, but in the last month of Jack's gestation, I began to produce the stuff on an industrial scale, filling row upon row of demi-johns with damson, plum, greengage, apple, pear, bullace, sloe and any other fruit I could lay my hands on. Finally, I purchased a wonderful globular, grape-shaped glass carboy, whose capacity was a majestic ten gallons. This noble vessel was duly filled with plum wine, and as Sally's belly swelled into a huge plum itself, the cloudy liquor slowly cleared to attain a magically translucent purple. Here was my baby, my alternative production (p. 36).

The programme of discussion groups run during pregnancy by the Tavistock Marital Studies Institute as part of a research programme suggested a similar diminution of difference in the couple relationship (Clulow, 1982). I well remember my sense of disbelief when a group of expectant couples discussed the part of London they were living in as if it were a rural retreat – complete with streams, green meadows and so on – whereas I saw only crowded buildings and congested traffic. I also remember the deafness that greeted my introducing difficult experiences that couples contend with once they have children. Had I said something wrong?

Ante-natal and birthing practices may unwittingly aid and abet identificatory processes between men and women in ways that blur the differences between them. Increasingly, from the late 1960s onwards, men have been introduced to childbirth preparation classes and allowed into delivery wards not simply as observers, but as an active part of the class or delivery team. Is this a modern version of the couvade syndrome, or an appropriate form of support for couples that enriches their partnerships and provides practical assistance? Are women having their babies delivered in hospital to take full advantage of medical technology, or have they surrendered control of their bodies to institutional procedures whose unconscious function is to manage male envy? Such processes have a long history (see Kraemer, 1995). What begin as permissive moves are sometimes institutionalized to the point that women – and men – find it more difficult to choose to do things separately and to acknowledge each other's distinctive differences.

The context of social change is relevant to these processes. Social values support equal opportunities for women in the workplace and the greater participation of men in childcare and family-based activities. It is true that practice lags behind intent. But, as Clifford Yorke suggested, the dividing line between the push for equality and denial of difference is not always clear-cut. This is particularly so during periods of transition when established patterns need rethinking. Couples have fewer reference points in managing their own transition-related uncertainties when these are taking place against a general background of social change and uncertainty.

Identificatory processes operate in other ways with often surprising and sometimes alarming effects on those involved. Past and present can be conflated, reinvoking memories of past conflicts and locating them as current dilemmas, plunging parents into a time warp where boundaries between child and adult dissolve. John Bowlby's (1990) biography of the naturalist Charles Darwin pays particular attention to his subject's attachment experiences as a child and his development in later life, including his hypochondriacal tendencies. Darwin had lost his mother at the age of 8 as a result of what is presumed to have been cancer of the stomach. The family did not talk about her after her death, so Darwin had little opportunity to understand what had happened to her or to mourn his loss. Bowlby analyses Darwin's experience of becoming a father for the first time in the following terms:

> The fact that Darwin was unwell through most of his first year of marriage and had a major breakdown at the end of it has led some to suppose it was due in some way to Emma's [his wife's] excessive cosseting. A far more likely explanation is that from April onwards he was aware of the pregnancy and that as the year progressed he became increasingly anxious about Emma's safety. There is much circumstantial evidence supporting this suggestion. First, his symptoms became noticeably worse as soon as she became pregnant. Secondly, his breakdown occurred immediately before she gave birth, when there were probably signs that it was imminent. Thirdly, writing to Fox six months later, after giving much detail of his troubles, he exclaims: 'What an awful affair a confinement is; it knocked me up almost as much as it did Emma herself'. Finally, it may be no coincidence that it was at this time that he first suffered from 'periodical vomiting', one of the symptoms that was to trouble him most during the following years. One possibility, which inevitably remains speculative, is that unconsciously he was linking Emma's abdominal changes with the months of abdominal illness that preceded his mother's death (p. 238).

Such confusions are not confined to pregnancy; they spill over into the whole child-rearing cycle. Parents frequently concertina their past experiences as children into their current experiences as parents. There are frequent unconscious attempts to slot the baby into the dynamic structures of the parents' personalities. Generational differences may be reversed so that children are perceived – and therefore related to – as parents or partners; partners, too, may be attributed with parental or childlike qualities. New parents may find themselves becoming unnervingly like the parents they knew as children and disowned as adults. Old scenarios may be replayed in contemporary settings. The pleasures and pains of parenthood derive in good measure from such identifications.

Difference and disillusion

If pregnancy draws couples together, children introduce difference into the parental partnership. This difference can be problematic. While there is plenty of evidence supporting the contention that the quality of the partnership between parents affects their abilities as individual parents, there is also, worryingly, a consistent body of research that equates the presence of children with a deterioration in the quality of marriage (Michaels and Goldberg, 1988). Typically, these 'satisfaction' studies depict a shallow 'U' or 'W' shaped graph when correlating reported satisfaction in marriage and the ages of children. The pre-school years and adolescence show up as particular troughs in the general dip.

The studies are not without their problems, and they can conceal variations within the overall pattern; for example, some studies associate children with enhanced satisfaction within marriage. It is certainly not possible to draw the conclusion that children cause marital disharmony or divorce; the evidence suggests that they are neither cause of nor solution to marital problems. They may widen already present rifts in a relationship, and they do test the capacity of the partnership to change. So how do we account for falling levels of satisfaction in those partnerships where it occurs?

An early hypothesis claimed an inverse relationship between levels of marital satisfaction following parenthood and the degree of role segregation in the partnership. Couples who shared many interests and enjoyed combined activities were described as having companionate partnerships, whereas those whose satisfactions came primarily from relationships and activities outside marriage, and whose roles were clearly demarcated, were described as having differentiated partnerships. Increases in marital satisfaction with children were associated with differentiated partnerships because the joint project of parenthood was seen as providing opportunities for partners to work together rather than separately, enhancing the rewards of the partnership. In contrast, companionate marriages were more likely to experience children as an intrusion into their shared life, however much they were wanted. Satisfaction from the marital relationship then declined.

The hypothesis is an interesting one given the social context of today where, as was evident in the companion volume to this book, *Women, Men and Marriage* (Clulow, 1995), companionate values in marriage have gained ascendancy over those that confer status on conjugal role – the institutional arrangement for regulating sexuality, and demarcating between 'providing' and 'homemaking' roles on the basis of gender. The more isolated a couple is, and the more partners depend on each other for self-affirmation, the more likely they are to experience children as an intrusion.

The problem with the hypothesis is that it conceives of partnerships in essentially static terms. There is no room for the same partnership to be both companionate and differentiated, and for change to occur over time. It may be more useful to think, instead, in terms of the developmental challenge that parenthood poses for couples and individuals.

Parenthood requires couples to redraw boundaries in their relationships with their social and economic environment, within their partnership as a couple, and within themselves as individuals. The experience of parenthood changes each of these dimensions as it resonates with both external realities and inner worlds of meaning. For some, the feelings associated with increased intimacy and interdependency in family relationships may be difficult at any or all of these levels. For others, the feelings associated with drawing apart and becoming more differentiated might be problematic. In other words, the transition to parenthood tests the capacities of couples to manage the boundaries between closeness and distance, intrusion and exclusion, sameness and difference in flexible ways that allow the balance between being together and being apart to change over time. The early stages of a love relationship invite and require what Plato's Symposium described as a 'merging and melting'. The relationship can then be established as special and distinct from other friendships. When children arrive, there must be some drawing apart. And when they leave home (if they ever do!), the couple must be able to manage being a pair again.

While it is too simple to describe the function of a partnership as facilitating coming together, creating something new and drawing apart again, it does capture the spirit of the processes by which the boundaries between family members are constantly being redefined along the axes of proximity and distance, sameness and difference.

The 'W' shaped graphs linking marital satisfaction with different stages in family life depict the pre-school years and adolescence as particular troughs. The psychological work going on for children and adults at this time is very much to do with issues of separateness, difference, autonomy and control. It may be that the dips do no more than record this work and the tensions associated with it.

The management of difference featured in Carolyn Pape Cowan's account of what has to change for couples when they become parents (Chapter 8). The 'Becoming a Family Project' that she describes highlights differences between men and women in terms of how they perceive themselves and how they perceive each other. With the arrival of children, women tend to see themselves less as a partner and more as a parent, whereas men's perceptions change only gradually. A man's sense of himself as a paid worker is likely to increase after birth, whereas the identity and social support derived from paid employment falls off sharply for women. Household tasks tend to be carried out along traditional gender-based lines, even when this was not the pattern before. The question of who does what at home is frequently a major source of conflict. Differences can create distance in partnerships, generating conflict, and affecting how satisfied partners feel together. They may also be more unsettling and difficult to manage than at other times of life. The physical and emotional exhaustion of taking on life and death responsibilities, and a general sense of being in an unfamiliar world with diminished resources, can add to the toll.

Present realities interact with past experience to raise fundamental questions about who is going to care for whom in the new family constellation. There are important gender differences in how these questions are answered, as Jennifer Johns made clear in Chapter 6. Writers offering a feminist perspective have drawn attention to cultural and interpersonal factors that predispose women to care for others and to deal with their own needs vicariously (see, for example, Orbach, 1995). The mother–daughter relationship is seen as the mechanism by which this pattern is handed down the generations. Mothers, disappointed by their partners (and this is a key aspect of the process), look to their daughters rather than their sons to provide understanding and support, thereby teaching the next generation of women that their role in life is to look after others, for whom mother is the prototype. Of course, as employment opportunities have expanded for women and diminished for men, solutions can change; the model of motherhood handed on to daughters is then also likely to change. Daughters may experience an absence in relation to their mothers as well as their fathers.

This view of development assumes that men hold out less potential than women as care-givers because their identity has been founded in opposition to their mothers on account of gender differences. The process of dis-identifying with mother (which provides for separateness) and counter-identifying with father (which provides for maleness) has been described as the *male wound* (Hudson and Jacot, 1991). While boys and girls are symbiotically connected with their mother, she is regarded as 'same' while father is regarded as 'different'. As male gender identity crystallizes (whether primarily as a result of biological or social process is unknown), boys experience a reversal in which what was 'same' (mother) is regarded as 'different', and what was 'different' (father) is regarded as 'same'. The developmental trajectories of boys and girls, it is argued, then depart from each other with profound consequences. The costs of the 'wound' are recorded in terms of personal insensitivity and misogyny; the benefits in terms of a sense of agency, a replenishing source of psychic energy, and a capacity for abstract passions: men have a capacity to relate to things as people and to people as things. They also have a capacity to displace private passions into public activities.

In contrast, girls can establish a secure gender identity without being 'wounded', and in consequence may have more difficulty in grasping the 'otherness' of others when focusing their desires. Desiring the 'other' of father may generate anxiety about rivalling mother, her 'sameness' then being experienced as a potential source of hostility and threat. According to Hudson and Jacot (1995): 'where heterosexual desire in the male promises a magical return to a state of primitive intimacy and connectedness, in the female it brings with it an incubus of identity-threatening anger and fathomless gloom'.

Both men and women struggle with a heightened need to be looked after that is excited by the arrival of children, but the options open to them for satisfying that need – and, in more adult terms, for contributing to the upbringing of their offspring – diverge as they become parents. As has been observed elsewhere, the *paradox of patriarchy* (Lewis and O'Brien, 1987) is that while fathers may be 'head of the family', they are not central characters within it. Men are most likely to respond to heightened attachment needs by turning to the world of work for compensation, a move that can usually be rationalized in terms of offsetting a drop in income caused by the woman giving up full-time employment. The male pattern of disconnection from mother, first practised in childhood, is then repeated in adulthood.

This analysis offers an explanation for the different life spaces occupied by men and women. They are solutions to the same problem: the problem for adults of satisfying their own attachment needs when these have been heightened by exposure to the responsibilities of caring for young children. As Andrew Samuels argues, in Chapter 7, such gendered solutions are a consequence of perceiving the distinctions between mothering and fathering in biologically based terms and uncritically accepting the socially constructed divisions between them as naturally ordained. They bypass a critical consideration of what is involved in the *roles* of mothering and fathering that could open the door to more flexible arrangements on the home front and at work. In so far as these solutions are considered to be problematic – by discriminating against women in terms of status, power and control of material resources, and by discriminating against men in terms of emotional sensitivity and a balanced life – they invite social policy that will reduce the gendered polarization of life by creating more opportunities for shared parenting and shared employment. One of the key resolves to emerge in the United Kingdom from the intense activity of 1994 – the year designated by the United Nations for supporting families – was to press for conditions that facilitate flexible patterns of parenting.

So far, I have been looking mainly at the ways children affect the partnership between their parents. Now, though, I want to consider the reverse direction of influence.

The function of the parental couple

In Chapter 9, Philip Cowan demonstrated how parenting patterns were linked with the quality of the relationship between the parental couple. He concluded that an important factor in determining whether conflict between new parents resulted in reduced marital satisfaction that might carry over into parenting behaviour was not the *degree* of conflict generated, but whether a spouse responded in ways that escalated or reduced it. This, in turn, was linked with levels of conflict reported by new parents in the parental partnerships within their own families of origin. Partnerships, especially those where the man was secure, were found to have a buffering effect against the transmission of conflict between one generation and the next.

These findings reinforce the marital psychotherapists' view of the potential of marriage to act as a psychological container (Colman, 1993; Ruszczynski, 1993) and the significance of the internalized parental couple for the way people operate in their adult lives and loves (Fisher, 1993; Di Ceglie, 1995). A secure internal couple creates the 'triangular space' that Joanna Rosenthall described in Chapter 11, allowing experience to be digested and reflected upon, and creating the conditions for giving up the illusion of ownership in relationships which, when clung on to, encourages separateness and difference to be regarded as betrayal. How does the couple relationship contribute to laying the foundations for individuals to be good partners and good parents? And how do children contribute to the development of their parents? Let's retrace the journey made in this chapter and retell a story.

Imagine, then, a couple who share friends, leisure interests and enjoy each other's company. According to the wishes and plans of both partners they succeed in conceiving a child without difficulty. During pregnancy, the woman becomes increasingly preoccupied with the unborn baby, organizing herself around this miracle of self and otherness that she carries around in her belly. She continues to smile at her partner, to hold his hand, and yet, imperceptibly, she also begins to draw apart from him. The baby is born. There are months – years – of feeding, cuddling, nappy changing, sleep deprivation, worry, relief, joy and pain, all requiring intense physical and emotional involvement with the baby. In a profound way the new mother may feel she has been filled by her baby, even fulfilled, or she may feel invaded and taken over by the new bundle of life and fear she is losing her grip on who she is as a separate person. Time for herself becomes paramount. She may not feel free to respond to emotional claims or sexual approaches from her partner, may not even want to hold his hand, so physically involved is she with another. The locus of intimacy within the family has changed.

Her partner may feel he has gained a son or a daughter, but lost the special relationship with his wife or partner. And so he has. The partnership that precedes parenthood is very different from the one that succeeds it. There is mourning to be done as well as celebrating. The couple are challenged to give up a previously enjoyed exclusivity in their relationship to make room for other possibilities. He may deny that the changes brought about by the baby are more than a temporary hiccup, and that life will soon 'get back to normal'. It never does. And so there follows a dawning realization of the need to adapt to a fundamentally changed life. In the meantime, he may be prone to oscillating feelings of rejection and belonging, envy and pride, pain and joy.

He has choices to make. Does he stay on the outside of the mother–baby dyad, perhaps throwing himself into work if he is fortunate enough to have a job, or into other activities outside the home? Does he move in on the baby, competing with his partner to be the mother and leaving her feeling like the 'crowd' in their threesome? The intrusive 'support' of some 'new' men can undermine the efforts of women to take up the mothering role, just as the gendered prejudices of 'old' women can deter potentially interested men in becoming involved fathers. Both strategies are ways of managing feelings of exclusion by exporting them to others. They heighten the possibilities of parents competing with each other and pairing with the child. As strategies they may stem from childhood experiences that make the prospect of being separate/on the outside or involved/ on the inside particularly difficult to manage.

There are other strategies. Do they as a couple delegate the task of parenting to a relative, a friend or paid employee, allowing them to continue their individual lives and time together as a couple with the minimum of disruption? This option binds the parents together, leaving the child to pick up the tab in the absence of satisfactory alternative arrangements. Or do they, as a couple, work out flexible ways of co-operating in the task of parenting that does not operate on a 'one in, one out' basis?

The classical significance of these options was recognized by the founder of psychoanalysis, Sigmund Freud, who formed it into one of the main building blocks of his overall theory. He looked at the dilemmas of parenting from the child's perspective when basing the Oedipus complex on Sophocles' best-known tragedy. In doing so, he introduced the child as an active, if unwitting, player in the triangular dramas of family life. Although his 'children' were adults, they continued to enact the child's dilemma in their adult lives, with him and in their other relationships – including those as partners and parents. The irony of the Oedipus legend is that the attempt of Laius and Jocasta to preserve their marriage against the intrusion of a child ultimately destroys not only their relationships as parents to their son but also, ultimately, their partnership as well. Oedipus was put out by his parents and left on a hillside to die. He survives – as a result of alternative care arrangements – and, with the passage of time, returns to destroy, quite unknowingly, his parents' marriage – with tragic consequences for family and community alike. And all the while, people turned a blind eye. An allegory for our times?

Contemporary thinking about the Oedipal situation highlights the significance of the parental couple for healthy child development. The argument runs that in the beginning there is only 'mother' (the quotes are used to signify the possibility of this role being taken by either sex). 'Father' may be there as a supporting presence, but the infant does not know it. If he is there as a substitute for 'mother', he does not exist in his own right. The process of individuation begins with the infant's recognition of the 'mother' as *other*, not as an extension of himself or herself. The first stage of developing a reflective self comes through the infant imagining himself or herself as being observed through the eyes of 'mother'. There is a metaphorical swopping of places with 'mother' to allow this new dimension to appear.

'Father', in the form of a separate third person, is more obviously *other* from the outset. He represents the world outside the family and the excitement and disturbance it can bring into the home. The infant will develop an attachment to him as well as to 'mother', and he will exert a positive push away from the regressive pull of maternal symbiosis. In describing this process, Kenneth Wright (1991) uses the image of Homer's Odysseus who ordered his men to strap him to the mast (phallus?) and to plug his ears (the process of male disconnection described by Hudson and Jacot, 1991) so that his voyage is not wrecked by the sweet siren voices luring him back to a fatal devouring embrace. He makes the point (in describing a journey that may be more linked to male than female development) that 'fathers' can be absent not only by being physically and emotionally removed, but also by being undifferentiated from 'mother'. In other words, if the parental partnership cannot tolerate difference, the couple environment does not encourage differentiation to occur for the child.

Occupying a third position outside the primary pair, 'fathers' create the conditions for a second stage in the development of a reflective self. The child now has an experience of there being a *couple* from which she or he is excluded. The child then takes up that third position, observing what goes on between the parents. To recognize the parental relationship, never mind the possibility that parents might have an exclusive sexual relationship (a boundary constituting the 'exclusion zone' of the incest taboo), involves giving up the illusion of having sole and permanent rights over 'mother'. This is both a profound loss and a substantial psychological achievement.

When the loss cannot be tolerated, as will often be the case with very young children, it must be defended against. In the polarized world of infancy, populated as it often is by fairies and witches, beasts and beauties, angels and devils, the psychologically threatened child may split the loved parent or parents into monster and saviour. The ability of the parent to remain connected within himself or herself, and of the parents to remain connected with each other, not only reduces the child's anxiety that to wish a parent dead is tantamount to murder (children have very omnipotent fantasies), but also allows for integrating loving and hateful feelings towards the same person. When things go well within and between parents, children can own and feel safe with powerful and contradictory feelings towards those most important to them. When they do not, anxiety may continue unchecked or go underground.

The parental partnership does something more. Being able to tolerate the link between parents provides children with a completely different perspective. They then occupy the third position described earlier, on the outside but not filled up with anxiety about being excluded. They can both observe and absorb the workings of the parental couple, and they can imagine themselves as being the objects of observation by the couple as other. As observers they learn how partnerships operate, how intimacy is handled and how differences are managed, without being central to the drama (which is not to say that they will not try to join in!); they can enjoy the liveliness of the partnership without feeling diminished, threatened, excluded, or impelled to intrude. As the ones observed, they develop a capacity for self-observation, for entertaining another point of view, and for independent thought and activity. In short, they develop a capacity to reflect on situations, to entertain differences without fearing annihilation, and to adopt a meta perspective – critically reviewing their own thinking and experience. The Oedipal situation then becomes the crucible in which the capacity to be alone and intimately involved with others – central ingredients of successful partnerships – are prepared.

But how adequate is this theory? Does it reflect a central truth or is it just another 'reproductive narrative', as Joan Raphael-Leff might describe it (see Chapter 5)? Theories have a habit of being culture-bound and ideologically driven. How necessary is what Andrew Samuels describes in Chapter 7 as 'the insertion metaphor' to describe the role fathers play in helping children develop a differentiated and separately viable sense of self, or is it simply an extension of patriarchal thinking? Do we, as he suggests, insult mothers and babies by implying they have no commitment and capacity within themselves to being and becoming separate, and without the paternal 'third' will simply languor in a state of psychotic fusion? Is the chronology right that the mother-infant duo must be firmly established before third parties such as fathers have a role, or do infants form multiple attachments from the outset? Observational studies question whether 'primary narcissism' is the natural state of early infancy, and suggest an interactive capacity that is not based on phantasy. Might one parent be able to embody enough of an 'internal couple' within themselves not to need an actual partner? The 'fucking thinking' that Britton's (1989) patient complained of in his analyst provides a vivid example of how the 'intercourse' of reflective thinking undertaken by one person can fulfil some of the functions of a parental couple.

These questions allow no final assertions, only hypotheses that need testing against experience. My hypothesis is that partner–parent dilemmas are essentially dilemmas of the triangle. Adult partnerships can enhance the abilities of adults to act as parents *and* they can diminish those capacities. They can check the impulses of children to 'divide and rule' in their dealings with others, *and* they can encourage patterns of relating that are deceptive, manipulative and exploitative. They can provide an environment within which parents and children are free to test themselves and develop new strengths, *and* they can confirm the worst that people fear about themselves, inhibiting further exploration. The subtle interplay between form and process allows no absolute judgement about the relative merits of two-parent families, only a developing awareness of the factors that affect how they and other family forms contribute to processes that are more and less healthy, and which will determine the social ecology of the next generation.

Christopher Clulow

| References

Alexander, K. and Entwistle, D., 'Achievement in the First Two Years of School: Patterns and Processes', *Monograph of the Society for Research in Child Development.* Vol. 53 (2), Serial No. 218, 1988.

Alexander, N., 'Male Evaluation and Semen Analysis'. In R. Ansbacher (ed.), *Clinical Obstetrics and Gynaecology.* Philadelphia: Harper and Row, 1982.

Badinger, E., *The Myth of Motherhood: An Historical View of the Maternal Instinct.* London: Souvenir, 1981.

Balint, E., 'Fair Shares and Mutual Concern'. In *Before I Was I.* London: Free Association Books, 1993.

Batchelor, J., Dimmock, B. and Smith, D., *Understanding Stepfamilies. What Can Be Learned from Callers to the Stepfamily Telephone Counselling Service?* London: Stepfamily Publications, 1994.

Baumrind, D., 'The Development of Instrumental Competence through Socialization'. In A. Pick (ed.), *Minnesota Symposia on Child Psychology.* Vol. 7. Minneapolis: University of Minnesota Press, 1979.

Belsky, J. and Kelly, J., *The Transition to Parenthood.* New York: Delacorte Press, 1994.

Berg, B., *Nothing to Cry About.* New York: Seaview Books, 1981.

Berg, B., Wilson, J. and Weingartner, P., 'Psychological Sequelae of Infertility Treatment: The Role of Gender and Sex Role Identification', *Social Science Medicine.* Vol. 33, No. 9, pp. 1071–80, 1991.

Berk, A. and Shapiro, J., 'Some Implications of Infertility for Marital Therapy', *Family Therapy.* Vol. 11, No. 1, pp. 37–47, 1984.

Bion, W., *Learning from Experience.* London: Heinemann, 1962.

Bion, W., *Elements of Psychoanalysis.* London: Heinemann, 1963.

Blyth, E., *Infertility and Assisted Reproduction: Practice Issues for Counsellors.* Birmingham: British Association of Social Workers, 1991.

Board of Social Responsibility, Church of England, *Something to Celebrate. Valuing Families in Church and Society.* London: Church House, 1995.

Bollas, C., *Being a Character. Psychoanalysis and Self-Experience.* London: Routledge, 1992.

Bongaarts, J., 'Infertility after Age 30: A False Alarm', *Family Planning Perspectives.* Vol. 14, No. 2, pp. 75–8, 1982.

Bowlby, J., *Attachment (Attachment and Loss Volume 1)*. London: Hogarth, 1969.

Bowlby, J., *Separation (Attachment and Loss Volume 2)*. London: Hogarth, 1973.

Bowlby, J., *Loss (Attachment and Loss Volume 3)*. London: Hogarth, 1980.

Bowlby, J., *Charles Darwin: A New Biography*. London: Hutchinson, 1990.

Brazelton, T. and Cramer, B., *The Earliest Relationships. Parents, Infants and the Drama of Attachment*. London: Karnac, 1991.

British Household Panel Survey, *Household and Family Change 1990–1992*. Colchester: University of Essex, 1994.

Britton, R., 'The Missing Link: Parental Sexuality in the Oedipus Complex'. In R. Britton, M. Feldman and E. O'Shaughnessy, *The Oedipus Complex Today: Clinical Implications*. London: Karnac Books, 1989.

Burghes, L., *Lone Parenthood and Family Disruption. The Outcomes for Children*. London: Family Policy Studies Centre, 1994.

Burgoyne, J., 'Afterword'. In D. Clark (ed.), *Marriage, Domestic Life and Social Change. Writings for Jacqueline Burgoyne 1944–1948*. London: Routledge, 1991.

Burgoyne, J. and Clark, D., *Making A Go Of It. A Study of Stepfamilies in Sheffield*. London: Routledge and Kegan Paul, 1984.

Butler, J., *Gender Trouble: Feminism and the Subversion of Identity*. London and New York: Routledge, 1990.

Campion, M. J., *Who's Fit to Be a Parent?* London: Routledge, 1995.

Carter, B. and McGoldrick, M., *The Changing Family Life Cycle: A Framework for Family Therapy*. Boston: Alleyn and Bacon, 1989.

Clark, D. (ed.), *Marriage, Domestic Life and Social Change. Writings for Jacqueline Burgoyne 1944–1948*. London: Routledge, 1991.

Clulow, C., *To Have and To Hold: Marriage, the First Baby and Preparing Couples for Parenthood*. Aberdeen: Aberdeen University Press, 1982.

Clulow, C., 'Partners Becoming Parents: A Question of Difference', *Infant Mental Health Journal*. Vol. 12, No. 3, pp. 256–66, 1991.

Clulow, C. (ed.), *Women, Men and Marriage*. London: Sheldon Press, 1995.

Cockett, M. and Tripp, J., *The Exeter Family Study: Family Breakdown and its Impact on Children*. Exeter: Exeter University Press, 1994.

Cohn, D., Cowan, P., Cowan, C. and Pearson, J., 'Mothers' and Fathers' Working Models of Childhood Attachment Relationships, Parenting Styles and Child Behaviour', *Development and*

Psychopathology. Vol. 4, pp. 417–31, 1992.

Colman, W., 'Marriage as a Psychological Container'. In S. Ruszczynski, *Psychotherapy with Couples*. London: Karnac, 1993.

Cowan, C. and Cowan, P., *When Partners Become Parents: The Big Life Change for Couples*. New York: Basic Books, 1992.

Cowan, P., Cohn, D., Cowan, C. and Pearson, J., 'Parents' Attachment Histories and Children's Internalizing and Externalizing Behaviour: Exploring Family Systems Models of Linkage', *Journal of Consulting and Clinical Psychology* (in press).

Cowan, P., Cowan, C., Schulz, M. and Heming, G., 'Prebirth to Preschool Family Factors Predicting Children's Adaptation to Kindergarten'. In R. Parke and S. Kellam (eds), *Exploring Family Relationships with Other Social Contexts: Advances in Family Research*. Vol. 4, Hillsdale, New Jersey: Lawrence Erlbaum, 1994.

Cox, M., Owen, M., Lewis, J. and Henderson, V., 'Marriage, Adult Adjustment and Early Parenting', *Child Development*. Vol. 60, pp. 1015–24, 1989.

Dennett, D., *Consciousness Explained*. Harmondsworth: Penguin, 1993.

Di Ceglie, G. R., 'From the Internal Parental Couple to the Marital Relationship'. In S. Ruszczynski and J. Fisher (eds), *Intrusiveness and Intimacy in the Couple*. London: Karnac, 1995.

Dollimore, J., *Sexual Dissidence: Augustine to Wilde, Freud to Foucault*. Oxford: Oxford University Press, 1991.

du Bois, P., *Sowing the Body: Psychoanalysis and Ancient Representations of Women*. Chicago: University of Chicago Press, 1988.

Dunstan, G. R., *Ideology, Ethics and Practice. The Second John Hunt Memorial Lecture*. London: The Royal College of General Practitioners, 1994.

Edelmann, R. and Connolly, K., 'Psychological Aspects of Infertility', *British Journal of Medical Psychology*. Vol. 59, No. 3, pp. 209–19, 1986.

Eekelaar, J. and Katz, S. (eds), *Marriage and Cohabitation in Contemporary Society*. Toronto and London: Butterworths, 1980.

Eliot, T. S., 'Little Gidding'. Reproduced in *The Complete Poems and Plays of T. S. Eliot*. London: Faber and Faber, 1969; originally published in 1942.

Etzioni, A. (ed.), *New Communitarian Thinking. Persons, Virtues, Institutions and Communities*. Charlottesville and London: University Press of Virginia, 1995.

Felman, S., *What Does a Woman Want*. Baltimore and London: John Hopkins University Press, 1993.

Fisher, J., 'The Impenetrable Other. Ambivalence and Oedipal

Conflict in Work with Couples'. In S. Ruszczynski (ed.), *Psychotherapy with Couples*. London: Karnac, 1993.

Forrester, J., *The Seductions of Psychoanalysis: Freud, Lacan and Derrida*. Cambridge: Cambridge University Press, 1990.

Foucault, M., *The History of Sexuality*. London: Allen Lane, 1979.

Freud, S., 'The Unconscious'. *Standard Edition Volume 14*, pp. 186–9. London: Hogarth, 1915.

Gelles, R., *Contemporary Families*. California and London: Sage, 1995.

Giddens, A., *Modernity and Self Identity*. Cambridge: Polity Press, 1991.

Gillis, J., *For Better or Worse: British Marriage 1600 to the Present*. Oxford: Oxford University Press, 1985.

Golding, W., *The Hot Gates*. London: Faber and Faber, 1965.

Goodnow, J. and Collins, W., *Development According to Parents: The Nature, Sources and Consequences of Parents' Ideas*. London: Lawrence Erlbaum, 1990.

Greil, A., Porter, K. and Leitko, T., 'Sex and Intimacy Among Infertile Couples', *Journal of Psychology and Human Sexuality*. Vol. 2, No. 2, p. 127, 1989.

Grossman, F., Eichler, L. and Winnickoff, S., *Pregnancy, Birth and Parenthood*. San Francisco: Jossey-Bass, 1980.

Harrison, F., *A Winter's Tale*. London: HarperCollins, 1987.

Haskey, J., 'Trends in Marriage and Cohabitation: The Decline in Marriage and the Changing Pattern of Living in Partnerships', *Population Trends*, No. 80. London: OPCS, 1995.

Heinicke, C., 'Impact of Prebirth Parent Personality and Marital Functioning on Family Development: A Framework and Suggestions for Further Study', *Developmental Psychology*. Vol. 20, pp. 1044–53, 1984.

Hermstein, R. and Murray, C., *The Bell Curve. Intelligence, Class and Structure in American Life*. New York and London: Simon and Schuster, 1994.

Hinde, R. and Stevenson-Hinde, J. (eds), *Relationships Within Families*. Oxford: Clarendon Press, 1988.

Houghton, P., 'Infertility: The Consumer's Outlook', *British Journal of Sexual Medicine*, Vol. 11, No. 1, pp. 185–7, 1984.

Hudson, L. and Jacot, B., *The Way Men Think. Intellect, Intimacy and the Erotic Imagination*. New Haven and London: Yale University Press, 1991.

Hudson, L. and Jacot, B. *Intimate Relations. The Natural History of Desire*. New Haven and London: Yale University Press, 1995.

Jordan, J., Kaplan, A., Miller, J., Stiver, I. and Surrey, J., *Women's*

Growth in Connection: Writings from the Stone Centre. New York and London: Guilford, 1991.

Kapstrom, A., 'Does the Career Woman Face Infertility?' *Supervisor Nurse.* Vol. 12, No. 7, pp. 54–60, 1981.

Kerig, P., Cowan, P. and Cowan, C., 'Marital Quality and Gender Differences in Parent–Child Interaction', *Developmental Psychology.* Vol. 29, pp. 931–9, 1993.

Kiernan, K. and Estaugh, V., *Cohabitation. Extra-Marital Childbearing and Social Policy.* London: Family Policy Studies Centre, 1994.

Klein, M., 'The Psychological Principles in Early Analysis'. Reprinted in *The Writings of Melanie Klein, Volume 1.* London: Hogarth Press, 1975.

Kraemer, S., 'A Man's Place?' In C. F. Clulow (ed.), *Women, Men and Marriage.* London: Sheldon Press, 1995.

Lacan, J., *Écrits.* Trans. A. Sheridan. London: Tavistock, 1977.

Lawrence, D. H., *The Rainbow.* Harmondsworth: Penguin English Library Edition, 1981; originally published in 1915.

Leach, P., *The First Six Months: Coming to Terms with Your Baby.* London: Collins, 1987.

Leach, P., *Children First: What Society Must Do – And Is Not Doing – For Children Today.* Harmondsworth: Penguin, 1994.

LeMasters, E., 'Parenthood as Crisis', *Marriage and Family Living.* Vol. 19, pp. 352–5, 1957.

Lewis, C. and O'Brien, M., *Reassessing Fatherhood. New Observations on Fathers and the Modern Family.* London and Beverly Hills: Sage, 1987.

Lord Chancellor's Department, *Looking to the Future. Mediation and the Ground for Divorce.* London: HMSO, 1995.

Macfarlane, A., *Marriage and Love in England 1300–1840.* Oxford: Basil Blackwell, 1986 p. 173.

Mahler, M., 'A Study of the Separation–Individuation Process', *Psychoanalytical Study of the Child.* Vol. 26, pp. 403–24, 1971.

Mahlstedt, P., 'The Psychological Component of Infertility', *Fertility and Sterility.* Vol. 43, No. 3, pp. 335–46, 1985.

Main, M. and Goldwyn, R., 'Adult Attachment System'. In M. Main (ed.), *A Typology of Human Attachment Organization Assessed in Discourse, Drawings and Interviews.* New York: Cambridge University Press (in press).

Mansfield, P. and Collard, J., *The Beginning of the Rest of Your Life?* Basingstoke: Macmillan, 1988.

Mansfield, P., Collard, J. and McAllister, F., *Person, Partner, Parent.* Basingstoke: Macmillan, 1996.

Marris, P., *Loss and Change.* London: Routledge and Kegan Paul, 1974.

Matte-Blanco, I., *The Unconscious as Infinite Sets: An Essay in Bi-Logic.* London: Duckworth, 1975.

Mattox, W., 'The Family Time Famine', *Family Policy.* Vol. 3, No. 1, 1990.

McAllister, F. (ed.), *Marital Breakdown and the Health of the Nation.* 2nd Edition. London: One Plus One, 1995.

McRae, S., *Cohabiting Mothers. Changing Marriage and Motherhood?* London: Policy Studies Institute, 1993.

Menning, B., 'The Emotional Needs of Infertile Couples', *Fertility and Infertility.* Vol. 34, No. 4, pp. 313–19, 1980.

Menning, B., 'The Psychology of Infertility'. In J. Aiman (ed.), *Infertility, Diagnosis and Management.* New York: Springer-Verlag, 1984.

Michaels, G. and Goldberg, W. (eds), *The Transition to Parenthood: Current Theory and Research.* New York: Cambridge University Press, 1988.

Miller, N., Cowan, P., Cowan, C., Hetherington, E. and Clingempeel, G., 'Externalizing in Preschoolers and Early Adolescents: A Cross-Study Replication of a Family Model', *Developmental Psychology.* Vol. 29, pp. 3–18, 1993.

Mooney, B., *From This Day Forward. An Anthology of Marriage.* London: John Murray, 1989.

Murray, C., 'Underclass'. In D. Anderson and G. Dawson (eds), *Family Portraits.* London: Social Affairs Unit, 1990.

Murray, L., 'Does Post-Natal Depression Matter When You Are 5 Years Old?', *Lecture given to the British Psycho-Analytical Society Research Group*, 15 February 1994.

Murray, L., Cooper, P. and Stein, A., 'Postnatal Depression and Infant Development', *British Medical Journal.* Vol. 302, pp. 978–9, 1991.

Orbach, S., 'A Woman's Place?' in C. F. Clulow (ed.), *Women, Men and Marriage.* London: Sheldon Press, 1995.

Osofsky, J. and Osofsky, H., 'Psychological and Developmental Perspectives on Expectant and New Parenthood'. In R. Parke (ed.), *Review of Child Development Research: The Family.* Vol. 7. Chicago: University of Chicago Press, 1984.

Pantesco, V., 'Non-Organic Infertility: Some Research and Treatment Problems', *Psychological Reports.* Vol. 58, No. 3, pp. 731–7, 1986.

Papernow, P., 'The Stepfamily Cycle: An Experiential Model of Stepfamily Development', *Family Relations.* Vol. 33, No. 3, pp.

335–363, 1984.

Pebley, A., 'Changing Attitudes Towards Timing of First Births', *Family Planning Perspectives.* Vol. 13, No. 4, pp. 171–5, 1981.

Pengelly, P., 'Working with Partners: Counselling the Couple and Collaborating in the Team'. In S. Jennings (ed.), *Infertility Counselling.* Oxford: Basil Blackwell Science, 1995.

Pengelly, P., Inglis, M. and Cudmore, L., 'Infertility: Couples' Experiences and the Use of Counselling in Treatment Centres', *Psychodynamic Counselling.* Vol. 1, No. 4, 1995.

Ramu, G. and Tavuchis, N., 'The Valuation of Children and Parenthood among the Voluntarily Childless and Pre-Natal Couples in Canada', *Journal of Comparative Family Studies.* Vol. 17, No. 1, pp. 96–116, 1986.

Raphael-Leff, J., 'Facilitators and Regulators: Vulnerability to Post-natal Disturbance', *Journal of Psychosomatic Obstetrics and Gynaecology.* Vol. 4, pp. 151–68, 1985a.

Raphael-Leff, J., 'Facilitators and Regulators, Participators and Renouncers: Mothers' and Fathers' Orientations Towards Pregnancy and Parenthood', *Journal of Psychosomatic Obstetrics and Gynaecology.* Vol. 4, pp. 169–84, 1985b.

Raphael-Leff, J., 'Fears and Fantasies of Childbirth', *Journal of Pre and Perinatal Psychology.* Vol. 1, pp. 18–25, 1985c.

Raphael-Leff, J., 'Facilitators and Regulators: Conscious and Unconscious Processes in Pregnancy and Early Motherhood', *British Journal of Medical Psychology.* Vol. 59, pp. 43–55, 1986a.

Raphael-Leff, J., 'Infertility: Diagnosis or Life Sentence?' *British Journal of Sexual Medicine.* Vol. 13, No. 1, pp. 28–9, 1986b.

Raphael-Leff, J., *Psychological Processes of Childbearing.* London: Chapman and Hall, 1991.

Raphael-Leff, J., 'The Baby-Makers: An In-Depth Single Case Study of Conscious and Unconscious Psychological Reactions to Infertility and Baby-Making', *British Journal of Psychotherapy.* Vol. 8, pp. 266–77, 1992a.

Raphael-Leff, J., 'Transitions to Parenthood: Infertility'. In *Infertility and Adoption.* London: Post Adoption Centre, 1992b.

Raphael-Leff, J., *Pregnancy: The Inside Story.* London: Sheldon Press, 1993.

Richards, M., 'The Companionship Trap'. In C. F. Clulow (ed.), *Women, Men and Marriage.* London: Sheldon Press, 1995.

Riviere, J., 'Womanliness as a Masquerade', *International Journal of Psycho-Analysis.* Vol. 10, pp. 303–38, 1929.

Robinson, M., 'Stepfamilies: A Reconstituted Family System', *Journal of Family Therapy.* Vol. 2, No. 1, pp. 45–9, 1980.

Robinson, M., *Family Transformation Through Divorce and Remarriage: A Systemic Approach*. London: Routledge, 1991.

Robinson, M. and Smith, D., *Step By Step: Focus on Stepfamilies*. London: Harvester Wheatsheaf, 1993.

Rose, P., *Parallel Lives*. London: Chatto and Windus, 1984, p. 5

Rowan, K., 'Meeting the Family', *The Guardian*. 8 January 1992.

Rubin, L., *Erotic Wars*. New York: Farrar, Straus and Giroux, 1990.

Ruszczynski, S., 'Thinking About and Working with Couples'. In S. Ruszczynski (ed.), *Psychotherapy With Couples*. London: Karnac, 1993.

Sadler, A. and Syrop, C., 'The Stress of Infertility'. In *Family Stress. Family Therapy Collections*. Royal Tunbridge Wells: Aspen, 1987.

Samuels, A., *Jung and the Post-Jungians*. London and Boston: Routledge and Kegan Paul, 1985.

Samuels, A., *The Plural Psyche: Personality, Morality and the Father*. London and New York: Routledge, 1989.

Samuels, A., *The Political Psyche*. London and New York: Routledge, 1993.

Schafer, R., *Retelling a Life: Narration and Dialogue in Psychoanalysis*. New York: Basic Books, 1992.

Seccombe, W., *Weathering the Storm: The History of Working Class Families*. London: Verso, 1993.

Sedgewick, E., *Between Men: English Literature and Male Homosocial Desire*. New York: Columbia University Press, 1985.

Shereshefsky, P. and Yarrow, L. (eds) *Psychological Aspects of a First Pregnancy and Early Postnatal Adaptation*. New York: Raven Press, 1973.

Slade, P., Raval, H., Buck, P. and Lieberman, B., 'A 3 Year Follow Up of Emotional, Marital and Sexual Functioning in Couples who were Infertile', *Journal of Reproductive and Infant Psychology*. Vol. 10, No. 1, pp. 233–43, 1992.

Smart, C., 'From Marriage to Parenthood. The Rise of the New Indissoluble Contract', *Sixth Annual Jacqueline Burgoyne Lecture*. Sheffield. 24 February 1995.

Smith, D., *Stepmothering*. London: Harvester Wheatsheaf, 1990.

Stern, D., *The Interpersonal World of the Infant: A View from Psychoanalysis and Developmental Psychology*. New York: Basic Books, 1985.

Stern, D., 'One Way to Build a Clinically Relevant Baby', *Infant Mental Health Journal*. Vol. 15, pp. 9–25, 1994.

Strindberg, J., 'The Dance of Death'. In *Strindberg Plays, Volume 2* (translated by Michael Meyer). London: Methuen, 1991.

Trevarthen, C., 'Communication and Co-Operation in Early

Infancy'. In M. Bullowa (ed.), *Before Speech. The Beginning of Interpersonal Communication.* New York: Cambridge University Press, 1979.

Utting, D., *Family and Parenthood: Supporting Families, Preventing Breakdown.* York: Joseph Rowntree Foundation, 1995.

Walker, J., *Family and Parenthood.* Paper 14. York: Joseph Rowntree Foundation, 1993.

Weeks, J., *Sexuality and Its Discontents.* London and New York: Routledge, 1985.

Wellington, K., Field, J., Johnson, A. and Wadsworth, J., *Sexual Behaviour in England.* Harmondsworth: Penguin, 1994.

Williams, R., 'Ideas and the Labour Movement'. In *Resources of Hope.* London: Verso, 1981.

Winnicott, D., 'What About Father?' In *Getting to Know Your Baby.* London: Heinemann, 1944.

Winnicott, D., 'Primary Maternal Preoccupation'. In *Collected Papers.* London: Tavistock, 1956.

Winnicott, D., 'Transitional Objects and Transitional Phenomena'. In *Through Paediatrics to Psychoanalysis.* London: Hogarth, 1958.

Winnicott, D., 'Mind and Its Relation to the Psyche-Soma'. In *Through Paediatrics to Psychoanalysis.* London: Hogarth, 1958.

Winnicott, D., 'Ego Distortion in Terms of True and False Self'. In *The Maturational Process and the Facilitating Environment.* London: Hogarth, 1960.

Winnicott, D., 'The Effect of Psychotic Parents on the Emotional Development of the Child'. In *The Family and Individual Development.* London: Tavistock, 1968.

Wirtberg, I., *His and Her Childlessness.* Stockholm: Karolinska Institute, 1992.

Wright, J., Allard, M., Lecours, A. and Sabourin, S., 'Psychosocial Distress and Infertility: A Review of Controlled Research', *International Journal of Fertility.* Vol. 34, No. 2, pp. 126–42, 1989.

Wright, K., *Vision and Separation Between Mother and Baby.* London: Free Association Press, 1991.

Yorke, C., 'Childhood and Social Truth. Five Talks for BBC Radio 3', *Bulletin of the Anna Freud Centre.* Vol. 18, No. 1, pp. 47–74, 1995.

| Index